The Virtue of Civility

Edward Shils (1910–1995)

THE VIRTUE OF
Civility

SELECTED ESSAYS ON LIBERALISM, TRADITION, AND CIVIL SOCIETY

Edward Shils

EDITED BY
STEVEN GROSBY

Liberty Fund

INDIANAPOLIS

1997

© 1997 by Liberty Fund, Inc.
All rights reserved
Printed in the United States of America
97 98 99 00 01 H 5 4 3 2 1
97 98 99 00 01 P 5 4 3 2 1

Library of Congress Cataloging-in-Publication Data

Shils, Edward Albert, 1911–
The virtue of civility : selected essays on liberalism, tradition, and
civil society / by Edward Shils ; edited by Steven Grosby.
          p.   cm.
Includes bibliographical references and index.
ISBN 0-86597-147-1 (h). —ISBN 0-86597-148-X (p)
1. Liberalism.   2. Civil society.   3. Liberty.   I. Grosby, Steven
Elliott, 1951–   .   II. Title.
          HM276.S525   1997
          301—DC20   96-31391

Liberty Fund, Inc.
8335 Allison Pointe Trail, Suite 300
Indianapolis, Indiana 46250-1687
(317) 842-0880

Contents

§

Introduction

§

THE LIBERAL DEMOCRATIC REGIMES of the twentieth century have without exception been beset by a number of severe problems. While some of the problems are external in origin, others are a result of the contradictory character—what Edward Shils called the *antinomy*—of liberalism. Still other problems arise from the imperfect relations among various truths of the human condition. Nonetheless, these regimes have shown themselves to be remarkably resilient.

Theorists of both fascism and Marxism have been one in their denunciation of liberalism. Their principal charge is that the individualism and pluralism fostered by liberalism are aimless and disorderly. They also charge that liberal democratic regimes are so weak that they are incapable of action so long as they insist on maintaining the form of representative government.

But the liberal democratic regimes have withstood and even defeated these challenges. In doing so, both the ultimate meaning and the order of human affairs upon which these regimes are based have been reaffirmed. This meaning and order arise from liberalism's belief in the sacredness of the individual human being, in the dignity and therefore the freedom of the individual to live in accordance with his or her own beliefs, and in the moral value of reason and civil discussion.

The existence, the success, and even some of the persistent problems of liberal democratic regimes lie in liberalism's acknowledgment of these foundational beliefs and the order of society that evolves from them. The following essays by the late Edward Shils on liberalism, tradition, and civility elucidate this contradictory character of liberalism. In doing so, these essays constitute an important defense of liberty and of the civility necessary to sustain liberty.

The beliefs that account for the contradictory character of liberalism are neither accidental nor capricious. They are grounded in nothing less than certain truths of the human condition. I wish to bring to the fore a few of the observations on the human condition and the nature of social life that are assumed by, and occasionally explicitly put forth in, these essays. These observations, on what Shils called "the fundamental proclivities of the human mind," are to be found throughout his work and they place his work in the best traditions of philosophical anthropology.[1] The bearing of these fundamental proclivities of the human mind on the contradictory character of liberalism and on civility is a recurrent theme of the following essays.

Time and again over a period of fifty-five years, Shils observed that the coherence and stability of any society depend at least in part on the existence of the image of that society; on the attachment of the society's members to that image; and, concomitantly, on the attachments that the members of that society form with one another. Such an image includes beliefs about the society, about the ultimate meaning of life, and about the order of the universe. Both the image and the body of beliefs that constitute the image are in large measure what Shils means in these essays by the terms "consensus" and "collective consciousness."

The fact that there are consensual beliefs about the ultimate meaning of life and of life lived within society suggests a number of things about the human mind. For example, it suggests that the mind of the

1. For example, see especially such essays as "Center and Periphery," "Primordial, Personal, Sacred, and Civil Ties," "Charisma," "The Sanctity of Life," and "Charisma, Order, and Status," all of which appear in Shils's *Center and Periphery: Essays in Macrosociology* (Chicago: University of Chicago Press, 1975); and his *Tradition* (Chicago: University of Chicago Press, 1981).

individual orients itself not only out of consideration to the pleasurable impulses of the body, or merely in response to or in anticipation of the actions of other individuals, but also to ideas. In other words, it suggests an imaginative capacity of the human mind to transcend the immediacy of the body and thereby to participate in, and to reflect upon, the meaning and order of human affairs. It further suggests the human need of what Shils called "cognitive order." By this term Shils meant that man is compelled to seek the meaning of his existence and to justify his actions and the order of society in accordance with that meaning. This is to say that the nature of man evidently requires the recognition of, and is in some measure expressed in, the order of his society.

There are, if you will, two bearers of life: the individual who makes choices and decisions, and the achievements—the language, traditions, laws—of the lives of many individuals of the larger collectivity. Determining the proper relation between these two bearers of life presents a great problem. This is true especially because human beings also exhibit the striking capacity—however limited or intermittent—to separate themselves from their participation in the consensus of the larger collectivity. Put succinctly, human beings have the capacity to say "no" to many sets of circumstances, including those circumstances that ought not to be denied. This ability to say "no" suggests that the human mind constitutionally exhibits not only a need for cognitive order but also a potential for independence. One can observe Shils's own acknowledgment of this truth of the human condition in his reference to one of his favorite quotations from Max Weber about the "magic of freedom" being "one of the most primordial dispositions of the human heart."[2]

Perhaps it is the uneasy combination of man's disposition to independence and his inexorable search for and participation in order that lies

---

2. See footnote 2 to the essay "Max Weber and the World Since 1920," reprinted herein.

at the basis of another truth of the human condition recognized by Shils, namely, man's ambivalent relation to authority; that is, man's propensity to be both awestruck by authority and yet resentful of it. The economist Frank Knight nicely captured this contradictory tendency of human nature when he observed that "man seeks to be inherently both a law-maker and a law-breaker."[3] Liberalism openly acknowledges this contradictory tendency of man.

Liberalism in its more classic sense, what Shils in "The Antinomies of Liberalism" calls the tradition of autonomist liberalism, acknowledges the openness of the human mind. Liberalism also acknowledges the freedom of the individual to live in accordance with his or her own beliefs, and it acknowledges the incommensurable plurality of ends that man pursues. Liberal democracy did not create this plurality. Rather, liberal democracy is an order of human affairs that is most prominent in the history of mankind in permitting the expression and the pursuit of different and at times conflicting ends. Liberal democracy affirms the legitimacy of this differentiation of ideals and the accompanying conflict of interests in human affairs. As Shils observed, these acknowledgments allow for the potential disaggregation of society itself. Even so, this potential disaggregation is the price that liberalism pays for the prominence it accords to liberty. Thus, there is an overt antinomy inherent in liberal democracy between the prominence accorded to the freedom of the individual and the consensual order that is necessary for freedom.

However, it would woefully misrepresent the relation between the freedom of the individual and the consensual order of society to conclude that it is merely a conflict-ridden dichotomy. The human mind's capacity for detachment is not only a natural prerequisite for individual freedom, it also is a precondition for that imaginative ability of the

3. Frank Knight, "Science, Philosophy, and Social Procedure," in *Freedom and Reform* (Indianapolis, Ind.: Liberty Fund, 1982), 253–54.

mind that makes possible a consensual order. The mind's very capacity for detachment therefore allows for the possibility of dispassionate analysis and rational conversation. Analysis and conversation allow, in turn, for the recognition of the common good along with individual self-interest. This is the capacity that Adam Smith recognized in *The Theory of Moral Sentiments* in his discussion of the "impartial spectator" and that Shils recognized as the capacity for disinterestedness. It is in the cultivated exercise of dispassionate analysis and rational conversation in pursuit of the common good that the virtue of the citizen is to be found. This virtue is in part what Shils meant by *civility,* the developed skill to be free. This is a skill that does not deny but artfully adjudicates between the consequences arising from the openness of the human mind, the pluralism in human affairs, and the meaning of life.

The violence against human nature perpetrated by ideology in all its various manifestations is in its denial of the plurality of ends that man pursues.[4] In the twentieth century, three of the more significant statements recognizing this plurality of orientations in human affairs are Max Weber's "Religious Rejections of the World and Their Directions" (1915), Michael Oakeshott's "The Voice of Poetry in the Conversation of Mankind" (1959), and Edward Shils's "Primordial, Personal, Sacred, and Civil Ties" (1957). In opposition to the totalitarian temptation of ideology stands liberalism's acknowledgment of a plurality of ends. Because this acknowledgment contains the potential for conflict, it is important that the virtue of a citizen—of civility—be cultivated in a manner that confines this potential.

Edward Shils is known to the world as a sociologist. But such a description requires an immediate clarification, especially at a time when sociology has come to mean for many people the pursuit of either what is not worth knowing or what already is known, and a pursuit

4. See "Ideology and Civility," reprinted herein.

that often is in the service of a technocratic manipulation of society. This was never Shils's understanding of the tasks of sociology. Rather, he understood the calling of sociology to exist in its contribution toward the self-understanding of society, and not in sociology's potential for direct, manipulated social improvement.[5] He argued that the best that sociology can offer is the cultivation of the dispassionate pursuit of truth through training in circumspection and imagination. Shils was a sociologist who understood sociology to be necessarily humanistic because, at its best, sociology attempts to comprehend whatever man does in categories that acknowledge man's humanity.

In this regard Shils described sociological analysis as "a variant in a contemporary idiom of the great efforts of the human mind to render judgment on man's vicissitudes on earth."[6] These of his essays on the nature of liberalism, its past, and its prospects for the future have for their foundation Shils's observations on man's vicissitudes on earth and the fundamental proclivities of the human mind: its need for order, its disposition to independence, and its plurality of orientations. These contradictory proclivities of the mind are at the basis of both the antinomy of liberalism and the ability of liberalism to ameliorate that antinomy, namely, civility.

STEVEN GROSBY

5. See "The Calling of Sociology," in Edward Shils, *The Calling of Sociology and Other Essays on the Pursuit of Learning* (Chicago: University of Chicago Press, 1980), 3–92.
6. Ibid., 32.

Editor's Note

§

FOR THE MOST PART, these essays of Edward Shils are reprinted as they originally appeared. Because of the autobiographical nature of the opening essay, "Observations on Some Tribulations of Civility," it was thought reasonable to ask Edward Shils to make a few additions to its previously published version. He made these few additions in the autumn of 1992. Two of the essays, "Civility and Civil Society: Good Manners Between Persons and Concern for the Common Good in Public Affairs" and "The Virtue of Civility," appear here for the first time in their original, longer versions.

In the preparation of these selections for publication, efforts were made to correct grammatical flaws and inconsistencies within the previously published individual essays. In particular, British spellings have been Americanized. Finally, where appropriate, a few footnotes have been added in the hope of clarifying Shils's references.

Acknowledgments

§

I WISH TO ACKNOWLEDGE the assistance of the John M. Olin Foundation, whose financial support allowed me to fulfill in a timely fashion my obligations as editor of this volume of Edward Shils's essays. I wish also to acknowledge three people whose efforts made this volume possible: Stuart D. Warner, of Roosevelt University; Charles H. Hamilton, director of the J. M. Kaplan Fund; and the late Elie Kedourie. Shortly before he died, Elie Kedourie reviewed with approval the proposal for this collection of essays. Many of us deeply feel the loss of Elie Kedourie, who was an unflinching defender of liberty and civility.

The Virtue of Civility

Observations on Some
Tribulations of Civility

❧

THE INSTITUTIONAL ARRANGEMENTS required for the freedom of expression of beliefs and the representation of interests and ideals—both of which can be divisive—can function effectively in society if those who use them for their own particularistic ends are at the same time restrained by an admixture of civility. Public liberties are conditions of the proposition, confrontation and persuasion of contending beliefs, of their cultivation in autonomous corporate bodies and of their presentation to public authorities. Representative institutions are the arrangements through which contending beliefs and interests are brought forward, considered and taken into account in the making of laws governing the territorially bounded society. The institutions in which beliefs and desires or interests are proposed and confronted in argument and the institutions in which beliefs and interests are taken into account and digested discriminatingly into law cannot work acceptably without some constituent civility and consensus of the contending parties. If the contending parties are vehemently irreconcilable and if effectively contending beliefs and interests are very widely disparate, one or another of the groups will resist physically or seek to impose its will by coercion and actual violence on the other. The representative institutions cannot, moreover, work effectively if they have too many tasks to master and if the different contending

Previously published in a slightly different form in *Government and Opposition* 15, no. 3/4 (1980): 528–45. Reprinted by permission.

parties within them are irreconcilable to the point where they deny the legitimacy of the institutions themselves, of the procedures for arriving at decisions, and the decisions themselves, should those decisions be uncongenial to their own beliefs and interests.

Civility is a belief which affirms the possibility of the common good; it is a belief in the community of contending parties within a morally valid unity of society. It is a belief in the validity or legitimacy of the governmental institutions which lay down rules and resolve conflicts. Civility is a virtue expressed in action on behalf of the whole society, on behalf of the good of all the members of the society to which public liberties and representative institutions are integral. Civility is an attitude in individuals which recommends that consensus about the maintenance of the order of society should exist alongside the conflicts of interests and ideals. It restrains the exercise of power by the powerful and restrains obstruction and violence by those who do not have power but who wish to have it. Civility is on the side of authority and on the side of those over whom authority would rule.

The argument that civility is necessary in any society which grows beyond the lineage as an adequate principle of social organization does not imply an expectation that it can ever be found in all the members of a society. It does require enough civility in enough persons in positions of power and prestige to restrain the conflicts arising from incompatible interests and widely diverging ideals. Civility is a virtue because it permits a variety of substantive interests and ideals or virtues to be cultivated and because it attempts to keep a balance among the parties to the conflicts by an example and an insistence on self-restraint. It is a restraint on the passions with which interests and ideals are pursued.

In a variety of ways, many of the tendencies which have become prominent since 1945 are injurious to civility. The main tendencies of belief and action about society of this period in Western countries are collectivistic liberalism, emancipationism, anti-patriotism, egalitarianism, populism, scientism and ecclesiastical abdication. Taken together they form a complex which I call progressivism. They are statements of what the members of society believe about authority in their society, about what it should be, and about the criteria by which to assess institutions of authority and in accordance with which these should be modified. These progressivistic beliefs are not universally shared in any one of these countries but they are very prominent on the public scene and they are very influential the nearer they come to the intellectual and political centers of society. All of these beliefs are in various ways very critical of and hostile to authority. Some, like emancipationism, will tolerate no authority over the expression of desires, sentiments and impulses which are directly injurious to it. Collectivistic liberalism is a menace to civility because it burdens government with unfulfillable tasks and thus brings its authority into discredit.

Towards the latter part of the first decade of our period, there set in an abatement of the attractiveness of Marxist ideology and no other ideology emerged to take up the slack created by its recession. But during the same decade, in a diluted or attenuated form, the rudiments of Marxism inherited from the people's front of the 1930s entered into collectivistic liberalism which ever since the revolution of October 1917 had shown an opening on that side. Disillusioned or intimidated fellow-travellers became supportive of collectivistic liberalism as the best they could hope for.

Until the end of the 1950s, ideological zeal was in a state of despondency, collectivistic liberalism followed the rule of "piecemeal social engineering," emancipationism was still moderate and content with privacy. The knowledge of the atrocities of the Stalinist regime had reached many intellectuals by the early 1950s, although the Soviet Union still had many intellectual supporters in all Western countries who denied those atrocities, explained them away or justified them. There were few exponents of a Marxism detached from Stalinism. The Frankfurt School was still in process of resettling the simplified Utopian Marxism which it masked under the name of "critical philosophy." It was the early springtime of "polycentric Communism." Socialist parties had reconciled themselves to a controlled capitalism. Conservative parties accepted the general rightfulness of most of the reforms which had been instituted in the recent past; in any case they accepted most of the achievements of social democracy and collectivistic liberalism as part of the tradition which they would support. Fascist ideologists and ruffians were discredited and discouraged.

The Western governments were committing themselves to the specific articles of the program of collectivistic liberalism, to policies of full employment, economic growth, unemployment insurance, old age pensions, etc., and in varying degrees these policies appeared not to be unsuccessful. In all countries the proportion of young persons over the age of 17 attending advanced secondary and higher educational institutions was increasing and there were corresponding increases in educational expenditures. McCarthyism had been brought down in the United States. The difficulties of British society did not yet appear to be as endemic as they have later shown themselves to be. Patriotic pride in British accomplishment in the Second World War was still very high. British intellectuals were enjoying the moral pleasure of reconciliation with their country and of the emancipation of the colonies; a sensible matter-of-fact social democracy moved forward, with the assent of the conservatives. In France in the middle of the 1950s the war in Indo-China was ending and the war in Algeria had not yet come to torment the country. The "Third World," then only in the process of formation, was still fairly quiet; the United Nations had not yet been made into its forum. The spirit of Bandung still had relatively few followers; "neutralism" was biased towards the Soviet Union but it was still not as virulently hostile to the Western countries as it later became. The developments in the "Third World" had not yet become ingredients in the bitter partisanship which later became so widespread in Western countries.

6

This was the setting of the brief "end of ideology." There was certainly an abatement of ideological fervor at this time. Raymond Aron and I were right when, in 1955, we discerned this abatement and affirmed it.[1] Neither of us said that ideological possession had disappeared forever from human history or even that it had disappeared for the rest of our century. We both saw that it was an inexpungible potentiality which is always present in society. What we did say was that the fervent self-confidence of its devotees had abated. We welcomed the diminution which had occurred and recommended that those who espoused any ideology should cease to do so. (This gave rise to a clamorous and confused attack by many would-be ideologists and their *bien-pensant* supporters who thought that we were digging away the ground from under their feet. After all, what could be more distasteful to them than to be told that they were participants in a losing cause, and one which was far from noble. The acrimony of their response formed what is now retrospectively called "the debate about the end of ideology.")

The disclosure of Khrushchev's speech of February 1956 at the 22nd Congress of the Communist Party of the Soviet Union was a further wound to the wavering forces of radical ideology. The "Polish October" and the uprising in Budapest which was followed by the armed Soviet invasion of Hungary immediately thereafter were severely disturbing experiences for many Communist intellectuals. The attachment of the ideologists to their idol was loosened, although not broken.

The fiasco of the attempted Anglo-French invasion of Egypt was a salvationary stroke for the disordered battalions of the Marxist ideologists. It compensated them for their losses from the now admitted misdeeds of the Soviet Union. While this collocation of events freed them from their subservience to the Soviet Union, the Anglo-French military action against Egypt vindicated their animosity against their

---

1. Edward Shils, "The End of Ideology?" *Encounter* 5 (November 1955): 52–62; Raymond Aron, *L' Opium des Intellectuals* (Paris: Calman Levy, 1955), specifically the concluding chapter, "La Fin des idéologies?" *(ed.)*.

own societies, the iniquity and weakness of which gave them courage to embark on a new course of radicalism. The "new Left" was the result.

The upshot of this devious course of ideology is the present condition in which there is ideological passion without a single authoritative ideology. The Marxism of the new Left was a very heterogeneous thing, having acquired infusions from psychoanalysis of an extremely emancipationist sort and from sociology; in addition, there was much disagreement, as various types of older Marxism, buried for years by Stalinist-Leninism, were exhumed. Having for the most part separated itself from the industrial working class, the new Left took refuge in the ivory tower of the university; this gave it a very effective way in which to carry on its "long march." The intellectual defenselessness of many students makes them a very easy field to sow; it is a self-expanding process since those already appointed help to appoint others like themselves.

The reborn ideology is not like the one which "ended" in the 1950s. Its intellectual content is widely and vaguely dispersed around a hollow core of negation of existing authority. The rudiments of an ideology are there in the shambles of Communist Marxism and the later accretions of hitherto unorthodox Marxism and emancipationism. Writers like Marcuse and Habermas have attempted to reconstruct this new ideological orientation but their achievements are more straws in the wind than solid and effective constructions. Hatred for the existing order of society and a conviction that reforms are hypocritical, impossible, trivial and undesirable are almost all that remains of the old ideology. Incivility of an extreme sort is coupled with exploitation of the potentialities afforded by public liberties and affluence—the new Left does not have to rob banks since its supporters often have sufficient wealth to support their publications and other activities. Unlike the ideological radicals prior to the invention of the people's front and the numerous institutions of fellow-travelling, the uncivil new Left addresses itself to and to some extent reaches a much wider audience.

Terrorism by small bands and a sympathetic attitude towards terrorism in larger circles have had a complex effect. It has shown governments to be in very difficult straits when they wish to observe legal norms in pursuing terrorists and it lays them open to objurgation if they disregard legal restraints in their efforts to repress terrorism. In either case, the efficacy and hence legitimacy of governments are placed in question by terrorism and the effort to deal with it—and all this before an audience as wide as the civilized world.

The reduction of the ascendancy of authority and the imposition of restraints on it were originally intended, by the spokesmen for the program of the enlightenment which supplied the basis of traditional liberalism, to elevate the subject into a citizen. This meant freeing the subject from the obligation of unquestioning obedience and of a self-derogatory deference to his betters. At the same time educational reformers and poets sought to enliven sensibility, to open the mind to the experiences and pleasures of the senses and to make the human being into a personality, into a "true individuality." In principle, individuality and the civil rights of the individual *vis-à-vis* authority seemed to go hand in hand. The belief in the realization of individuality through the enrichment of experience was in fact held in check except among educational reformers whose plans were effective only within very narrow limits; the emancipationist outlook and practice were absorbed much more in literary and artistic bohemias, but these were segregated from the rest of society.

In the period since the end of the Second World War, the emancipation program has gained in force and in following, consequent on the successes of collectivistic liberalism and social democracy in the curbing of private authority. Under the protection of collectivistic liberalism and social democracy, the proponents and practitioners of emancipationism left the reserve of privacy and came forward into the public scene. There they have carried on a steady and effective campaign on behalf of the derogation of restraints on sexual conduct and on the pattern of moral standards which accompanied sexual restraint. A limitless ethical relativism, and the location of the vital center of existence within the experiencing ego have further enfeebled the legitimacy of authority. This enfeeblement of the legitimacy of authority has not diminished demands on government for service, provision and regulation. Emancipationism extends the paradox of collectivistic liberalism which would turn authority entirely into an instrument without inherent legitimacy while at the same time demanding more and more benefits from the exercise of authority. Egoism is not conducive to civility; the dissolution of society into an aggregation of demanding individualities is not conducive to civility.

Patriotism was in the first line of fire of collectivistic liberalism and social democracy, at least in theory. It had already been ridiculed for its irrationality and for the heavy expenditure of life and fortune which its military expression consumed. The establishment of an association between patriotism and private business enterprise was one of the achievements of socialist theory in the latter part of the nineteenth and the early twentieth centuries and collectivistic liberalism absorbed much of this belief—insofar as it did not itself promulgate it.

Patriotism in the sense of attachment to national territory and to the national society became tarred with the brush of imperialism, militarism, wasteful expenditures on armed forces and armaments and with all the vices of ideological nationalism. With all the distaste of intellectuals for patriotism, it has not been expunged from Western societies in recent years. It has had few articulate spokesmen; the support which it offered to civility in many subtle ways has been reduced.

There was always a trace of egalitarianism in traditional liberalism. It aimed to dim the glory of earthly majesty and the ascendancy of prelates. It put the private owners of property to the test of the rationality of the investment of their resources. It extended the franchise. Traditional liberalism was never wholly consistent; it intended to leave intact a considerable degree of inequality in the distribution of property and income and it intended to maintain the basic framework of authority through representative institutions and the rule of law.

It never went as far as the egalitarianism which is now—not by any means consistently—espoused by collectivistic liberalism and social democracy. Collectivistic liberalism began by contending for raising the floor; it now seeks to bring down the roof of society. "Anti-elitism" has become its battle-cry; "anti-elitism" is the touchstone of many of its policies and it does not even leave its leadership free of the charge of "elitism." A zealous egalitarianism which will tolerate no criticism is at the same time committed to an ethical relativism which denies the legitimacy of moral rules, of public authority and of a commensurate relationship between achievement and reward. It denies such rules and arrangements because they raise some human beings higher than others.

There is an easy step between this type of substantive egalitarianism and populism. Populism used to be a laudation of the peasantry, then it was transformed under the auspices of Marxism into a laudation of the working classes. In the United States it became a praise of the *Lumpenproletariat.* But in other Western countries where the *Lumpenproletariat* has not been large enough to gain the sympathy and to dominate the imagination of radicals and collectivistic liberals, to say nothing of social democrats, participatory democracy has appeared. It is a variant of plebiscitary democracy.

In principle, participatory democracy could be an extension to wider circles of the practice of civility. Nevertheless, it is at least as often a program for the diminution of the legitimacy of institutional and governmental authority. It is invoked to justify "extra-parliamentary opposition," "citizen-initiatives," etc. What it is, in fact, very often, is the propaganda of members of peripheral elites seeking to dominate the center. It is carried on in a fiercely polemical manner, refusing to admit the legitimacy of its adversaries and it is thus deeply inimical to civility.

Scientism, in its latter-day forms, is another denial of civility. Again, there is nothing inherent in the scientific knowledge of the physical

11

world which is incompatible with civility. Decisions in the making of policies which entail scientific technology can certainly be made in accordance with the criteria of civility. Nonetheless, in a number of forms, scientism is injurious to civility. For one thing, its proponents would remove responsibility from politicians and transfer it to scientific technologists. It also fosters the illusion that the decisions which have to be made by persons in positions of authority can be made entirely on the basis of the results of scientific research. The practical judgment of experienced politicians is placed in a position of inferiority to allegedly scientific knowledge.

The rise of a scientistic outlook has paradoxically weakened the legitimacy of secular political authority although it certainly has not contributed to the weakening of the powers of government. It has weakened the legitimacy of secular authority by reducing the standing of the clergy and by diminishing the self-confidence of the clergy. In response to their weakened religious faith, they have become critical of authority. They criticize both ecclesiastical and secular authority and deny their legitimacy on the same grounds that secular collectivistic liberalism, social democracy and radicalism criticize them.

I do not wish to portray the Western societies of the past third of a century as having fallen from grace into perdition. That is not the case. There were many imperfections before our period began and some of the vices of our period have arisen from efforts to repair those imperfections. And many of our present vices are such because they are immoderate extensions of genuine virtues.

Nevertheless, I think that the unreasoned and rancorous hostility towards authority in one's own society is a serious flaw in our present moral constitution and it is storing up further trouble for the future. No society can exist without a belief in the legitimacy of indispensable authority within the framework of that consensus. Coercion is the only alternative to the war of each against all if this moral consensus is lacking. A society which possesses it can be an effective pluralistic and individualistic society. A society which is pluralistic and individualistic but which lacks that moral consensus will descend into the state of nature and will emerge from it only through coercion legitimated by ideology.

On a number of occasions over the past thirty-five years, I wrote that modern Western societies since the French and American revolutions had begun to germinate the rudiments of civility in contrast with their predecessor-societies, which had been dominated by dynastic interests, class, lineage, and property interests, ecclesiastical interests, and local attachments.[2] The new type of society, predominantly liberal and increasingly democratic in Western Europe and North America, seemed to veer towards the production of a stratum of persons who "spoke for the whole" and who acted on behalf of that ideal.

The idea of disinterested service to and care for the whole of society, which had been adumbrated in the past by political philosophers and historians, seemed to have taken a firmer, deeper and thicker root in the liberal nineteenth century, above all in Great Britain and to some extent in France, the United States, the Low Countries and Scandinavia. It appeared marginally in Italy and Spain, and, even more peripherally, it made a feeble but estimable appearance in Tsarist Russia.

Civility seemed in the nineteenth century to have "caught on" in the rhetoric of publicists and politicians. It seemed even to have made an impression on the conduct of citizens and politicians, although it never dominated or gained exclusiveness in any country. It did however become established as an actual and indispensable ingredient of public life; the societies of the West could not have worked as well as they did without that ingredient.

It was too much to hope that civility would become the sole or even the dominant feature of public life. Class and regional interests, occupational interests, ecclesiastical interests and sheer individual self-interest and familial interests were too strong. Nevertheless, it was

2. See, for example, Shils's essays "Center and Periphery," "The Integration of Society," and "Charisma, Order, and Status," which are included in *Center and Periphery: Essays in Macrosociology (ed.)*.

finding a substantial embodiment in the thought and action of a modest number of politicians and publicists in more civilized countries, and it was also finding a more attenuated existence in the outlook and public conduct of a much larger number of ordinary citizens in the working and middle classes. The self-interestedness of individuals and families, of regions and classes, the particularism of religious communities and ethnic groups and the partisanship of doctrinaire fanatics were to some extent attenuated and to some extent held in check by the presence and activities of the civil component of the society. They were inhibited in expression and in action by the presence of civility more than they might otherwise have been; their influence was limited by the contrary influence of civility. The existence of civility made the pluralistic societies of the liberal democratic age practicable. It prevented them from degenerating into a "war of each against all."

Civility and ideological radicalism are irreconcilable. Ideological radicalism is at war with the rest of society, seeking its support at the periphery or among those who have deliberately or by mischance gone from the center to the periphery. The very notion of a common interest, of a concern for society as a whole, is abhorrent to ideological radicalism. In contrast, civility is, in principle, compatible with collectivistic liberalism and democratic socialism although it has not worked that way. Populism which extols the virtues of one part of the society against all others is about as inimical to civility as is ideological radicalism. Populism is susceptible to reinterpretation in an ideological direction but even when it is not, its preference for demonstrative and plebiscitary political procedures is at odds with representative institutions. Civility has suffered from all of these. It has not been flatly and explicitly rejected. It has in fact become sufficiently established for its rivals to contend that they are indeed meeting its standard. The Communists justified the situation in the societies over which they ruled tyrannically and ineptly as a transition to a fuller realization of a society in which "the interest of each is the interest of all." Flattering though it might have been to the proponents of civility for Communists and collectivistic liberals and radicals to claim that they act on behalf of the ends of civility, the truth is otherwise.

Indeed the Communists and other ideological radicals and emancipationists have endangered what little there has been of civility. They endanger it when they agitate to change society "totally," so as to annul the ideals and interests of all the sections except the one which they wish to promote above all others. They endanger it when they claim that the traditional equilibrium of society as it has existed should be brought to an end. They endanger it above all when they assert that there is an unbridgeable gap between themselves and their adversaries. They endanger it when they conduct their politics without regard to the representative institutions which bring the different parts of society together. Civility is an outlook which attempts to do justice to all the interests—which involves also holding them in check—and thus maintaining the traditional pattern of plurality within a common society which is of intrinsic value.

Although the abdication of the Communist regimes of Central and Eastern Europe has discredited and discouraged adherents of the Communist parties in the West, it has not by any means had such devastating effects on ideological radicalism or collectivistic liberalism. The devotees of such ideals had for some years been keeping themselves at a distance from the Soviet Union and the "peoples democracies"—the movement away from support for the Soviet Union began in 1956 and continued following the publication of *The Gulag Archipelago* and the banishment of Sakharov; their main article of faith was their hatred of their own societies and that has not diminished. As a matter of fact, hostility to their own societies has been strengthened by the efflorescence of emancipationism. Emancipationism, which has its own tradition in anarchism and bohemianism, has received much support from collectivistic liberalism. The program of sexual emancipation, i.e., the prizing of sexual experience as the highest good, with heterosexuality and the traditional family of husband, wife and children as the obstacles to be eliminated, has been joined by the hostility to persons of European

15

ancestry ("whites") and hatred of capitalism. Civil society is of no value to the emancipationists; it is no more than the opportunity to work against the liberal democratic order of society. Marxism and animosity against the great works of Western civilization are both important components of the emancipationist coalition. Collectivistic liberalism, which for many decades took the Soviet Union under its protective wings, now extends its benevolence to emancipationism. Emancipationism, taking advantage of this support, has developed a powerful momentum of its own.

The intensification of emancipationism, which is disregardful of the pattern of society and which is concerned above all with the gratifications of individual desire, is injurious to civility. An interpretation of collectivistic liberalism which turns it into a governmentally imposed egalitarianism and which attempts to promote certain strata at the expense of traditional liberal principles, thereby deforming the traditions of society and the patterns they maintain, also diminishes the sphere of civility.

Tocqueville said more than a century and a half ago that the presence of the black race on American soil was the "most formidable evil threatening the future of the United States." The chapter devoted by Tocqueville to the future of the black race is one of the most somber things written about the United States over its whole history; the fact that it was written by a well-wisher makes it all the more to be taken seriously.

In some important respects, Tocqueville has been proved wrong. The weakening of animus of white Americans against Negroes over the past half century is one of the most heartening achievements of American society. The "civil rights movement" has been a great success partly in consequence of the courage and dignity of many blacks, famous and obscure, and partly because large parts of American society decided that the situation hitherto obtaining was wrong and had to be righted. But alongside this success is the very tangible presence of the young black *Lumpenproletariat*. The combination of the restless

idleness of having no steady occupation, their own propensity to violence and criminality, and the protection given them by the white
academics, publicists and black civil leaders sustains a great gap in the
civility of the United States.

Civility is more than liberalism; it is not just humanitarian concern
for the poor and the outcasts of society; it is greater than the desire
for tidiness and honesty in politics and public administration. Civility
is not the same as democracy. It is much more than nationalism, which
has usually been more concerned about the position of one's own
country in competition with other countries than it has been about
the internal pattern of that country. Civility is nevertheless a function
of a sense of membership in a national society coterminous with the
boundaries of the state. The society which is the object of civility is a
national society; the state within which it operates is a national state.
Nationality and civility seemed at one time to grow apace; they were
not identical but they were intimately intertwined because civility was
focused on the national society. When nationality becomes nationalistic, it usually has become uncivil as well; the demand for complete
national solidarity has often involved uncivil suppression.

These are the deeper tendencies which have helped to bring the
world of societies to its present condition. They did not produce nuclear
weapons; they did not directly make our societies dependent on oil as
their chief form of fuel for the energy needed for industrial production
and transportation. Scientific and technological imagination were the
instigators of the discoveries of nuclear physics and the invention of
the internal combustion engine. Nevertheless, they have contributed
to the shaping of the most recent situation of Western societies.

Collectivistic liberalism itself is a product of humanitarianism, bits
of traditional liberalism, such as the idea of progress and public liberty,
freedom of association, the right of public dissent, and a dislike of
private business enterprise, a dislike which is antithetical to traditional
liberalism. Collectivistic liberalism has always had an opening towards
democratic socialism and in Great Britain these two traditions have

become nearly indistinguishable. As social democratic parties have become less committed to Marxism, they have moved in the direction of collectivistic liberalism. This was not necessarily damaging to civility, even though it has had other disadvantageous effects.

There has also been a disposition in collectivistic liberalism towards sympathy with ideological radicalism. This sympathy first was manifested in the attitude of Western intellectuals and socialists towards the Bolshevik Revolution of 1917 and the Soviet Union. A residue of this sympathy still exists. When the agitating students took up a radical line, the sympathy of the collectivistic liberals went out to them. The attitude of *Die Zeit* and *Le Monde* towards the students who were disrupting the universities in Germany and France was a characteristic expression of this sympathy. The benefits which radicals have gained from this sympathy may be seen in the long hesitation of the Labour Party leadership in Great Britain to take action against the Trotskyists in the constituency parties, despite the report of the national agent of the party, and in the success of the campaign in the United States by collectivistic liberals inside the government and outside it on behalf of radicals against the Federal Bureau of Investigation and the Central Intelligence Agency. The weak Communist Parties of the German Federal Republic and the United States have also attempted to rehabilitate themselves by clinging to the coat-tails of the new Left and to gain thereby the protection afforded by collectivistic liberalism. Fortunately, these Communist Parties are not a danger to the constitutional order in these countries.

Collectivistic liberalism has also been drawn into an alliance with emancipationism; this is evident in the legislation regarding pornography, homosexuality and abortions and the campaign to change the legal status of the use of marijuana. In the United States, the First Amendment to the Constitution, which guarantees freedom of speech and prohibits the establishment of a state church, has been extended to afford protection to subversion, obscenity and pornography. The unbounded right of abortion is justified by the invocation of the right of privacy. Some of the particular objectives of the emancipationists taken singly are quite compatible with traditional liberalism and with civility. As a bundle of demands and as a set of procedures for bringing about their objectives, carried on through very active and far-flung movements, emancipationism is uncongenial to civility.

The sphere of representative institutions has been markedly constricted by the increased power of the executive bureaucracy and the courts on the one side, and by the pressure of plebiscitary opinion on the other. It is not that the legislature is blameless in this respect. Bureaucracy does not act entirely without regard to the legislation which is enacted. But by the enactment of such a volume of collectivistic legislation, bureaucracy is forced to have more power. It is not an opportunity which is rejected. Public opinion polls have increased the direct influence of the electorate over the elected representative; the mandate has gained at the expense of the responsibility of an elected representative to act in accordance with his own considered judgment within the framework of loyalty to his party and to the country as a whole. "Extra-parliamentary" opposition and "citizen-initiatives," regarding, for example, the production of nuclear energy, have infringed on the efficacy of representative institutions. Of course, local and sectional interests continue to be considered but legislators who consider only these abdicate the civility necessary for a decent society; this was so in the past and it is still so. Pressure groups have always been a feature of democratic societies; they have however increased in their range and intensity of activity in the most recent period. Most of them drive in the direction of more governmental activity while at the same time giving expression to a distrust of representative institutions and of governmental authority.

The one belief which has become central both in collectivistic liberalism and radicalism is that which attributes a residual and inexpungible virtue to communistic governments. Stephen Decatur's reference to "our country right or wrong" has often been derided by progressivistic critics as a characteristic expression of the irrationality of patriotism; they have however accepted it as valid in their attitude towards the Soviet Union. As a result, the Soviet Union retained in wide intellectual, publicistic, and political circles an overtone of moral superiority— despite its recognized misdeeds. Thus, for example, in the discussion about *détente,* many Western publicists who were not ideological suggested that critics of the Soviet Union wished to revive the "cold war," while they averted their eyes from the conduct by the Soviet Union of the same policies which it carried on during the "cold war." The "cold war" became in their eyes a unilateral war. In the name of "proletarian internationalism," the Soviet Union continued, not without local, sometimes successful, resistance, to extend its influence in Africa, Asia and Latin America, including the Caribbean Islands. It extended its influence among the "non-aligned" bloc, which, despite the recalcitrance of some of its members, continued to be markedly biased towards the Soviet Union and against the West. The discussion of Salt II in the United States drew on this disposition to attribute good intentions to the Soviet Union and malignant intentions or simple-minded prejudice to those who oppose the treaty. The impotence of the treaty as a means of restraining Soviet armament is acknowledged; nevertheless its ratification has been demanded in order to demonstrate to the Soviet Union the good faith of the United States; the good faith of the Soviet Union was never in question. The common reluctance in a number of West European countries to support the North Atlantic Treaty Alliance was a consequence of distrust of their own government on the part of intellectuals and of the diminished patriotism of the most articulate and more forceful sectors of society; so were the demands for more welfare services at the cost of expenditures on the armed forces and the wide-spread tendency to regard arguments for stronger defense as having aggressive intentions against a Soviet Union which self-evidently had no such aggressive intentions.

This is how I see the world as it has developed since the end of the Second World War. Have these developments caused me to change my ideas about the society and its right order? Of course, my views have developed in response to these developments. My views seem to have moved more slowly than the times but they too have moved. They have not moved with the times but rather against them.

This has not been to my taste. I do not like to be against my fellow-countrymen or against the civilization to which I owe my existence. I have never wanted to be a Cassandra—it is much too easy to make dark prophecies—but I fear that I have more of a sombre outlook now than I had at the end of the Second World War. Such changes as have occurred in my picture of society and societies have occurred gradually so that I have not been aware of any rapid or drastic change in my outlook.

Yet when I think back over my writings of the beginning of this period, I am mortified by what appears to me now as callowness and the will to believe. I must acknowledge that for at least five years after the end of the Second World War, I thought that knowledge gained through the methods and theories of the social sciences might develop sufficiently so that it would contribute to the wisdom of the public and the governments of Western societies. I was not very sanguine, as an atrociously printed paper in *Philosophy of Science*, written in about 1948, would show, but I was not entirely unsympathetic with the idea, nor was I unreservedly pessimistic.[3]

To take another example, I thought—not, it is true, with much confidence—that it might be possible to establish a system of international control to limit and even abolish the production of nuclear weapons. I did not believe this very long, but even for that short time I should have known better. I avoided the naïve and ingenious optimism of my friend Leo Szilard and the naïve scientism of Eugene Rabinowitch. I did not foresee that Jacob Viner's prediction of and recommendations for a "balance of nuclear terror" were more correct than any of the other responses to the existence of nuclear weapons and would indeed

---

3. "Social Science and Social Policy," *Philosophy of Science* 16 (July 1949): 219–42 (*ed.*).

help to keep the peace and to avoid war better than the scheme for the international control of nuclear weapons which I put forward for a while in 1945 and which I then supported in the modified form of the Acheson-Lilienthal report. I thought then that it had little chance of acceptance by the Soviet Union but I thought nevertheless that I should argue its merits as if it did have some chance of acceptance and then successful realization.

Having read Waldemar Gurian's *Der Bolschewismus* and Bertrand Russell's *Theory and Practice of Communism* in about 1930 and Arthur Rosenberg's *Geschichte des Bolschewismus* in about 1933 and a great deal of the writings of Marx and Engels and especially the *Briefwechsel* in Riazanov's edition, I was well prepared to withstand the fellow-travelling deluge of the 1930s. (I should add that my brother worked as an engineer in the Soviet Union throughout the first half of the decade and I learned a lot about it from him. Incidentally I did not envisage, until after the end of the Second World War, that the numerous falsehoods spread by the Communist Parties through their fellow-travellers from 1935 to 1945 would be precipitated into such a laudatory image of the Soviet Union that it would become the touchstone of right conduct through much of the world.) I knew that the accounts spread in the West about the Soviet Union were false, that the Soviet Union was an appalling country and that it was ruled by harsh and unyielding men. I was aware of the hostile and irreconcilable attitude of the Soviet Union and I was not unaware of the inhibitions on our side. But thinking, in those five years at the end of the 1940s, that there was even a small chance that a scheme for the international control of nuclear weapons might be accepted and in view of the dangers of not having such a scheme, I espoused it. This attitude was characteristic of my way of thinking. I supported proposals which I thought were important and right even though I was skeptical about their chances of adoption. This intellectual ambivalence left much room and opportunity for my ideas to develop.

I anticipated by the end of the war that the emancipation of the colonies would occur but I did not anticipate that it would occur as rapidly as it did. I foresaw that when it did happen there would be difficulties of all sorts in store. Yet in what I wrote in the early 1960s about the new states of Asia and Africa on the basis of my studies in India and of considerable reading about it and a number of visits to Africa, I emphasized the potentialities for a better course, even though I was doubtful whether that course would be followed and I even thought that I knew the reasons why. In a discussion with Mrs. Elspeth Huxley in *Encounter* in about 1961 about the new states of Black Africa, I argued that these states might develop democratically and liberally although I knew that her pessimistic prediction was more likely to turn out to be right than my own.[4] I did not want to add a discouraging voice so I gave them the benefit of the doubt—which I had. The same was true when I drafted several chapters of the report of the National Education Commission of the government of India about the reform of the Indian universities. I put too good a face on the possibilities of improvement about which, with one half of my mind, I knew better.

I knew that there was a danger that the rulers of the Western European countries might become deficient in self-confidence to be followed later by the United States, and I said this in a lecture at the Royal Society of Medicine in 1947, but I did not permit the idea to become prominent in my mind and I did not follow out its implication. I foresaw the growth of collectivistic liberalism, with the early manifestations of which I was not entirely out of sympathy, but I did not foresee the speed and fullness of its triumph in public opinion or the extent to which it would become governmental policy. I did not predict that the Christian Churches would so hastily and eagerly abdicate their convictions and their authority even though, as early as 1947, I was aware of their faltering self-confidence. In general I thought that the

4. "The False Prospero: Observations on Mrs. Elspeth Huxley," *Encounter* 17 (July 1961): 82–87; "Further Observations on Mrs. Huxley," *Encounter* 17 (October 1961): 44–49 *(ed.)*.

tenacity of the traditions of European and American societies was sufficiently great so that changes would occur more slowly than they have in fact occurred and that they would not occur to the extent that they did. I had an intellectual premonition that these things might happen but I did not bring it forward in my mind until after the shades of night began to fall.

Ideology and Civility

§

I

AN IDEOLOGICAL OUTLOOK encircled and invaded public life in the Western countries during the nineteenth century, and in the twentieth century it threatened to achieve universal dominion. The intellectual classes which concerned themselves with politics were particularly affected. The intensity of the attack has varied from country to country. It has been least severe in the United States and Great Britain; in France, Germany, Italy, and Russia, it possessed an overwhelming power. Wherever it became sufficiently strong, it paralyzed the free dialectic of intellectual life, introducing standards irrelevant to discovery and creation, and in politics it inhibited or broke the flexible consensus necessary for a free and spontaneous order. It appeared in a variety of manifestations, each alleging itself to be unique. Italian Fascism, German National Socialism, Russian Bolshevism, French and Italian Communism, the Action Française, the British Union of Fascists—and their fledgling American kinsman, "McCarthyism," which died in infancy—have all, however, been members of the same family. They have all sought to conduct politics on an ideological plane.

What are the articles of faith of ideological politics? First and above all, the assumption that politics should be conducted from the stand-

Previously published in a slightly different form in *Sewanee Review* 66 (July–September 1958): 450–80. This version of "Ideology and Civility" also appears in Edward Shils, *The Intellectuals and the Powers* (Chicago: University of Chicago Press, 1972) *(ed.)*. © 1972 by the University of Chicago. All rights reserved. Reprinted by permission.

point of a coherent, comprehensive set of beliefs which must override every other consideration. These beliefs attribute supreme significance to one group or class—the nation, the ethnic folk, the proletariat—and the leader and the party as the true representative of these residences of all virtue, and they correspondingly view as the seat and source of all evil a foreign power, an ethnic group like the Jews, or the bourgeois class. Ideological politics have not been merely the politics of a dualistic faith which confines itself to the political sphere. The centrality of this belief has required that it radiate into every sphere of life—that it replace religion, that it provide aesthetic criteria, that it rule over scientific research and philosophic thought, that it regulate sexual and family life.

It has been the belief of those who practice politics ideologically that they alone have the truth about the right ordering of life—of life as a whole, and not just of political life. From this has followed a deep distrust of the traditional institutions—family, church, economic organizations, and schools—and the institutional system through which politics have been conventionally carried on in modern society. Ideological politics have required, therefore, a distrust of politicians[1] and of

---

1. The hostile attitude toward politicians, toward the "parliamentary talking shop," with its unprincipled compromise of interests, and the petty quality of the personnel of civil politics are continuing themes of the ideologist. Hitler said that politicians were "people whose only real principle was unprincipledness, coupled with an insolent and pushing officiousness and shamelessly developed mendacity" (*Mein Kampf* [Munich, 1941], p. 72). "Parliament itself is given up to talk for the special purpose of fooling the 'common people' " (Lenin, "State and Revolution," in *Towards the Seizure of Power,* book 2, *Collected Works,* vol. 221 [New York, 1932], p. 186). At the other pole of intellectual sophistication, Edmund Wilson, during his own ideological phase, once wrote, "Our society has . . . produced in its specialized professional politicians one of the most obnoxious groups which has ever disgraced human history—a group that seems unique in having managed to be corrupt, uncultivated, and incompetent all at once" (*New Republic,* 14 January 1931, reprinted in *The Shores of Light* [London, 1952], p. 529). The antipolitical literature of the ideological intellectual is vast: Hilaire Belloc and G. K. Chesterton, *The Party System* (London, 1911), is representative.

the system of parties through which they work. Insofar as ideological politics have been carried on by organizations calling themselves political parties, it has only been because that term has become conventional for organizations actively concerned with politics. It has not signified that their proponents were ready to participate constitutionally in the political system. Extra-constitutionality has been inherent in their conceptions and aspirations, even when their procedures have seemed to lie within the constitution—and by constitution, we mean not just written constitution, laws, and judicial decisions, but the moral presuppositions of these. Ideological politics have taken up a platform outside the "system." In their agitation, ideological politicians have sought to withdraw the loyalty of the population from the "system" and to destroy it, replacing it by a new order. This new order would have none of the evils which make up the existing system; the new order would be fully infused with the ideological belief which alone can provide salvation.

Ideological politics are alienative politics. They are the politics of those who shun the central institutional system of the prevailing society. Ideological politicians feel no affinity with such institutions, and they participate in them for purposes very different from those who have preceded them in the conduct of these institutions.[2]

For the ideological politician, membership in a parliamentary body

---

2. Aneurin Bevan, who had within him, together with other gifts, a powerful ideological strain, wrote of the radical's entry into the House of Commons: "Here he is, a tribune of the people, coming to make his voice heard in the seats of power. . . . The first thing he should bear in mind is that these were not his ancestors. His ancestors had no part in the past, the accumulated dust of which now muffles his own footfalls. His forefathers were tending sheep or plowing the land, or serving the statesmen whose names he sees written on the walls around him, and whose portraits look down upon him in the long corridors. . . . In him, his people are here for the first time and the history he will make will not be merely an episode in the story he is now reading. It must be wholly different, as different as the social status he now brings with him" (*In Place of Fear* [New York, 1952], p. 6).

or the acceptance of office involves only an opportunity to overthrow and destroy the system rather than to work within it and improve it.[3]

Ideological politics are the politics of "friend-foe,"[4] "we-they," "who-whom."[5] Those who are not on the side of the ideological politician are, according to the ideologist, against him.

Thus, moral separatism arises from the sharp, stable, and unbridgeable dualism of ideological politics which makes the most radical and uncompromising distinction between good and evil, left and right, national and unnational, American and un-American. Admixtures are intolerable, and where they exist they are denied as unreal, misleading, or unstable.[6]

Ideological politics have been obsessed with totality. They have been obsessed with futurity. They have believed that sound politics require a doctrine which comprehends every event in the universe, not only in space but in time. To live from year to year and to keep afloat, to solve the problems of the year and of the decade are not enough for ideological politics. Ideological politicians must see their actions in the context of the totality of history. They must see themselves moving toward a culmination of history, either a new epoch, totally new in every important respect, or bringing to a glorious fulfillment a condition

3. See Leon Trotsky, *Whither England?* (New York, 1925), pp. 111–12: "We Communists are by no means disposed to advise the . . . proletariat to turn its back on Parliament. . . . The question . . . is not whether it is worthwhile to use the Parliamentary method at all, but . . . is it possible to use Parliament, created by Capitalism, in the interests of its own growth and preservation, as a lever for the overthrow of capitalism."

4. Carl Schmitt, *Der Begriff des Politischen* (Munich, Leipzig, 1932), pp. 14 ff.

5. Striking evidence of the separatism of ideological politics may be found in N. Leites, *The Study of Bolshevism* (Glencoe, Ill., 1953), pp. 291–309, 384–90, 430–42.

6. See Raymond Aron, *The Opium of the Intellectuals* (New York, 1957), chap. 1, "The Myth of the Left." The deep-rootedness of the mythology of left and right among intellectuals of the Marxist tradition, and its penetration even into allegedly scientific research in sociology and social psychology, are treated in my essay "Authoritarianism 'Left' and 'Right,' " in Richard Christie and Marie Jahoda, *Studies in the "Authoritarian Personality"* (Glencoe, Ill., 1954), pp. 24–49.

which has long been lost from human life. Whether totally without precedent or a renewal of the long lost, the ultimate stage will be sometimes unique in history.[7] Everything else is a waiting and a preparation for that remote event.

II

What are the grounds for thinking that the age of ideological politics is passing? How can we summon the naïveté to think such a thing, when the world is frozen into a menacing division engendered and maintained by Bolshevik ideas, when the communist parties of France and Italy are among the largest in their countries, when in the Middle East, in Africa, and in Asia passionate nationalist and ethnic ideologies continuously encroach on rational judgment and reasonable moral action.

Yet the expectation is not simply frivolously optimistic. The very heart which has sustained ideological politics among intellectuals over the past century is gradually losing its strength. Marxism is decomposing. The mythology of Bolshevik Marxism, the true nature of which was seen at first only by Bertrand Russell, Waldemar Gurian, and a handful of European Social Democrats and liberals, began its own self-deflation in the mid-1930s, at the moment of its maximum appeal to

---

7. The Communist Manifesto declared that in place of a class society with its classes and class antagonisms there would be a new free society "in which the free development of each is the condition for the free development of all." In the first edition, this was regarded by its authors as an entirely unique condition: "The history of all hitherto existing society" being "the history of class struggles." In 1888, Engels added a footnote which corrected this view, saying "all written history" was the history of class conflict. There had been a prehistorical period of communally owned property which was free of class conflict. Communism would thus be a renewal on a higher plane of what had been lost since the beginning of history (Marx and Engels, *Historisch-kritische Gesamtausgabe*, part 1, vol. 6 [Moscow, Leningrad, 1933], pp. 525–26, 546).

29

the world's intellectuals. The Moscow Trials were the first major step in the breakdown of the communist claim that in the Soviet Union the ultimate stage of human history, the true realm of freedom, was being entered upon. The Berlin uprising of 17 June 1953 was a step further. The realm of harmony through which mankind would transcend its conflict-ridden history was unveiled as a phantasm when Russian tanks shot down German workingmen in the streets of Berlin. According to Marxism, there could only be harmony between socialist societies bound together by the solidarity of the proletariat, but the Soviet Union showed no compunction about suppressing the East German workers by force. The eagerness with which Hungarian and Polish intellectuals greeted their prospective emancipation from a compulsory Marxism and the Russian repression of the Hungarian Revolution of 1956 also contributed to the demythologizing of Marxism.

Political events alone have not discredited Marxism. Perhaps more important is its sheer unresponsiveness to the multiplicity of life itself. People still have a need to believe, but Marxism cannot satisfy it. Its formulae are too simple, and it offers nothing to those who are attempting to establish their intellectual individuality in the face of large-scale organizations and their accompanying professional specialization. The humanitarian element in Marxism—its alleged concern for the poor—can have no appeal when there are still many very poor people in communist countries, and the poor in capitalist countries can now be seen to be much better off than their opposite numbers in communist countries. Marxist utopianism has lost its power of conviction—the world is too tired and even, in this respect, too wise to be aroused by promises of a future which might be spurious and which would not be much different from the present. Journals like *Dissent* in the United States and the *Universities and Left Review* in Great Britain have been valiant and touching efforts to save something of the ideological heritage. But they show how much ideological politics are now on the defensive, and how uncertain they are of the validity of their position. They know that their myth has faded, and that with good grounds, the intellectual spirit of the times is running against them. In every sphere of intellectual life, in economic theory, in history, and in sociology, Marxism has lost its power to attract because it is too simplistic, too threadbare intellectually and morally, and too often just wrong or irrelevant to the problems of the contemporary mind.[8] The emergence of the social sciences as major subjects of university research and teaching—even though they have their serious limitations and even though they sometimes bear a Marxist imprint—constitutes a major factor in the tarnishing of Marxism.

Nationalism too has lost its doctrinal grip on the intellectuals of the West. Its deeper, primordial hold is very strong, but it does not reach into the plane where it could provide for political judgment and action, and even less does it provide a criterion for regulating other spheres of life. In the twentieth century among Western intellectuals doctrinal nationalism has never been long preponderant, although in France among the followers of Maurras and Barrès there has been a persistent and virulent minority. In Germany, it for a time suffocated reason, and in Italy under fascism it found many willing proponents. Now, however, it is dormant. It might even be said that it is at its lowest ebb in Europe and America since the Risorgimento and the movement for the unification of the Reich. The hideous example of National Socialism, the terrible national intoxication, and the monstrous deeds committed in the name of the nation have for the time being at least exhausted the ideological passions of the German people—intellectuals and laity. The fatigue and waste of the past world wars and the ominous possibility of an even worse war to come add themselves to all the other elements in the constitution of the intellectual outlook to render nationalistic enthusiasm one of the least attractive of all the available alternatives of the present time.

---

8. Even Professor Merleau-Ponty, against whose ingenious efforts to fuse existentialism and early Marxism Professor Aron directed an unsparingly detailed and devastating criticism, lost some of his confidence in Marxism in his last years.

Moreover, the asperities of the debate between socialism and capitalism seem to be fading. The achievements of the American and Western European economies since the war, together with the political equivocality of centrally planned economies, the failures of economic planning in the Soviet satellite states, the reintroduction of the principles of the market economy into their economies by some of the communist states, and the modest and by no means glamorous achievements of nationalized industries in England and France, have cooled the fires of a century-long dispute between the proponents of socialism and the advocates of capitalism.

The more valid aspirations of the older humanitarian elements which were absorbed into Marxism have been more or less fulfilled in capitalist countries. The socialist and communist countries have neither realized their more grandiose ideals at all nor achieved their more reasonable aspirations any better than the capitalistic countries.

The Negro problem in the United States of course arouses passions, but no doctrines, no principles offer an apparently easy way out. The "woman question" has settled down to being a perennial headache, curable by no enunciation or espousal of clear and unambiguous principles. The ideology of egalitarianism has left the fundamental precipitate of moral egalitarianism from which it originally arose, but as a universally applicable principle it has lost its glamor. It seems almost as if what was sound in the older ideologies has been realized and what was unsound has demonstrated its unsoundness so obviously that enthusiasm sustained by reason can no longer be summoned.

Of course, ideological politics, Marxist, Islamic, Arabic, Hindu, Pan-African, and others, still exist in the new states outside the West in a vehement, irreconcilable form and often with great influence. But many in the West who sympathize with the desires and deplore the excesses are inclined to believe that they too will pass when the new states in which they flourish become more settled and mature. Looking back from the standpoint of a newly achieved moderation, Western intellectuals view the ideological politics of Asia and Africa, and particularly nationalism and tribalism, as a sort of measles which afflicts a people in its childhood but to which adults are practically immune.

There seems to be no alternative ideology for the intellectuals to turn to now, nothing to absorb their intelligence, nothing to inflame their capacity for faith and their aspirations toward perfection. The conservative revival, though genuine, is moderate. People take Burke in their stride. They have become "natural Burkeans" without making a noise about it. The *National Review*, despite its clamor, is isolated and unnoticed, and the effort to create a "conservative ideology" which would stand for more than moderation, reasonableness, and prudence has not been successful.[9]

There seem to be no good grounds for ideological politics. Thus, it appears reasonable to think that the age of ideological politics is gradually coming to its end. The flurries of romantic enthusiasm of the late 1960s do not belie the deeper trend.

III

One of the grounds for believing that the age of ideological politics is ending is its modernity.

Professor Aron has put forward the view that ideological politics originated in the French Revolution.[10] There is much truth to this contention. Ideological politics did indeed come into the forum of public life only at the end of the eighteenth century in an outburst not hitherto experienced by the human race.

The reason for this relatively recent appearance of ideological politics on a grand scale is not far to seek. Until recent centuries politics

9. See Irving Kristol, "Old Truths and the New Conservatism," *Yale Review* (Spring 1958): 365–73.

10. Aron, p. 42. The same view was put forward by Professor D. W. Brogan in his most interesting essay, "Was the French Revolution a Mistake?" *Cambridge Journal* 1 (October 1947): 43–55.

were not public. In the aristocratic republics and in the ancient city democracies, politics did not engage the attention of the mass of the population. Politics were the concern of rulers and of those who aspired to become rulers. The aspiration was, however, spread over a relatively small section of the population. Tribal, feudal, and dynastic interests, which were uppermost in the political life of societies before modern times, did not nourish the ideological outlook. There was, moreover, no intellectual class as a major factor in politics. Where the educated were taken into the civil service, as in China, in ancient Rome, and in the European Middle Ages, the bureaucratic ethos and personal dependence on the prince, to say nothing of the type of education preparatory for the civil service career, discouraged the emergence of an ideological orientation. The intrigues of court politics did not foster the success of the ideologically minded man. There was no class of independent professional literary men and journalists, free of patrons and of the need to remain on the right side of the authorities.

The violent political struggles of the Greek city-states and of the last decades of the Roman Republic, even where they involved the bitterest class antagonisms, did not become ideological. They were fought on behalf of "interests." The notions of "justice" and of the "good social order" did not enter into them except peripherally.

The ideological orientation toward life existed, of course, as it must exist wherever human society exists. It passed judgment on all things, and so it passed judgment on political things. It censured the existing political order as a realm of iniquity, and counseled and predicted its destruction. This ideological attitude toward politics did not, however, enter the sphere of political activity, because the kinds of persons who espoused it or came under its influence were not admitted into the circles which discussed and decided on succession to political office and on the actions of governments.

As long as politics were not an instrument of justice or of the realization of the right social order and were concerned with the mere maintenance of order, the conservation of the power of dynasties and classes which already had or sought it, there was no room for ideological politics. Those who practiced politics were not susceptible to them, except on rare occasions, and they found no following even where great individual personalities were moved by ideological—above all, religious—considerations.

The invention of printing and the possibility arising therefrom of diffusing arguments to a wider public, the Protestant belief that the Bible and not the priesthood is the vehicle of the sacred, and the slow and gradual rising of the mass of European populations from their torpor—all of these had much to do with the creation of the necessary conditions for ideological politics. The crucial element, however, was the creation of a class of intellectuals no longer dependent exclusively on patronage or inheritance for their livelihood.

The body of intellectuals which came into existence in the sixteenth century was a new phenomenon in world history. It consisted of men whose sensibility, intelligence, and imagination carried them beyond the standards and requirements of everyday life; they were no longer forced to depend on church or state or princely, aristocratic, or mercantile patronage for their existence. Their capacity for loyalty thus liberated, they were endowed with the freedom to attach themselves to symbols beyond those embodied in existing ecclesiastical and governmental institutions. The steady growth in the scale and importance of this stratum of the population in modern European societies is perhaps the decisive factor in the "ideologization" which, on its better side, has been called the "spiritualization of politics." The intellectuals—who before the development of specialized technical training were coterminous with the educated classes—have lived in a permanent tension between earthly power and the ideal, which derives from their nature as intellectuals. They have not, however, created from within themselves the imagery and passion of ideological politics. The numerous traditions which they have developed, e.g., the romantic tradition, the scientistic tradition, the bohemian tradition, important though they have been in disposing intellectuals toward ideological politics, would scarcely have been sufficient to give to such politics their extraordinary attraction and compellingness.

35

Ideological politics are rooted in an ideological tradition which lives in our midst through invisible radiations coming down from the depths of our Western past. They are sustained by our Judaic-Christian culture, by passions which are part of our souls, and by the nature of human society.

The millenarian tradition which is the oldest source of the ideological outlook is an ever-present potentiality in Christian teaching and experience; it is usually maintained, for most persons, most of the time, in a state of latency. It has a living existence in the life of the Protestant sects and in the records of the saints of every Christian society. Even where religious belief has become attenuated or has evaporated, the millenarian expectations and judgments have persisted in an aromatic tradition which, on occasion, becomes crystallized in a sensitive and receptive person. Religious enthusiasm, as the late Ronald Knox[11] showed with such compassionate understanding and as Professor Cohn,[12] writing from a very different point of view, has corroborated, has never been absent from Western civilization. As early as pre-Exilic times, Jewish prophets foretold the cataclysmic end of time and the world as we know it, a Day of Wrath and a Last Judgment, when sinners, individual and corporate, would be cast down, and a regenerated Israel would populate Palestine and a second Eden.

The expectations of a Last Judgment on a sinful temporal order took a deep root in the early Christian communities. The tradition did not die out as the Church settled down to live on as an institution. Manichaeism, with its basic distinctions between light and darkness and its conception of the universe as a field of irreconcilable struggle between the forces of light and the forces of darkness, found hospitality in the Christian circles where this chiliastic tradition persisted. No church, indeed, no established institution, could survive if its members

11. *Enthusiasm: A Chapter in the History of Religion, with Special Reference to the XVII and XVIII Centuries* (Oxford, 1950).
12. *The Pursuit of the Millennium* (London, 1957).

expected an imminent end of the world and its subsequent replacement by the Kingdom of God. It was to meet this view that Saint Augustine elaborated his conception of the Church itself as the Kingdom of God on earth. But for those with a great sensitivity to the sacred, and disciplined intellect, no living church could ever represent the Kingdom of God. Insofar as it refused to preach the proximate realization of the Kingdom of God, it rendered itself subject to their most anguished and harshest criticism.

Professor Cohn, who was not concerned either to support the Marxist view that millenarian sectarianism was merely the ideology of a class conflict expressed in a religious idiom or to espouse the anti-Marxist view which argues that millenarianism was solely an expression of a hypersensitive and perhaps disordered religiosity, was at his best when he showed how it fused with the animosities of class, of ethnic hatreds, and of fantasies of national glory. The hatred-filled fantasies of princes, lords, wealthy merchants, the pope, Jews, Turks, Italians, Saracens were amalgamated with the frightful images of Satan and the Antichrist. In its meandering and tragic history, full of misery, persecution, and violence, rabid and deluded yearnings, false messiahs, deranged visions, hostility, and pitched battles, a single complex theme runs unbrokenly. This is the central theme of the ideological orientation toward existence.

The ideological outlook is preoccupied with the evil of the world as it exists; it believes in the immiscibility of good and evil. It distinguishes sharply between the children of light and the children of darkness. It believes that no earthly action can ameliorate or attenuate evil. It exhibits a violent hatred of the existing cosmic order, and especially of its earthly beneficiaries, governmental, economic, and ecclesiastical authorities, indeed, of authorities of any kind. It regards authority as an agent of evil and as a compromise with evil.

The mass of mankind lives in constant temptation and seduction by evil; the petty concerns of daily work and commerce, attachment to family, loyalty to friends, and the quest of private advantage are all inextricably involved with evil. Those who take upon themselves to rule the world as it is, are either corrupt in their very nature to begin with, or become so through their contact with authority, which is diabolical by nature.

The ideological outlook expressed by millenarianism asserts, however, that the reign of evil on the earth is of finite duration. There will come a moment when time and history as we know them shall come to an end. The present period of history will be undone by a cosmic act of judgment which will do justice to the wronged and virtuous by elevating them to eternal bliss, and equal justice to the powerful and wicked by degrading and destroying them for all time to come. The order which will be ushered in by the cosmic last judgment will be a new realm of perfect harmony and peace, in which all men will live in accordance with the ultimate criteria of justice and mutual love. No conflict will mar their existence; there will be no scarcity to degrade and cramp them.

To usher in this glorious epoch requires heroism on the part of the small number of consecrated persons who live strictly in accordance with the dictates of the highest judgment. Heroism is required, above all, to give witness to the truth of the standards which ultimately will come to prevail and to help to inaugurate this totally new phase of existence.

Despite its extraordinary persistence, the millenarian tradition has been no ordinary tradition transmitted by the elders of a society to their next generation. Its reception is not the ordinary reception of tradition as something given, but a search and a yearning. There is no evidence of continuity of the movement of this tradition from person to person, and it is not commonly taught in any society. It is a phenomenon of the sinks and corners of society, and it creates groups which, in a state of inflammation, are remarkably short-lived as compared with the long history of the churches. The tradition, however, has a long and continuous history.[13] From the Near Eastern seedbed of

13. See LeRoy Edwin Froom, *The Prophetic Faith of Our Fathers. The Historical Development of Prophetic Interpretation* (Washington, D.C., 1948), vols. 1–4; Steven

enthusiastic religiosity, millenarian Christian sectarianism spread into Southeastern Europe and North Africa, from Bulgaria into Northern Italy, from Northern Italy into Southern France, from Southern France into the Low Countries, from the Low Countries into Germany and Central Europe and then into England. Yet the mechanism of its transmission remains a mystery. There is some evidence of personal links of the founders and spreaders of particular variants of millenarianism, but this does not explain why the soil was so fertile for their labors.

Similarly, although the inner affinities of millenarianism and modern revolutionary politics are now perfectly obvious,[14] the lines of filiation are more difficult to trace. The German Marxists' discovery of their own ancestry in the Anabaptists of Munster, in the Levellers and the Diggers of the English Civil War,[15] is an acknowledgment of the affinity, but is not evidence of a directly received influence.[16]

Runciman, *The Medieval Manichee: A Study of the Christian Dualist Heresy* (Cambridge, 1947); Dmitri Obolensky, *The Bogomils: A Study in Balkan Neo-Manichaeism* (Cambridge, 1948); Knox, *Enthusiasm*. I should like also to call attention to a very sympathetic article by Storm Jameson, "The Dualist Tradition," *Times Literary Supplement,* 6 August 1954.

14. Aron, chap. 9, "The Intellectuals in Search of a Religion," pp. 264–94; Erich Voegelin, *Die politischen Religionen* (Stockholm, 1939), pp. 39–42; Fritz Gerlich, *Der Kommunismus als Lehre vom tausendjährigen Reich* (Munich, 1920), esp. pp. 17–78.

15. See Friedrich Engels, *The Peasant War in Germany* (New York, 1926); Karl Kautsky, *Communism in Central Europe in the Time of the Reformation* (London, 1897); Edward Bernstein, *Cromwell and Communism: Socialism and Democracy in the Great English Civil Revolution* (London, 1930); Ernst Bloch, *Thomas Münzer als Theologe der Revolution* (Munich, 1921).

16. The German working class movement of the 1840s and British working class radicalism did, it is true, thrive in areas which had been the scenes of Protestant sectarianism from the sixteenth to the eighteenth centuries. It is a plausible hypothesis that the ideological traditions of sectarian life made for a receptivity to revolutionary and radical ideas by virtue of their correspondences; in turn, aided by theorists more deeply dyed by the revolutionary traditions of the French Revolution and the Hegelian (and ultimately Christian) idea of history, the tradition of religious enthusiasm was transformed into an apparently secular heroic doctrine of ideological politics.

Perhaps the continuity of the millenarian outlook through many different situations arises not from a continuously handed-down tradition but from the recurrent attachment to its sources—the Book of Daniel, the Book of Revelation, the Sybilline Books, and the Johannine prophecy, which are available on the edge of our culture to all those who have a need for them. To these, time and again, persons with a yearning for the end of earthly injustice and the transcendence of time in a new and purer realm resplendent with harmony and love, have turned. In the past century, they have not had to go back to the original sources. Through the heirs of these sources, their transformations into the doctrines of contemporary ideological politics have been available in an idiom more acceptable to the contemporary mind.

Now, if this is no ordinary tradition, transmitted in the way ordinary traditions are transmitted, why then does it persist as such a recurrent theme in Western history? The answer must be sought in Christianity, which contains among its manifold potentialities the ever-present promise of a Second Coming and the unchanging imminence of the ultimate catastrophe which precedes the second coming of a Messiah. Although the central institutions of modern societies, out of the very necessities of their continuing existence and the nature of the human beings who live in them, preclude the widespread practice and observance of the ideological orientation, there are always some persons in these societies to whom the ideological orientation has an especial appeal. It is always there for those who have the ideological need to be in saving contact with the ultimate. Every society has its outcasts, its wretched, and its damned, who cannot fit into the routine requirements of social life at any level of authority and achievement. Max Weber said that salvationary religions are most commonly found among declining strata of handicraftsmen and small enterprisers. This proposition is capable of generalization. Those who are constricted, who find life as it is lived too hard, are prone to the acceptance of the ideological outlook on life. A society in which the lot of the many becomes more constricted, in which they feel more deserted and more uncared for as a result of the failure of their rulers, will encourage this proneness to seek realization.[17]

Naturally, not all those who live in a broken and disadvantaged condition are drawn equally by the magnet of the ideological orientation. Special personal qualities are required.[18] It takes a hypersensitivity to ultimate standards, to the sacred, and this is a quality which although rare in all populations, is found in some measures at all times and particularly at times of crisis. There are human beings who, by personal constitution, are sensitive to the ultimate grounds of existence, just as there are human beings with a need for and a capacity for abstract reasoning, for understanding the mysteries of the universe in accor-

17. Bengt Sundkler, *Bantu Prophets in South Africa* (London, 1948); Georges Balandier, *Sociologie actuelle de l'Afrique noire* (Paris, 1955), pp. 417–86; and Peter Worsley, *The Trumpet Shall Sound: A Study of "Cargo" Cults in Melanesia* (London, 1957), show the connection between salvationary, messianic religion and the deprivations arising from the disruption of traditional institutions.

18. Professor Cohn declared that paranoid tendencies are a necessary condition for the expansion of millenarianism. His view is supported not only by the content of millenarian imagery and aspirations which his book so richly describes, but by contemporary experience of millenarian groups, religious and political. He does not claim that all members of such groups must be paranoid, but that the leaders must be such. "There are always very large numbers of people who are prone to see life in black and white, who feel a deep need for perfect saviours to adore and wicked enemies to hate; people ... who without being paranoiac yet have a strong tendency towards paranoid states of mind. At a time when such tendencies are being encouraged by external circumstances, the appearance of a messianic leader preaching the doctrine of the final struggle and the coming of the new age can produce remarkable results—and that irrespective of whether the leader is a sincere fanatic or an imposter or a mixture of both. Those who are first attracted will mostly be people who seek a sanction for the emotional needs generated by their own unconscious conflicts. ... These first followers, precisely because they are true believers, can endow their new movement with such confidence, energy and ruthlessness that it will attract into its wake vast multitudes of people who are themselves not at all paranoid but simply harassed, hungry or frightened" (pp. 311–12). There is much truth in this well-balanced picture, but it seems to me that he omits the religious or ideological sensitivity—the sensitivity to remote things—which is not necessarily connected with paranoia, any more than imagination or curiosity is connected with it.

dance with the powers of their reason. Some become mystics, some become scientists, other philosophers. Others who are filled with the sense of injustice and of grievance against the earthly order in its various manifestations, political and ecclesiastical, as well as familial and sexual, reach out toward and seek fusion with the symbols of apocalyptic fulfillment. That is why the ideological orientation so frequently draws to itself madmen full of hatred and fear—the paranoids who play such an important role in Professor Cohn's interpretation. Ideological sensitivity, even if it did not draw on the accumulated hatred and aggressiveness of its followers, would be separatist and in tension with the "world" of normal traditional society. Its utopianism and its quest for perfect harmony would put it at odds with the world of conflicting interests, half-measures, and self-seeking. The addition of the hatred and fear of those who feel injured and neglected adds a highly combustible fuel to its fire. For this reason, the ideological outlook is full of the imagery of violence and destruction, and its practice is often crowded with actual acts of brutality and a heartless asceticism, while preaching a message of an ultimate condition of love and peace enveloping all human beings.[19]

Ideological politics have their nerve in this need to be in contact with the sacred. They live from grievance and the feeling of injustice, and no conceivable society can attain the condition in which everyone could be permanently free from grievance and the feeling of injustice, any more than any society could live up to the standards affirmed by the most saintly prophets and maddest zealots of the apocalypse.

The tendency of intellectuals in modern Western countries, and latterly in Asian and African countries, to incline toward ideological

19. One need only read the pacifist press to see how the preaching of peace and love is combined with a pleasure in the contemplation of maimed bodies and universal destruction. Mazzini once wrote, "I am inclined to love men at a distance . . . contact makes me hate them." Bolton King, *Life of Mazzini* (London [Everyman edition], 1912), p. 55.

politics does not, however, derive only from this permanent feature of the Judaic-Christian religious culture, which affects even those who do not accept its explicit articles of faith.[20] As intellectuals, they also live in the flowing stream of other traditions which are particular to them as intellectuals.

It is probably not an accident that most of the traditions of modern intellectuals seem to dispose them toward an ideological outlook. It seems to be almost given by their attachment to symbols which transcend everyday life and its responsibilities. Some of these traditions have arisen as effluvial by-products of specific intellectual activities, as, for example, scientism has arisen from scientific research and analysis. Others, like the tradition of bohemianism, have arisen from the age and mode of life of persons whose inclinations drive them toward an effort to be independent of traditions and conventions and on whom their devotion to the symbols of artistic and literary creation, and the restricted market for the sale of their creations, enforces material poverty and uncertainty. And still others, like the tradition of romanticism, are the complex products of a profound movement of the human spirit, so intricate and multifarious that it seems almost inexplicable.

Let us consider some of these traditions of the intellectuals with regard to their contact with the ideological outlook and their inherent disposition toward ideological politics. Let us consider scientism first. Scientism entails the denial of the truth of tradition. It asserts that life, if it is to be lived on the highest plane, should be lived in accordance with "scientific principles," and that these principles should be achieved by the rigorously rational examination of actual experience, systematically confronted through the elaborate and orderly scrutiny and experi-

20. Is it entirely an accident that communism in India has achieved its greatest success so far in an area where previously Christian missionary education had reached a larger proportion of the population than in other parts of India? It is not intended, however, to explain Indian leftism solely by an ultimate derivation from a secularized Christian outlook.

ment which constitute scientific research. It regards the generally accepted traditions of society as impediments to the attainment of these
principles, which are ultimately the principles immanent in the universe.
As such, therefore, scientism constitutes a vigorous criticism of traditional and institutional life, and a refusal to accept authority on any
grounds except those of scientific principle. It holds before mankind the
ideal of a society in which scientists, and administrators and politicians
guided by scientists, will rule and in which the ordinary citizens will hold
no beliefs and perform no actions which are not sanctioned by scientific
principles.[21] This rejection of the prevailing order and its central institutions and traditions, and the appreciation of an ideal order governed by
the ultimate principles of science, obviously possess close affinities with
certain features of the millenarian outlook. The hostility toward the barrier which received tradition raises between the human being and the
ultimate principles of the universe, the dispraise of the authority of institutions, and the vision of an ideal order (infused by and conducted in
accordance with the ultimate principles of universal existence) are only
a few of the lines of affinity which link these two traditions. It is therefore
not difficult to understand how the acceptance of the scientistic tradition
can prepare the way to the acceptance of a secularized millenarianism
and thus lead on to ideological politics.

21. See F. A. Hayek, *The Counter-Revolution of Science* (Glencoe, Ill., 1952), which
provides the best account of one of the most important sources of scientism, that
which derives from Descartes and which reaches its fullest elaboration in the work of
Saint-Simon and Comte. B. F. Skinner, *Walden II* (New York, 1948), is an extreme
contemporary statement of the scientistic position, to which there are numerous
approximations, not the least the Marxist. Marxist scientism is best represented by
Professor J. D. Bernal, who has written, "Science has put in our power the means of
transforming human life to a degree at least as great as those provided by the technical
developments of the origin of civilization but the change differs in one crucial respect
in that they can be consciously undertaken. What we can see straight away is the
possibility of the removal of most of the hindrances to full human and social life that
exist in our civilization." "Science and Civilization," in C. Day Lewis, *The Mind in
Chains* (London, 1937), pp. 194–95.

Romanticism too flows in the same direction, feeding into and swelling the sea of ideological politics. Romanticism too views any existing order as repugnant because it mediates, compromises, and deforms the ideal. The ideal of romanticism is the spontaneous and direct expression of the essential nature of the individual and the collectivity. Both the individualistic and the collectivistic variants of the romantic tradition placed great emphasis on the direct and full experience of the ultimate value of individual creativity or of the spirit of the community (folk or national or local). Like the millenarian outlook, romanticism regards immediate experience of the sacred as a touchstone of the good. Whatever is mediated by calculation or contrivance, by organization or compromise is antithetical to it. That is why modern large-scale society as it has emerged since the end of the eighteenth century is abhorrent to those who live in the tradition of romanticism. Civil society, which allows so much space for private concerns, and which permits neither the single individual nor the total community the complete realization of their essential potentialities, is seen by romanticism as a system of arbitrary repression in contrast with some ideal realm of freedom and fulfillment. Civil society requires compromise and reasonableness, prudent self-restraint, and responsibility, and these are all deviations from the unqualifiedness and spontaneity which romanticism demands of all action. Romanticism is, as a result, at war with civil society.

The influence of romanticism on the outlook of intellectuals runs far beyond those circles who knowingly acknowledge its sovereignty over them. It has become universally pervasive. It is a major determinant of the attitude of the intellectuals toward politics and the authority of institutions. And different though it is in content from the frightful and dazzling visions of millenarianism, they both work to the same end—the rejection of the existing order in the name of a pattern of existence more infused with the sacred.

In their spiritual genealogy, the tradition of bohemianism and populism are closely related to romanticism. Bohemianism had an older history before it developed an ethos of its own. The restless scholars of the medieval universities[22] and the homeless minstrels and minnesingers who lived from begging, thieving, and the hope of selling their artistic wares were the ancestors of the modern bohemian. They were footloose; they were not incorporated into the routines and responsibilities which filled most of the medieval European social structure. They would not accept the burdens of family and vocation, and sought only to serve their own creative impulse and pleasure.

The development of printing and the appearance of a body of writers trying to maintain themselves from the sale of their written product added a substantial body of persons in Western Europe whose uncertain existence and whose intellectual sensitivity forced them into an irregular course of life. Bohemian practice and bohemian ethos were well under way in London and Paris before the beginning of the nineteenth century. The widened range of education and the increased reading public, fed by the romantic idea of the creative man, the lonely genius who knows no law, made the café intellectual, the bohemian writer and artist into a major figure of life in all the great capitals of the Western countries. Paris was the center of this life, but London, Berlin, Munich, Saint Petersburg, Rome, and New York all had their bohemias. The traditions of the French revolutions of 1789, 1830, 1848, and the commune of 1871, and the tradition of anarchism, doctrinal and practical, found a warm reception in the Parisian bohemia, and, with varying degrees of attenuation and adaptation to national political traditions, they found acceptance in the bohemias of the other countries as well. Antinomianism— moral, aesthetic, and political—was at home there, and the political police kept their eyes peeled for revolutionaries in bohemian intellectual

---

22. Miss Helen Waddell, describing these forerunners of bohemianism, quoted the Council of Salzburg: "They go alone in public naked, lie in bake-ovens, frequent taverns, games, harlots, earn their bread by their vices and cling with inveterate obstinacy to their sect, so that no hope of their amendment remaineth." *Wandering Scholars*, 7th ed. (London, 1942), p. 188.

circles. Bohemians were at war with society,[23] some on well-thought-out grounds, seeking a free life less encumbered by traditional standards, others out of an incoherent and impulsive aggressiveness against any sort of authority, cultural or institutional, and an inability to live in a settled routine of work or life. There were many points at which bohemianism and millenarianism diverged. Bohemianism was usually against the Church as well as against Christianity; millenarianism was Christian and only hostile to the authority of the Church. Bohemianism was usually opposed to asceticism; millenarianism was often ascetic. They had in common, however, their repugnance for *mere* tradition and for the constituted authorities who were associated with it.

Populism—the belief in the wisdom and the supreme moral value of the ordinary man of the lower classes—is a new phenomenon. In some respects it was a creation of romanticism, but it was also an outgrowth of the moral egalitarianism of the Christian sects and of life at the peripheries of Western culture. By its praise of the uneducated and the humble, it places itself in opposition to the great and mighty of the earth; it denies their cultural creativity while imputing true creativity to the lower classes. Populism charges academic science and scholarship with a preoccupation with bloodless symbols unconnected with the essence of life. When it becomes political, populism asserts that the standards of the ordinary people should prevail against the standards represented by the authoritative institutions of society—the state, the law, the church, the universities. Thus the populistic tradition, too, like the other traditions cited, expresses a deep alienation from traditional culture and from the society ruled through civil politics and the equilibrium of power.

Populism and millenarianism share many significant features. Both repudiate the official traditions of learning, millenarianism declaring

23. Baudelaire once wrote, "Usefulness to the community always seemed to me a most hideous thing in man." *The Essence of Laughter and Other Essays, Journals and Letters,* ed. Peter Quennell (New York, 1956), p. 178.

THE VIRTUE OF CIVILITY

that the prevailing interpretation of sacred texts falsifies their true meaning, and populism charging the learned with the transfiguration of authority and with enmity toward the truth expressed in the popular will. Both oppose the mediation of contact with the highest values, by authoritative institutions, by priests, professors, and parliamentarians. Both are against the cold-blooded and impersonal rules of institutions; both are responsive to charisma. The conceptions of the people and of the proletariat easily merge, as do those of people and nation; so populism can turn without difficulty into an ideological political orientation.

These are not the only traditions of the modern intellectual, but most of the others have the same tendency. Of course, these traditions are not accepted equally by all intellectuals. They are most widely accepted among men of letters and academic scholars and scientists. Nonetheless, although an increasing proportion of intellectuals in the broader sense, i.e., persons who have passed through colleges and universities, are engaged in practical tasks in administration and technology which curb their ideological predispositions, the atmosphere in which they acquire their qualifications, and the traditions which adhere to their professions, give to many of them some impulsion in this direction. The impetus to an ideological outlook inherent in the very constitution of intellectual activities would probably not be enough to account for the upsurge of ideological politics of the past century and a half. It has required the confluence of numerous traditions and their common confrontation with the situation of modern society to release the flood.

IV

Traditions seldom die. They recede very slowly, yielding before new traditions which replace them by incorporating elements of their predecessors and assimilating them to new elements. The new traditions can grow only by attachment to older traditions which they expand and elaborate.

It seems excessively sanguine, therefore, for us to congratulate ourselves on the end of the ideological age. We would be more realistic to speak of its subsidence, rather than of its end. Old traditions, such as millenarianism, deep in the marrow of our intellectual bones, traditions such as romanticism, which are at the very heart of the modern age, are not likely to disappear so soon after the fury and the disillusionment of the first fifty years of this century.

What we may legitimately hope for in the coming decades is a condition of quiescence of ideological politics and of the ideological disposition from which it springs. This quiescence can be sustained only if an effective alternative is available. Civil politics are this alternative.

Civil politics are based on civility, which is the virtue of the citizen,[24] of the man who shares responsibly in his own self-government, either as a governor or as one of the governed. Civility is compatible with other attachments to class, to religion, to profession, but it regulates them out of respect for the common good.

Civil politics do not stir the passions; they do not reveal man at the more easily apprehensible extremes of heroism and saintliness. They involve the prudent exercise of authority, which tries to foresee the consequences of that exercise while appreciating the undeterminable limitations of human powers and the uncertainties of foresight. The civil politician must be aware of the vague line between the exercise of authority and the manipulation of human beings as objects outside his moral realm. He must shun that line and yet on occasion go over

---

24. Civility has meant more than good manners, and it is an impoverishment of our vocabulary as well as a sign of the impoverishment of our thought on political matters that this word has been allowed to dwindle to the point where it has come to refer to good manners in face-to-face relationships. Two recent books by eminent British writers—*Traditions of Civility*, by Sir Ernest Barker (Cambridge, 1948), and *Good Behaviour: Being a Study of Certain Types of Civility*, by Sir Harold Nicolson (London, 1955)—show no awareness of the older meaning of the term.

it, realizing the moral costs of such crossing over and the difficulties and the necessity of crossing back into the domain of legitimacy. He must maintain a sense of affinity with his society and share with his fellow citizens their membership in a single transpersonal entity, while bearing in mind their unresponsiveness to the ideal and their incapacity to sustain a continuous and intense relationship with the sacred. He must maintain this sense of substantial affinity while being aware of their lesser willingness to be responsible for the common good and while keeping his own feeling of responsibility for it alive and taut.

The difficulties of civil political conduct are great in democracies. Their large size and the impossibility of direct contact between politicians and their constituents are strains on the sense of moral affinity which, lacking the support of personal relationships, must be self-sustaining. Civility was rare in aristocratic societies, partly because aristocratic virtue—the virtue of the warrior—and civil virtue—the virtue of the citizen—are so far apart in their inner constitutions, and particularly because aristocratic systems by their nature restrict man's development of the empathic sense of affinity. Liberal democratic regimes place great burdens on the civil sense because they permit open conflict and acknowledge and thus encourage partisanship. The common good is always hard to define, but it is rendered even harder when it must gratify and reconcile opposing interests and simultaneously attempt to guard values for which no strong partisan contends, but which, nonetheless, are essential to a good society. The politician must be partisan himself, while civility requires a partial transcendence of partisanship as well as an empathic appreciation of the other parties within the circle of the civil political order. Partisanship must be carried on with the simultaneous perception of the civil and moral order which embraces both one's opponents and one's allies.

Civil politics—which are by no means identical with democratic politics—are especially difficult in contemporary society. The complex tasks which governments undertake and which nearly everyone thinks they should undertake, make so great the amount of material that a politician who devotes himself to the matter must master, and so many the obligations to which he must attend, that reflection is deprived of the quiet and leisure which it needs to mature. The complexity of the tasks renders easy understanding of them beyond the power of most of the citizenry and encourages a depreciatory attitude toward the capacities of the electorate, thus inhibiting the vitality of the sense of affinity between citizens and leaders that is essential to civil politics. The deep and increasing penetration of populism in all countries results in a greater pressure on the politician for the immediate satisfaction of class and sectional ends. The development of techniques of mass communication and of chemical, surgical, and psychological modes of controlling human behavior presents continuous temptations to the politician to respond to the incessant demands by manipulation. Not that he always by any means yields or that the techniques would be successful if applied, but the mere existence of the putative possibilities creates an atmosphere which impedes the cultivation and practice of civility.

Civil politics entail judging things on their own merits—hard enough in any case where the merits and demerits in any complex issue are so obscure and intertwined—and they also require respect for tradition. Civility requires respect for tradition because the sense of affinity on which it rests is not momentary only but reaches into the past and future. As to the past, civil politics appreciate the factual reality of past achievements as well as the human quality of those who, by virtue of having once been alive, command our respect for their names and the things they valued; as to the future, civil politics see the unity, in essence, of the present generation and those which are to follow, not just in a biological sense, but in the order of value as well. The population of a civil polity is in its fundamental being a continuous procession of those living in the present, preceded by those who have lived, shading off into the obscurity of time past, and to be followed by those who have still to live, shading off into the even more shadowy obscurity of time still unelapsed.

The traditional consciousness is not, however, one which encourages the direct contemplation of the merits and demerits of things as they are. The utilitarian mind usually has little patience with the pastness of things and is even disposed to assume that the mere fact of having been appropriate to the past is a disqualification for relevance to the present and future. Yet both the need for continuity—i.e., the maintenance of affinity with the past—and the need to draw on the benefits of the intelligence and artfulness exercised in the past, render imperative an appreciation of tradition.

Above all, civil politics require an understanding of the complexity of virtue, that no virtue stands alone, that every virtuous act costs something in terms of other virtuous acts, that virtues are intertwined with evils, and that no theoretical system of a hierarchy of virtues is ever realizable in practice. It has been a major fault of ideological politics that they have made the mistake of thinking that a coherent systematic doctrine could guide conduct unfailingly along a straight line which made no compromise with evil. Ideological politics believed that the more strictly one adhered to a virtue, the more intensely one was attached to it, and the more completely one fulfilled it, the better would be one's actions.

This was the basis of the idea of the political spectrum which ran from the pole of virtue—be it left or right—to the other pole, the extreme and complete negation of virtue. The realism and circumspection of civil politics cannot accommodate such a simplification.

Practicing politicians do indeed manage to avoid the excesses which are inevitable in such simplifications. Professor Aron once said French politicians in the nineteenth and twentieth centuries, in one of the countries of the most extreme ideological politics among intellectuals, have in practice usually not been dominated by this distinction between "left" and "right."[25] Indeed, this has been one of the reasons why French

25. The avoidance of ideological politics is not synonymous with the practice of civil politics. Politics practiced in accordance with the prevailing constellation of

intellectuals have been so alienated from the political practice of their country.

The practice of politics imposes some measure of civility, but it also stirs the temptation of demagogy and offers the easy solution of satisfying the most clamorous sectional interests. If intellectuals could settle down to a more reasonable political outlook, their concern for the more general and for what transcends the immediate advantages of particular "interests" would infuse a most precious ingredient into political life.

V

Is it plausible to expect intellectuals to renounce their attachments to antipolitical traditions in which they have lived for centuries? Can it be expected that intellectuals will be drawn down from the heights of the ultimate ideal so that they could, while still remaining intellectuals, tolerate the burden imposed by the vicissitudes of maintaining themselves as politicians who have invested their future in the unpredictabilities of politics, and by the task of keeping a society going? Can intellectuals be brought to appreciate politics which are concerned to keep society on a steady course, as much concerned to keep it from becoming worse as to make it better? Can they be expected to affirm a political practice which provides no final solution and which does not promise to bring society or the human race to a resting point of perfect fulfillment?

The civil politics which must replace ideological politics in the affections of the intellectuals have many competitive disadvantages. Their traditions are fewer and frailer. Cicero, who preached and tried to practice the virtues of civil politics, has been called an opportunist,

---

interests is a third alternative, and it is one which is most commonly pursued by politicians. If the "interests" are intractable, then the civil order can be as badly damaged as it would be by ideological politics.

and his assassination by the side with which he compromised has been regarded as evidence of his failure as a politician. Tacitus spoke on behalf of civility through his censure of its degradation in the Empire.[26] Clarendon's civil wisdom was put on paper in the rueful melancholy of exile and with the distrust of power which is the destiny of the disappointed and disregarded counselor to princes. The fate of More and Raleigh and the disillusionment of the humanists who sought to guide the conduct of princes have left bitter memories of the tribulations of the intellectual in politics. On the other side, the image of politics reflected by those "advisers to princes" whose names stand out in our minds, Machiavelli above all, Halifax, and others like them, have given an appearance of justice to the condemnation of politics which the intellectual, devoted to the ideal of his calling, has often expressed.

The intellectual who seeks the path of civil politics has little to cheer and fortify him in his quest. He has many of his own prejudices to overcome—the whole complex of the traditions of ideological politics, and, in America, his traditional aversion for the politics of the pork barrel and the patronage lists, and his image of the 42nd Ward Young Men's Democratic Club, with its smokers and its belching boorishness, and of the harsh selfishness of the Union League Clubs.[27] He has no feeling of standing in a great intellectual tradition. There is no equivalent civil tradition to counterpose to the subterranean pervasiveness of the

26. "So corrupted, indeed, debased was that age by sycophancy that not only the foremost citizens who were forced to save their grandeur by servility but every ex-consul, most of the ex-praetors and a host of inferior senators would rise in eager rivalry to propose shameful and preposterous motions. Tradition says that Tiberius as often as he left the Senate House used to exclaim in Greek, 'How ready these men are to be slaves' " (*Annals*, book 3, section 65).

27. This is by no means confined to capitalistic America or to bourgeois politicians. Ferdinand Lassalle once said, "I have a real horror of workers' delegations where I always hear the same speeches and have to shake hard, hot and moist hands" (David Footman, *The Primrose Path* [London, 1946], p. 183). The intellectuals' attitude toward politicians, regardless of their class, is epitomized in: "I met Murder on the way. He had a mask like Castlereagh."

millenarian tradition, to provide an atmosphere in which he can breathe. He has the memory of Woodrow Wilson and Thomas Masaryk, Disraeli and Gladstone, and Guizot, to set alongside the far more numerous intellectuals approving of bomb throwing and assassination, themselves engaged in wire pulling and plotting, impatient and contemptuous of the political profession.

If civil politics depend on an acceptance of the limitations of human powers, their establishment in the second half of the present century will not be rendered easier by scientific developments. The advances in physiology, biochemistry, neurology, applied mathematics, cybernetics, and the foolish propaganda made by some of the enthusiasts of psychology and the social sciences, can hardly induce a feeling of modesty in man, nor can they be expected to promote that fellow feeling necessary to civil politics.

Nor, for that matter, can the specialization of education which accompanies this scientific progress bring much support. Quite the opposite. It is not that the humanistic education of the past has provided much of a bulwark against the ideological outlook. Extreme specialization, however, adds a further strain to the weak sense of affinity. It is true that extreme specialization which reduces the contact of the intellectual with the broad range of traditions of the intellectual life of the past also restricts his relationship with many of the ideological elements in the traditions of the intellectuals. In many fields, however, and particularly in those of increasing importance, it exposes him more fully to the scientistic tradition. Thus, while it increases his matter-of-factness, it also increases his pride, his contempt for the past, and his confidence in the boundless superiority of the future, and these are not so congenial to civility.

If ideological politics thrive in conditions of danger, what are we to think of the chances of civil politics in an age in which peace is maintained by a conscious fear of cataclysmic destruction by nuclear weapons? These awful possibilities cannot avoid stirring up latent apocalyptic images and expectations. These real dangers make the sober, moderate, small-scale measures of civil politics appear excessively puny alongside the monstrous tasks which nuclear weapons impose on governments.

It should not be thought that civil politics can be stifled only by ideological politics, or that millenarianism is the decisive determinant of radical alienation. Radical transformations in society can be undertaken without millenarian impulsion. Western and Oriental antiquity have known revolutions without ideologies. Every social order, even the most just, will have some victims, and every population will contain antinomian personalities. These alone instigate tendencies toward a sort of proto-ideological politics, even when there are no ideological traditions living in the open or under the surface.

Finally, civil politics are not the only alternative to ideological politics for the intellectuals. They have in some instances entered upon political careers like professional politicians, given up their intellectual concerns and attachments, and devoted themselves to the conventional round of vote getting, interest representation, self-preservation, and self-advancement. They could yield to the customary temptations of the vain and egocentric, demagogy, flattery, and opportunism. They could, in short, conform to their own prevailing image of normal political life.

This, however, is not likely. What is far more likely is withdrawal—angry withdrawal or sad and serene withdrawal. The traditions of withdrawal among the intellectuals are among the profoundest in our intellectual inheritance. One can be antipolitical without being ideological. This was the dominant trend among American intellectuals from the Jacksonian revolution until the Russian revolution; and it is unfortunately, despite the charges of conformity, of "other-directedness," and of being "organized men," still prevalent among American intellectuals today. The valiant effort to embrace "our Country and our Culture" is not a resounding success as far as civil politics are concerned.[28] The

28. See Newton Arvin et al., *America and the Intellectual*, Partisan Review Series no. 4 (New York, 1953).

repudiation of ideological politics has not led to the espousal or practice of civil politics. The life of American society is affirmed, but its political life and the civil element in its political life are not.

The situation in Great Britain is not very different. Great Britain has a better record in civil politics than any other country in the world, and its intellectuals have their proper share in that record. What is the situation today? The post-war idyll has ended in disenchantment. "Butskellism" has retreated. The "angry young men" are on the rampage. Even the most amiable Mr. Kingsley Amis, who said that he is, when he has to choose, a Labour Party man, cannot take politics seriously. His heart is not in it.[29] He, like those with whom his name is coupled, is distrustful of the "professional espouser of causes." The humiliation of the Suez fiasco and the danger of the hydrogen bomb have seriously damaged the British intellectuals' capacity for civil politics. Even a sober, responsible intellectual of long and honorable political experience, Mr. Christopher Hollis, told his fellow intellectuals that the main task before the British electorate is to discredit the two major political parties, even though he expects no serious "Liberal revival."[30] Mr. John Osborne, who has no such background of experience of political responsibility, is far harsher in his anti-politics. "I can't go on laughing at the idiots who rule our lives. . . . They are no longer funny because they are not merely dangerous, they are murderers . . . they are stupid, insensitive, unimaginative beyond hope, uncreative, and murderous."[31]

VI

Can the intellectuals reeducate themselves to a civil state of mind? Can they keep the traditions of ideological politics quiescent while they modify their own outlook? Can they bring forth and fortify the incipient

---

29. *Socialism and the Intellectuals,* Fabian Tract 304 (London, 1957).

30. "What Shall We Do Next Time?" *Spectator* (21 February 1958): 225–26.

31. "They Call It Cricket," in Tom Maschler, ed., *Declaration* (London, 1957), p. 67.

impulses of civility which the harsh experiences of the past half-century stirred into movement?

One condition of the success of this effort at "self-civilization" is that we should not think that we can or should completely extirpate the ideological heritage. There are valuable elements in that inheritance which are worthy of conservation in any political outlook which lays claim to our respect. The demand for moral equality, the distrust of authority and of the institutions which it conducts for its own continuance, the insistence on justice, and the call to a heroic existence, even the belief in the earthly paradise and the realm of freedom, all have some validity in them. To deny them will only lay civil politics open to the charge—not unjustified—of being philistine politics in the worst sense, without feeling or sympathy, unimaginative, timorously clinging to what already exists. The ideological element in our intellectual classes will not die out so easily and so soon that its successors will be able to escape unscathed while conducting politics which, while called civil, are merely concerned with the maintenance of order and keeping things as they are.[32]

These impulses in the human heart will not be disregarded. The fact that they have been forced to an extreme and cast into the framework of unrealizable hopes does not mean that they are in themselves immoral. The discredit into which their doctrinaire proponents have deservedly fallen should not be extended to them. Life would be poorer without them, and a political system which sought to proceed entirely without them or entirely against them would find the most sensitive spirits of its society once more drawn up in embittered and irreconcilable opposition.

It has not been the substantive values sought by ideological politics which have done such damage. Rather it has been the rigidity, the

32. One of the dangers of the New Conservatism is that it fails to see that civil politics are as eager for improvement as they are ready to conserve what has come down from the past. See Charles Parkin, *The Moral Basis of Burke's Philosophy* (Cambridge, 1956), chap. 6, pp. 109–30; also Mr. Kristol's perspicacious essay in the *Yale Review*, mentioned earlier.

exclusiveness, and the extremity with which particular values have been sought. There is nothing evil about loyalty to one's community, national or ethnic or cultural, nor is there anything wicked in the appreciation of equality or the devotion to any particular ideal. What is so malign is the elevation of one value, such as equality or national or ethnic solidarity, to supremacy over all others, and the insistence on its exclusive dominion in every sphere of life.[33]

Civil politics therefore will have a better chance to obtain more enduring devotion among intellectuals if their proponents do not disavow all continuity whatsoever with the substantive values of ideological politics. Correspondingly, their chances for success will be enhanced if the prudence they extol is exercised in finding a just balance among the contending values rather than in merely seeking self-maintenance, which will degenerate into unprincipled opportunism.

A complete disavowal of every line of affinity between civility and ideology will not only be false in fact but would turn civility into an ideology. Civility would become an ideology of pure politics concerned with no substantive values except the acquisition and retention of power and the maintenance of public order and with absolutely no other interest. Civility would take upon itself the onus of the very same moral separatism for which it criticizes ideological politics, if it denied its affinity with the substantive values which the ideological outlook holds and distorts.

VII

How can intellectuals retain those elements of romanticism which prize spontaneity and genuineness of expression, and which aid the

33. Few writers have made this criticism of ideological politics, while retaining a compassionate sympathy for their ideals, as well as Conrad. Natalie Haldin says at the end of *Under Western Eyes*, "I must own to you that I shall never give up looking forward to the day when all discord shall be silenced ... and the weary men united at last ... feel saddened by their victory, because so many ideas have perished for the triumph of one. ..."

cultivation of individuality, while curbing their expansiveness? By excessive demands for individuality and the consequent exaggeration of the restrictions which institutional life imposes on it, romanticism will discredit any social order and turn the intellectuals against it and arouse the custodians of order against the intellectuals. The "imperialism" which the late Baron Ernst Seillière bemoaned in so many volumes can disrupt any social order, and above all a liberal order. A way must be found to retain many of the values of romanticism while restricting their expansiveness.

A renewal of the old idea, fundamental to modern liberalism, of a separation of the spheres is needed. It can, of course, be realized only very incompletely; economic life cannot be completely independent of government and politics, and vice versa; religion and politics cannot be completely separated; culture and politics cannot be completely separated. Nonetheless, while acknowledging and accepting their necessary collaboration and affinity, it is very important that the guardians, practical and intellectual, of each of the spheres should be aware of the desirability, in principle, of their separateness. This would be a bulwark against the romantic—and ideological—insistence on the universal application of a single set of standards. The separation of the different spheres of life would not please those ideological politicians and intellectuals who seek complete consistency. Without it, however, civility would be extinguished and our best intellectual traditions would be frustrated.

It should be quite possible in practice to realize a far-reaching separation of the spheres while maintaining their overlaps and affinities. This is in fact done to a large extent in societies of the West, however imperfectly and unprincipledly. The real difficulty is to bring about the intellectual's acceptance of it as a reasonable policy. There is not such a completely unbridgeable antinomy between individuality and institutions as romanticism insists on although there must inevitably be some tension. The intellectual's distrust of the ongoing life in the spheres outside his own arises from the defects in his sense of affinity.

The nature of the sense of affinity which binds the members of a society together is a mystery. It seems somehow connected with the empathic capacities of the individual—not just his empathy for persons whom he encounters in concrete form, in person, or through written or plastic symbols, but for classes of persons who must necessarily remain anonymous. Up to a certain point, it goes hand in hand with individuality, and societies which do not know individuality also live without a sense of civil affinity. It is shriveled and shrunken by fear, and when it is restricted, it is in its turn conducive to fear of one's fellow men. If somehow the intellectuals could be got over their almost primordial terror of and fascination for authority, which, they fear, crushes their individuality, the movement for civility would make a tremendous advance.

Modern Western societies have witnessed a diminution in the moral distance separating the higher and the lower classes. This has in part been a result of the changes in the distribution of national income which have raised the lower strata and diminished the upper strata, so that standards of life are now very much nearer to each other than they have ever been before, however considerable the differences remain, and should, to some extent, still remain. But more significant, I think, is the change in the civil consciousness which has taken place in Western societies. This is in some measure a result of the inner development of the potentialities of the Protestant idea—the same complex of ideas and sentiments which has aggravated the millenarian disposition. The notion that every man has a spark of divinity in him, that all men participate in a common substance—sacred in the last analysis but civil in its concrete and mediated forms—has grown out of the conjunction of the modern national state and Christian protestantism. From this conjunction grew the idea of the citizen, and from it our modern idea of the civil order as a stratum of being in which all the members of a state participate.

The modest flowering of civility in the modern world is a new thing in history. Pericles' Funeral Oration foreshadowed its program. The great Roman forerunners were, however grandiose, no more than adumbrations of a human possibility, rather than indications of a well-functioning civility in ancient times. The growth of civility has been halting and very imperfect. Its growth has been attended by an exacerbation of ideology—and the two seem in the modern epoch to have some obscure and intricate interdependence. Yet it does seem that with the spread of individuality—imperfect now and never perfectly realizable—in the wider reaches of the population, the sense of civil affinity has increased its scope and power among the lower strata, who previously existed as objects of authority and economic power but did not dwell within the same moral and civil domain as their rulers. There is now in all strata, on the average, a higher civil sense than earlier phases of Western society have ever manifested—and this despite class conflicts and ideological separatism and irreconcilability. Even ethnic barriers seem slowly to be yielding to the rising tide of civility. Is it too much to hope that the intellectuals, who have provided such illustrious antecedents in the true "civilization" of politics, will themselves come more fully into this process, and thus, by one of the great continental drifts of history, bring the age of ideology to an end?

Civility and Civil Society

GOOD MANNERS BETWEEN PERSONS
AND CONCERN FOR THE COMMON GOOD
IN PUBLIC AFFAIRS

I

MANY YEARS AGO, I tried to put into a broader context the notion of ideology.[1] By ideology I meant a set of ostensibly systematized beliefs, referring to all aspects of life, and asserted with dogmatic fervor and moral rigorism in the assessment of actions and institutions in the light of those beliefs, the consistent application of the beliefs to action in all spheres of social and cultural life, and the sharp disjunction between "we"—the usually organized adherents of the ideology—and "they"—those who do not adhere to it in all its details. Ideology entails an irreconcilable conflict between the proponents of the ideology and "the others," i.e., those persons and groups who do not share it. Ideological politics apply Carl Schmitt's distinction between "Freund/Feind." (Those who are not completely with us are our enemies!) Ideologists think in large perspectives. Ideologists are apocalyptic. They think of a "final struggle" and last judgment.

A much shorter and different version of this essay was previously published in Edward Banfield, ed., *Civility and Citizenship* (New York: Paragon House, 1992). Reprinted by permission of Professors World Peace Academy.

1. See the previous essay in this volume, "Ideology and Civility" *(ed.)*.

I certainly did not mean by "ideology" just any constellation of beliefs shared by many individuals. I did not mean beliefs of a conservative "backward looking" sort in contrast with progressivistic beliefs. Nor did I mean just any beliefs which were closely consistent with or contributory to the achievement of the "interests" of the individuals and collectivities which espoused them. Nor finally did I mean any set of erroneous beliefs widely shared. I make these points in order to try to clear up the confusion left by Marxists, by Karl Mannheim and by anthropologists, sociologists and political scientists who habitually make a muddle of the whole matter, indiscriminately amalgamating several of the usages and never specifying in what sense they use the term. I should add that when they use the term "ideological" adjectivally, they usually mean something closer to my definition of ideology than to their own usage.

At that time, the Second World War had not been long over. I had before my mind's eye the beliefs espoused by official spokesmen of the Soviet Union and by the Communist parties which were agents of the Soviet Union throughout the rest of the world. I had in mind also the inner core of the German National Socialists and the German political sects from whose midst the National Socialists emerged. This was also the period when Senator Joseph McCarthy was ascending in the United States, and expressing certain features of the ideological outlook. There were many instances of this ideological picture of "the war between the children of light and the children of darkness."

What were the alternatives to ideological politics? One alternative was the "machine politics" and the associated "spoils-system" which had preoccupied American reformers and intellectuals since the 1880s.

In the United States, before the federal government became so preponderant, local and state politics were more visible and more important on the political scene than they later became. Local and state politics in the United States were clearly the preserve of the political "machines." These added corruption for self-enrichment to the vices of the representation of private and local interests at the cost of the interest of the whole.

Another form of "machine politics" was the bureaucratization of the leadership of political parties; it was this variant which was the object of Robert Michels' analysis and criticism of European social democratic parties. "Machine politics" were not always associated with bribery but they were nevertheless looked upon as offering to kinsmen and members of the politicians' own ethnic group opportunities for income from jobs and contracts poorly executed. It was the revulsion against these particular alternatives of bureaucratic "machine politics," of the "spoils-system" and the association and corruption, and against the democratic regimes in which they flourished which prepared the way for the espousal of the ideological politics which began to spread among Western intellectuals after the Russian Revolution of October 1917 and even more during the economic depression of the 1930s. (The revulsion against bourgeois society was not aimed only at the political life of that type of society but also against its philistine conventionality, its constrictive morality and the etiquette of its private relations.)

The several variants of "machine politics" did not offer appealing alternatives, even though in some respects they were regarded as unavoidable and even useful in large societies with universal suffrage. In Europe, "machine politics" were marked by the subservience of the ordinary member of the legislature to his party's leaders, individual self-seeking and the representation and promotion of particular interests through legislation and administration. Max Weber thought that "machine politics" were inevitable in large parties and that large parties were inevitable in "mass democracies" with universal suffrage. Max Weber, although he was brutally pessimistic in his friendly criticism of Michels about the chances of escaping from the bureaucratic machine in politics, was not content with the simple alternatives of the ethics of conscience in politics—*Gesinnungsethik* or *Gesinnungspolitik*—and "machine politics," which was the politics of bosses and party-bureaucrats concerned with offering and taking spoils—the profitable or comfortable sinecures and favoritism in the award of contracts for the supply of goods and services to governments. He thought that there was a possibility of a politics of responsibility, of *Verantwortungsethik* or *Verantwortungspolitik*.[2]

By the "ethics" or "politics" of "responsibility," Max Weber meant choices made by weighing the costs and benefits of pursuing a variety of alternatives, each of them entailing values incommensurable with or irreducible to each other and not standing in a relationship of logical subsumption with each other. Yet a decision had to be found which would be better than any other decision. Weber did not think that any decision was as good as any other decision. Some were better than others, although no formula for making such decisions could be found. To make such decisions required courage—it required a charismatic political leader who could withstand the party bureaucrats and the bureaucrats of the civil service and would make decisions in the national interest, not just the interest of any particular sector of German society.

Max Weber never said what the national interest was, but he was inclined to think of it as ascendancy on the world scene. I would substitute the term "the interest of the whole society" because I would like to give more prominence to the practice of the politics of responsibility on behalf of the entire society in its internal affairs as well as in its position in the world. It is not easy to define "the interest of the whole society" in specific and concrete terms. It is easier to do so negatively than positively. For example, some measures taken by politicians clearly represent parochial interest of the most evident sort; a

2. Max Weber's contrast between the *Gesinnungsethik* and the *Verantwortungsethik* occurs in his 1918 essay "Politics as a Vocation." Shils translates the contrast as between the "ethics of conscience" and the "ethics of responsibility." Many readers in English know the first term as the "ethics of ultimate (or absolute) ends" from the translation of "Politics as a Vocation" by Hans Gerth and C. Wright Mills, *From Max Weber* (New York: Oxford University Press, 1946) *(ed.)*.

legislator who votes to maintain a military air base in his constituency because 1500 of his constituents are employed in it and because the air force spends X millions of dollars in purchases from local shopkeepers. All this despite the demonstrated fact that there is no military value in that particular air base, either directly or indirectly, and that two billions of dollars would be saved if the air base were closed down and its military operations, etc., assigned to other bases. It is clear that the decision of the legislator to vote to retain the base in his constituency is an action in disregard of the common good. This is a very simple instance.

At the third angle of this triangle of alternatives—the first two are machine-and-spoils politics and the politics of parochial or sectional interest—are the politicians of the ethics of conscience, who calculate and weigh nothing against anything else. For them, certain actions are intrinsically good and right and it is absolutely imperative that they be performed. A message from God or a ruminative obsession or simply a powerful passion or an all-transcending ethical obligation requires the performance of an intrinsically valuable action. (Max Weber called it value rational action.)

There are some scholars who accept "interest politics" as inevitable and reasonable. They assert that it is impossible to transcend particular interests. They fail, however, to recognize that the particular interests which they regard as internally homogeneous and as irreducible are in fact heterogeneous in composition. What they think is a single homogeneous interest is in fact a common denominator of a host of more particular and often quite divergent interests. The representation of a partisan interest is invariably the construction of an ostensibly single common interest from a number of diverse interests, the proponents of which are willing to renounce some of their anticipated advantages or interests on the behalf of the common interest of the whole partisan bloc. Interests too require the composition of conflicting and incompatible elements. In their logical structure, parochial or group interests are not wholly unlike the common good which is borne in mind by those who act according to the idea of the politics of responsibility. They require compromise and a common denominator.

"Interest politics" are at the opposite extreme from ideological politics. Ideological politics care only for an end or a object remote in time and meaning from the immediate present. "Interest politics" care only for what can be achieved in the very near future and for identifiable beneficiaries—mostly the "interest politician" himself and his identifiable clients and patrons. There is no ideal in interest politics, nothing transcendental. It is the most secular, the most earthly, the most self-seeking of political actions. It is concerned with the more or less calculable "here and now."

Only recently have political theorists tried to work out a general theory of interest politics. Not surprisingly, they have found the economic theory of the market the most appropriate mode of analysis.

II

There are similarities between interest politics and ideological politics. Both aim to realize the objectives of a particular group within the larger society. The practitioners of interest politics have no transcendental justification for their actions on behalf of a particular group. Their aim is to satisfy the demands of that particular group. The politicians who attempt to do that on behalf of the particular group might do so because they expect benefit for themselves in the form of votes in a subsequent election, or in an indefinite series of subsequent elections, or in the form of financial support for the campaign for votes for themselves or their party in the next election or the subsequent elections. They might also believe that it is ethically right that the demands of that particular—parochial—group should be satisfied or because they expect to receive some financial gain or they see in it a political advantage for themselves in return for their efforts to satisfy that group's demands. Parochiality or partiality of objectives is the mark of "interest politics."

Interest politics resemble machine-*cum*-spoils-politics in that both aim to satisfy particular groups. The machine politicians aim to benefit themselves and their supporters; interest politicians do the same but in the former case the benefits are intra-governmental while in the latter extra-governmental. These two types of political action often overlap; they differ primarily in the locus of the beneficiaries and in the nature of the benefits—employment in government and contracts from government in the one case, and economic advantages outside government in the other.

Ideological political sects or parties and their representatives are also very parochial in their immediate objectives although they claim that ultimately their objectives will serve the entire society or the entire human race. They justify their immediate exclusive parochiality on the ground that they alone know what must be done for the attainment of the larger ideal and that everyone who is not in their sect is a part and agent of the present sinful regime. The ideological sect has to keep itself clear of these pernicious persons or groups in order to be able to redeem their entire society from some social, moral, metaphysical or biological defects or dangers. They claim that ultimately the beneficiary of the ideological politics of their particular sect or party will be the entire society or all of mankind. On themselves alone rests the responsibility for the realization of the highest end, which is a purified and perfected society or the kingdom of God on earth. In the meantime, however, they divide the politically or religiously active sector of society into two fundamentally irreconcilable parts—themselves and all the others. The other part is irredeemably and completely defective; there is no remedy for the defects of this group or groups except extirpation, suppression or exile.

The individual politician who is wedded to the course of interest politics is often indifferent to the moral value of his opponents and even to the moral values of those whose demands he is attempting to fulfill; he is interested in future benefits in exchange for the services performed. If he takes the view that the "devil take the hindmost," it is not because he is hostile towards those to whom is left the hindmost; he is simply uninterested in them. He does not regard them as evil. This is, in principle, in marked contrast with the beliefs of an ideological sect or party which seeks the realization of its ideal.

Because of its orientation towards an ideal, ideological parties or sects have something in common with civil politics, which also have an ideal in view. The former wishes to achieve a complete realization of the ideal, which is remote from existing circumstances. The ideal of civil politics is closer to present reality, it has less specific substantive content and it is concerned with compromises among a plurality of values and with compromises of the demands of parochial parts of the society with the interest of the society as a whole.

III

Let me say here that civil society and liberal democracy are not identical, but they overlap with each other. A liberal democracy might be very little of a civil society, but if it contains very little of civil society its future as a liberal democracy is in danger. Liberal democracy is a set of institutions. Civil society comprises the institutions of liberal democracy but it contains other institutions as well. It also comprises a pattern and standard of judgment without which the institutions of civil society cannot flourish. When that pattern of judgment and the relations it sustains are lacking, it is scarcely possible for civil society to exist at all.

The practices which are appropriate to this mode of political conduct and which are characteristic of civil society, I call civil politics. The attitude and ethos of this conduct, I call civility.

A liberal democratic society which is also a civil society is one in which there is enough civility to keep the partisanship of ideological politics, "interest politics" and machine politics in check. The criterion by which civil politics operates is a solicitude for the interest of the whole society, or in other words, a concern for the common good.

A civil society is not a primordial community. A primordial community is one in which members are significant to each other because they believe that they are linked with each other by their having a common biological ancestor; they are also linked with each other by their common residence in a locality of short radius. They are seen by each other as kinsmen, or as members of the same putative lineage; this is reinforced by derivation from ancestors of long residence in the narrow locality. Ethnic collectivities, even where they no longer reside in a common locality of short radius, still think of themselves as having a common biological ancestry. In an ethnically heterogeneous civil society, ethnic collective self-consciousness is held in check by the preponderance of the civil collective self-consciousness. Likewise, in civil societies in which there are lineage and local collective self-consciousnesses, these too are held in check by preponderance of the civil collective self-consciousness.

In contrast with the primordial collectivity—called *Gemeinschaft* by Tönnies—the civil collectivity or the civil society is constituted by a collective self-consciousness in which the important referent is the civil quality of its participants, i.e., their being members of a society under a common authority, common laws and living in a common, more or less bounded territory. Each participant in the civil collective self-consciousness sees his fellow participants as fellow-citizens, not as fellow-kinsmen. Participation in a common civil collective self-consciousness engenders a sense of obligation to the other participants simply by virtue of their quality as members—mainly anonymous members—of the same civil society.

It is their civil quality which is the focus of the tie which binds the members of a civil society to each other. Primordial qualities lose much of their significance as referents in the collective self-consciousness. Civil qualities become the dominant referents. The civil person, the bearer of civility, sees his fellow-citizens taken all together—not just his kinsmen or his neighbors—as entitled to his obligations. In the civil society, the authority rules over the whole society; the bureaucracy administers whatever in the society is regarded as being in need of administration without consideration for the primordial properties of those ruled.

It was in this spirit that the civil service reformers of Great Britain, British India and the United States desired a civil service which was recruited without regard to primordial properties—kinship, clientage or ethnicity—and which would administer the whole society for the advantage of the whole society. (The designation as civil service is a very good name, although it was not chosen with that idea in mind; the term "civil" in that context was intended as a differentiation from military and ecclesiastical.) The judiciary—if it behaved civilly—applied the law without concern for the primordial properties of kinship or race or locality but only with concern for the actions the defendants have performed and to which the rule of law is to be applied. That is the nature of the rule of law. It applies equally to all who are members of the civil collectivity, i.e., those who reside in the territory of the civil society; this includes those who are in positions of governmental authority.

Thus, the civil person, when he has to decide and act in a situation in which there is a conflict, is one who thinks primarily of the civil society as the object of his obligations, not the members of his family, or his village, or his party or of his ethnic group or his social class, or his occupation.

Hegel's idea of "civil society" (*bürgerliche Gesellschaft*), as he treated it in *The Philosophy of Right*, requires extension to a wider range of objects than the market economy. There are wants and desires which might seek satisfaction for the individual in institutions and situations other than the market. The striving for status, the organization to advance the interests of a section of society, a class, etc., may seek satisfaction through organization, monopoly and abstention or boycott, etc., and these phenomena do not occur only in markets. The entire institutional system for the collection and transmission of information, and scholarly and scientific knowledge, are also parts of the civil system. The institutions which compete for influence over the state, political parties, the formation of public opinion also belong in the civil sphere. These are not sufficiently treated by Hegel.

The state is not the market. The state is the sphere of the rights and duties of the citizen, of the authority which legitimately rules, in limited spheres, over the population of the bounded territory. That authority is the government. The state also comprises the citizenry with its rights and duties. The rights of the citizens are rights *vis-à-vis* the government and their fellow-citizens. Their duties likewise. They are duties to government and their fellow-citizens. The citizen is not only a bearer of rights and duties *vis-à-vis* the government and his fellow-citizen. He is also a participant in the family and the market. There are important spheres of action outside the state; they are not exhausted by Hegel's account in *The Philosophy of Right* of the family and of bourgeois society.

There is a zone of social life outside civil society (*bürgerliche Gesellschaft*) in Hegel's sense and the state. That zone is the extended zone of civil society. (This is also Hegel's view in his essay on "The German Constitution.")

A civil society is in my terms a society in which civility enfolds both "civil society" as understood by Hegel and the state; it also enfolds but does not saturate the family—anymore than it pervades the *bürgerliche Gesellschaft* and the state. Civility is a broader phenomenon than citizenship in the state. The state comprises the government and that part of civil society which is oriented towards it. Citizenship is a phenomenon of the state; it is the complex of actions of submission to, criticism and active guidance of the government. If there is no civil society of the sort I delineate here, the government is subject to no higher authority than itself and there are no rules which transcend the positive laws of the state. If there is a civil society—not just the market—the government itself is the higher authority in society, guided or constrained only by the higher law which is present in civility—outside itself and over it. Civil society is the governor which regulates both the economy and the government although both are, to some degree, autonomous. A totalitarian society is the antithesis of civil society.

Membership in the civil society, i.e., in the part of the society which realizes the condition of effective civility, is, in one fundamental aspect, participation in a collective self-consciousness which "transcends" or is "preponderant" over more numerous special, more partial and narrower collective self-consciousnesses, which can co-exist with it. It also comprises within itself the collective self-consciousness of the state itself. Membership in the state as a collectivity in a civil society is the same as citizenship. It entails participation in the civil collective self-consciousness of the state. This participation in the collective self-consciousness of the state, i.e., this citizenship, bears within itself the dignity of the individual as a bearer of rights and duties within the state, of a share in the rulership of the government and of the differentiation of the state into rulers, legislators, civil servants including judges, and citizens. Civil society carries within itself an awareness, i.e., knowledge, of the limits of the state as a collectivity *vis-à-vis* the economy and *vis-à-vis* society.

A society differentiated with respect to occupation, region, religion, ethnic origins, status, etc., is bound to experience conflicts among its various sectors; the conflicts are conflicts of particular, divergent interests and of particular, divergent ideals. Any society with public political life and with relatively widespread participation cannot avoid some degree of segmentally differentiated organization in its political activities. Once organizations and differences in intensity of participation exist, the necessities of organization render inevitable and useful a measure of bureaucracy and a measure of "bossism" within the organizations. That cannot be avoided. Unorganized participatory political life, in a territorially extensive and numerous society, such as is envisaged by proponents of "participatory democracy," is a phantom. Even if such a political life existed in the initial stages of a small society, it would soon yield to "machine" and "interest politics" as soon as the polity increased in size and as its society became more differentiated.

Nor can ideological politics, even in the most civil societies, be entirely avoided. No society, however decent, is perfect in the light of exigent standards; there are always imperfections discernible when such exigent standards are applied to it. There are always some persons who are attracted by such exigent standards, even though they themselves do not conform with them, and there is enough of a tradition of ideological politics to offer to such "perfectionists" a dignifying intellectual and moral legitimation.

IV

Any large society which is not simply a system of imperial rule over small, largely self-contained, primordial societies, but in which the society is more or less coextensive with the territory, is inevitably a differentiated society, differentiated not only in the numerous primordial societies, which retain their own traditions to a considerable extent, but also by a division of labor (insofar as there is an exchange or market economy) and stratification of property ownership, political power and social status. Each sector of a differentiated society has "interests," i.e., ends, actually conceived or potential, which are frequently in conflict with the "interests" of the other sectors of society. The conflicting parties see that their own benefits would be endangered by an increase in the benefits of the others. This is bound to happen when desires, in the aggregate, exceed the supply of the objects which would satisfy those desires. Conflicts are therefore inevitable; even where there is peace or harmony with a society, the conflicts are potentialities. Where they are experienced as conflicts, they may be suppressed by the more powerful or they may be open. All large differentiated open societies stand in need of civility. They must contain a substantial degree of civility; otherwise they will be in danger of severe conflict and disorder.

Civility is an attitude and a mode of action which attempts to strike a balance between conflicting demands and conflicting interests. Liberal democracy is especially in need of the virtue of civility because liberal democracy is more prone to bring latent conflicts into actuality, simply because it permits their open pursuit.

Liberal democracy has opened the political field to the demands of all sectors of society and it has tended to attribute legitimacy to the demands of those classes and groups who previously had no continuously open way to give voice to their demands. Liberalism provided the institutions of representative government and the prerequisite public liberties through which such demands could be made public; democracy brought into those institutions the classes whose demands were hitherto unspoken in public or, when spoken, were unheeded by others.

No society has ever had a complete "harmony of interests." Liberal democracy has made the disharmony of interests more visible and audible to all other parts of the society. The sight of interests, asserted and realized, has heightened the individual and collective self-consciousness not only of the exponents of those interests but of those who are, within their own society, spectators of these conflicts. The differentiation and stratification of functions and positions are not only among the referents of the collective self-consciousness of each sector of society, they are also a source of contention and a stimulus to demands. The growth of wealth, the increased desires of the electorate, their increased awareness of government and their increased turning to government for the satisfaction of these desires, and the increased readiness of governments to attempt to satisfy those desires, have combined to make it appear that their demands are realizable. The belief in the realizability of a demand encourages the further articulation of demands and more forceful insistence on their gratification.

The freedom of the press and of assembly and petition have given more opportunity for demands to be expressed in public and to become known to most parts of society. Their expression has encouraged the emergence of new demands from previously relatively undemanding parts of the population.

Intellectuals, with their hostility towards their respective societies and particularly towards the centers of those societies and their belief in the rightness of the demands of any group at the periphery against the center, have given resonance to demands and have thereby fostered their intensity and insistence.

There has been an antinomy at the heart of liberal democracy throughout the period since the Second World War. On the one side, demanding groups seek satisfaction for their demands through the exertions of government. On the other, since the demands are insatiable, indeed have grown with their partial satisfaction, the capacity of the government to satisfy those demands is diminished relatively to the demands. Therewith, the authority of a government is put into question because the legitimacy of government is to a large extent dependent on its effectiveness in realizing its intentions. Government is regarded almost exclusively as an instrument for the satisfaction of demands. Its legitimacy is not acknowledged unless it satisfies particular parochial demands. The press—the printed press and television—contributes to the undermining of the legitimacy of government. It denies to governments the prerogatives of sovereign power to exercise discretion in the choice of alternatives in their compromise and to refuse demands out of concern for the common good. It strengthens the tendency towards interest politics.

The illegitimacy of authority weakens its effectiveness—just as weakness or ineffectiveness reduces belief in its legitimacy. The ineffectiveness and illegitimacy of authority have a solvent effect on the more inclusive collective self-consciousness of the various sectors of the pluralistic society. The process strengthens the individual self-consciousness of many individuals but it does not "atomize" society into an aggregate of separate self-interested individuals. It does produce a tendency in that direction but only to a limited extent. The chief immediate beneficiaries of the weakening of the collective self-consciousness of the society are the numerous particular sectors of the society. Their particular collective self-consciousnesses are fortified by the weakening of the collective self-consciousness of the entire society. The collective self-consciousness of the entire society is, in any case, never completely ascendant in the constituent sectors of society. It is always mixed with the respective particular collective self-consciousnesses of those sectors. No society can ever be a completely civil society, concerned only about the common good.

Civil politics, in accordance with its concern for the common good of society as a whole, assumes a belief that there is such a thing "as society as a whole." Civil society is not the market, although it has a place for the market. It is also not a political market of different, distinct and disjunctive interests, competing and incompatible or conflicting with each other. Since the idea of the good of the whole cannot be rigorously determined, there are inevitably different conceptions at any one time regarding the substance of the good of society as a whole.

In civil society and in civil politics, some of the politically active persons act civilly, i.e., for the good of the whole. This does not mean that they are entirely lacking in partisanship. It does, however, mean that they are less partisan than some of their fellow-partisans and their opponents and that they speak and act more frequently and more visibly for the good of the larger society. They appeal to the recessive or latent civility of their fellow-partisans and opponents and they sometimes succeed in arousing it and thereby strengthening it.

Civility entails civil conduct towards other parties, those which represent other conceptions of the common good of all, as well as those which are not concerned with the common good but which are clearly interested in the good of particular parts of the society.

Civility is not only a policy of action on behalf of the whole society; it entails a cognitive account of the structure or pattern of the whole society and a normative prescription to act for its benefit. It is also a procedure of political or public action. It is the procedure of good manners in the public or political sphere.

V

It is at this point that public civility and good manners, which have at times been regarded as the substance of civility,[3] come together. The use of the term civility for good manners is perfectly respectable; there are many good historical precedents for it. Nevertheless, this usage of civility is much narrower than the usage I am employing in this essay. The two usages are not however wholly disjunctive.

Civility in private life and civility in the face-to-face relations of participants in public life are not entirely different from each other. Good manners are a feature—unfortunately not a universally realized feature—of the direct contacts of individuals in each other's presence or at a distance through writing, telephonic communications, etc. Good manners might be highly elaborated, conventional or even idiosyncratic; they express respect or deference and avoid offensiveness. Good nature or temperamental amiability ("natural good manners") also restrict offensiveness.

There is not enough good nature or temperamental amiability in any society to permit it to dispense with good manners. Good manners are like uniforms and discipline which hide slovenliness, poor taste and unpleasing eccentricity. Good manners repress the expression of ill nature, but not invariably.

In political and public institutions, good manners, i.e., civility in the sense of courtesy, permit the collaboration of persons of diverse and often inimical dispositions. A wise politician, Sir William Harcourt, once said, according to T. S. Eliot, "the survival of a parliamentary system requires a constant *dining with the opposition*."[4] In legislative bodies which practice the politics of interest, antagonists can frequently work together easily because they are courteous towards each other,

3. See Ferdinand Mount, "The Recovery of Civility," *Encounter* 41 (July 1973): 31–43; Harold Nicolson, *Good Behaviour, Being a Study of Certain Types of Civility* (London: Constable, 1955).

4. *Notes Towards the Definition of Culture* (London: Faber and Faber, 1948), p. 84.

even when the realization of the intentions of one of the parties is incompatible with the realization of the intentions of the other parties. Their incompatibility notwithstanding, the contending individuals remain in courteous relations with each other. Sometimes even the practitioners of ideological politics develop civil qualities in their relations with those who, in accordance with the fervently held convictions of the ideological politicians, are doomed to go down in a final struggle.

VI

Nevertheless, good manners in direct relationships of individuals in the public sphere are not civility. Poor manners might aggravate incivility or be a part of it. Good manners, courtesy, temperate speech in relationships face-to-face, cannot be identical with the civility which is a part of civil society. In contemporary liberal democratic societies, even the smallest of which—omitting eccentric exceptions—contains about five million persons, face-to-face relationships occupy very small zones of any society and altogether they cover only a small part of the images and relationships which are integral features of the constitution of the entire society. The larger the society in territory and numbers, the smaller the fraction of relationships conducted in face-to-face situations. In such societies, political collaboration and contention and the making of political decisions are very intensively carried on in situations in which allies and antagonists see each other face-to-face, but the contentions and decisions refer to and affect parts of the society which the politicians do not see and with whom they are only in very infrequent contact and then only with a tiny minority of the persons referred to and affected. Furthermore, those persons who are in relationship to each other face-to-face make up, for every member of the society, only a small part of the politically active population. With the large majority, the civility of good manners and public civility have very different objects. Their good or poor manners in their immediate dealings with other persons make a difference in the quality of the daily life of the members of society but they are not directly important in politics. The referents of public civility in the collective self-consciousness of any sector of society are far more widely dispersed than are the individuals who are the objects of private civility or good manners in face-to-face relationships. Relationships with anonymous persons and classes or categories of anonymous persons over large distances are major features of liberal democracy in large societies. The public civility of those remote peripheries in their orientation towards centers of society and towards the other peripheries of their respective society do indeed make a considerable difference to the political order. They sustain civil society.

In a liberal democratic society in which literacy and affluence are widespread and the technology of communications makes possible and stimulates a widespread attention to and interest in the center and participation in an inclusive collective self-consciousness, political activity is not confined to a tiny minority comprising the head of government, cabinet members, legislators, and high officials in the government and of publicists, lobbyists, and agitators. Even though many individuals do not vote, very large numbers, including "non-voters," have opinions which they express and their opinions are often markedly touched with strong emotions. Public opinion polls have given prominence to a type of political participation which was previously lacking; it is a participation which makes desires known through means other than direct communication through speaking or writing. Experienced politicians in liberal democratic societies often have the gift of apprehending the views of their "silent" constituents. These "silent views" are also a form of political participation; I call it "participation by emanation." It is fostered by participation in the collective self-consciousness of the civil society. It is a bond between the representatives and the represented; it binds both of them. Such "participation by emanation" has never been wholly absent in liberal democracy. Such "participation by emanation" is the matrix of representation.

VII

The leaders of parties are often not very civil when there is an opportunity to gain an advantage over their rivals, often within their own party and especially of the rival party. As was pointed out by Gustave LeBon and Henry Sumner Maine and other critics of democracy in the course of the nineteenth century, speech in public becomes demagogic proportionately to the size of its audience. Politicians are often more civil to each other within the chambers of the legislature and within the committees and sub-committees of the legislative body than they are when they speak about each other while addressing a large audience beyond the boundaries of the legislature. Large anonymous audiences foster demagogy and encourage incivility. Discourse on the floor of a legislative chamber or in the committee rooms of parliamentary bodies is also often discourse before a larger public which works back upon discourse in face-to-face situations.

It is perhaps the least civil manifestations of the conduct of politicians which come to the attention of the mass of the population through the media of mass communication. The demagogy of politicians and the eagerness of journalists and commentators, including broadcasters, to seek out what can be dramatically presented and what will cause a sensation in the audience over the wrongdoing of public figures has resulted in an uncivil portrayal of the political sphere. Much of the conduct of the press, even of the "quality" press, in most liberal democracies acts in this uncivil way. This diffuses incivility in the society. It undoubtedly fosters uncivil attitudes in the population at large or at least in some parts of it. It is an impediment to civil society.

Nevertheless, in the middle, lower-middle and working classes, active incivility is held in check by indifference, distraction, skepticism and patriotism, the latter being an attachment to the entire society—or at least most of it.

Nationalism, especially extreme nationalism, is frequently uncivil because it not only embodies a hostile attitude towards foreign countries but also because it is accompanied by hostility to other sections of the population in the same society who do not share the intensity of feeling and the exclusiveness of attachment which accompany nationalism. Nationalists are frequently uncivil; they are often hostile and persecutory towards groups within their own society who are not as nationalistic as they are themselves. But it is important to bear in mind that nationalism is not identical either with nationality or patriotism; the latter can turn into nationalism and hence they have the potentiality of becoming uncivil. Nevertheless, nationality and patriotism are often sources of civility in the public sphere.

Intellectuals are often more uncivil than politicians who, despite their rhetorical exaggerations and their efforts to gain advantages for their parties, constituents or patrons, are often ready to make prudent compromises. Many of the most eminent intellectuals in most countries in modern times—England was an exception for much of the nineteenth century—and especially the most eminent literary intellectuals, have regarded themselves as outsiders in their own societies. The tradition of romanticism was a powerful impetus to incivility because it reinforced the tendency of literary intellectuals to regard themselves as neglected, unappreciated geniuses, neglected and unappreciated by a society of philistines. The French Revolution left behind a tradition of insurrectionary sects, which being doctrinaire, attracted a handful of intellectuals. The socialist movements, St. Simonian, Proudhounist and then Marxist and Christian, also attracted and supported small numbers of influential intellectuals in a melodramatic view of the corruption of contemporary society and its moral and aesthetic unworthiness. Although there were great proponents of civility among intellectuals in the nineteenth century—Tocqueville far more than any other— by and large intellectuals were, whatever their genuine intellectual and artistic merits, prominent models of incivility.

The Russian Revolution of October 1917 gave them a positive rallying point. The Soviet Union from its very beginning declared itself to be an enemy to the death of the Western liberal democratic societies;

classical Marxism was very uncivil, Leninism was even more so. The Bolshevik doctrine and the time and circumstances of its origin rendered it inimical to Western liberal democratic societies. Those Western intellectuals who took the side of the Soviet Union became more sharply focused and more sustained in their uncivil animosity towards their own societies, even though they themselves seldom attempted to carry out revolutionary actions.

It should be pointed out that the hostility of the Soviet Union towards the Western liberal democracies was not, as the apologists of the former in the 1920s used to claim, a defensive reaction to the horrible experiences of the civil war and the intervention by the Allied forces. The uncivil hostility to bourgeois society was a matter of principle central to Leninist Marxism, and had been promulgated long before the collapse of the Tsarist Russian armies towards the end of the First World War.

It would be too long a story to write here about the history of the incivility of Western intellectuals. It is certainly a broad penumbra of intellectual history since the French Revolution. It is not just a product of Marxism; it long antedates Marxism but Marxism added greatly to it. In any case, it has been a profoundly uncivil tradition; indeed, it has made incivility into a doctrine, although incivility is not inevitably doctrinaire.

VIII

It is in the nature of liberal democratic societies to accept, as given, the division of labor which occurs in any territorially extensive society in consequence of the working of a market economy. Governments and reformers might seek to increase the fraction of the population in the lower middle classes through education and propaganda but the fact of occupational differentiation is accepted as determined by the nature of things in a market economy. However egalitarian collectivistic liberals might be in their protestations, they generally accept this fundamental fact, which makes heterogeneity inevitable. They might seek to obliterate ethnic heterogeneity but they accept heterogeneity of occupation and even income. Once heterogeneity exists, there are bound to be conflicts. There are other sources of conflict as well. If the life of a liberal democratic society is to be peaceful enough and orderly enough to allow its citizens to go about their various businesses, the different sectors must be in a peaceful equilibrium with each other. It is not possible for this balance or equilibrium to be achieved or maintained only by rational bargaining in the market and by explicit rational compromise in political institutions. Differences of interest can usually be bargained over and fixed by contract, within the setting of a civil society. Differences of ideals usually cannot be reconciled, harmonized and made universally acceptable by a rational application of a clear criterion of the common good.

Of course, it would be very good if this could be done, but it is not likely. The belief that this is possible is one of the shortcomings of one popular current of contemporary academic social science. It is a worthy ideal but it is not realizable. It assumes that there is a fundamental common interest which is inherent in society and which, once disclosed, will supervene over all other interests of the respective parties; it assumes rigorously persuasive rationality and relevant empirical knowledge of a high degree of precision and reliability. There are also assumptions that evaluations can be very exactly formulated and compared with each other. If these modes of settling disagreement by contract, ratiocination and the adduction of empirical knowledge cannot be practiced, the only alternative to disintegrative and rancorous conflict is some trans-parochial solidarity which is capable of holding the disagreements in check so that they do not become excessively wide or acute. I know that this is a bit like saying that the best way to overcome illness is to be well. I think that there is more to it than that.

There must be a more or less society-wide collective self-consciousness which, coexisting alongside the various sectional collective self-consciousnesses, imposes limits on the demand for the realization of the divergent ideals and interests, and which, on occasion, can supersede them. The referent of the inclusive collective self-consciousness is the civil society. The attachment to an ideal of the civil society is decisive. The pattern of judgement and conduct which enters into and which is formed, or sustained, by this inclusive or society-wide collective self-consciousness and which is represented in this attachment is civility.

How much civility is needed for a society to be civil? And what are the conditions under which this modicum of civility can be achieved? We can only draw on what is already there. It is not a matter of creating it *ab ovo*; it is rather a matter of nurturing already existing dispositions and not cultivating the weeds of conflict which can suffocate it.

Not everyone in a civil society needs to be completely civil in his relations with the rest of society or to a particular group other than his own, and at all times. Even if it were desirable, it is neither necessary nor possible. The centers of society must be more civil than the peripheries, although the latter too must possess some civility. There must be sub-centers of high degrees of civility scattered throughout the peripheries of society.

It is dangerous for the internal peace and good order of a society if the centers are very uncivil internally and in their relations with each other. A civil society is imperilled if there is a low degree of civility within and between its centers. Their conflicts are broadcast in amplified form through society and their example encourages uncivil attitudes in other parts of the society. Incivility within the centers and among them breeds incivility in the citizenry, especially among young persons who have no significant experience of their own in public matters. It demoralizes a society when the centers are internally uncivil and are uncivil in their relations with each other.

IX

In 1895, Max Weber delivered his inaugural lecture at the University of Freiburg on "Der Nationalstaat und die Volkwirtschaftspolitik." In it, he reviewed the civil capacities of the main strata of German society with regard to their readiness to "face facts," to make hard decisions and to lead the society in a unifying way which would realize those decisions. I would like to do approximately the same with regard to the civil capacities of contemporary liberal democratic societies.

Before doing so, however, I should emphasize that the institutions of civil society—representative government, competitive political parties, periodic or regular elections, secret ballot, universal suffrage, a free press, freedom of association, assembly and petition or representation, independent institutions of learning and institutions of private property and freedom of contract—are absolutely necessary for a civil society. Without these institutions, there is no such thing as civil society. The institutions themselves do not guarantee a civil society; public civility is indispensable.

In which sections of the population can civility, rudimentary or highly developed, be found? Let me begin with the institutions and the professional custodians of those institutions which have in the past been regarded as the witnesses to transcendental values and as superior to partisanship. At first thought the universities might appear to be the most likely institutions of civil society.[5] The universities should, in principle, be as disinterested among the contending interests and ideals as devotion to truth permits. The teachers in the universities should offer to society an authority standing outside the political struggle. They have performed these functions rather poorly in recent years.

Generally, universities as corporate bodies and their higher administrators have usually been neutral on public issues other than the scale of financial support by government. Universities, as corporate bodies, usually do not make declarations of their attitudes and recommendations regarding actions taken or to be taken by governments. This is far from true of individual university teachers, particularly in certain fields of study and especially so lately. Large numbers of them espouse one or another partisan attitude and, in the United States, at least,

5. See "The Modern University and Liberal Democracy," reprinted herein *(ed.).*

the frequency with which they have attempted to persuade university administrators and sometimes the higher governing bodies of their universities to espouse a partisan policy has increased over the past few decades. University teachers are often partisans on behalf of their own pecuniary interests but they are no less often public partisans on behalf of the demands and what they regard as the interests of other parochial groups. In their teaching within the university, some of them espouse incivility and deny the existence of civil society.

The idiom and substance of the teaching of literature nowadays have in many Western universities become uncivilly partisan. Many teachers now assert that "oppression" is inherent in language and in works of literature. The teaching of literature has in many universities become politically partisan and inimical to civility. The hostility of teachers of humanities in the United States towards "the canon" is justified on ideological grounds. The teaching of sociology has been similarly affected. In political science and anthropology, the "unmasking of oppression," "demythologization," the analysis of the "construction of tradition," etc., are less intellectual activities than they are political activities. They do not contribute to the order of civil society.

Nor is a great deal of help to be expected from the churches. Churches as such belong to the boundary between the earthly and transcendental realms. They are not in themselves parts of civil society; their society is the sacral society. But they also exist in the earthly realm of society, and in that role, they are or can be parts of civil society, although much of their history has been passed in societies which have not been civil societies.

The churches in Western societies have traditionally preached a single religion for all sectors of society; their deity was the deity of the entire society and of all mankind. Whereas the churches once behaved uncivilly in their espousal of the interests of the royal house and the aristocracy and great landowners and later of the class of wealthy private businessmen against the rest of the society—there were always some exceptions of clergymen who spoke on behalf of the entire society—

now the churches, especially the more prominent clergymen of the major Protestant churches, share the political and social views of the more or less antinomian secular intellectuals. Similar attitudes are spreading among Roman Catholic intellectuals and priests. The sects and denominations—disparaged as "fundamentalists" by the intellectuals of the major churches, sects and denominations—are also in an aggrieved and resentful state of mind. Many of their members are patriots but they seem to be unbridgeably separated from those whom they think of as ravaged by secularist views about many very important matters. An uncivil strife is rampant among the churches and sects; this strife is aggravated by the partisanship of more or less secularist collectivistic liberals, with an infusion of radicalism and of anguished very conservative believers. None of the antagonists contributes to civility in the earthly religious sphere or in the political sphere.

At one time, the upper classes, inheritors of great wealth, the land-owning aristocracy, prosperous merchants and industrialists produced a small number of public-spirited men and women who devoted much of their energy and some of their wealth to the protection of the common good; they also produced active as well as passive and vigorous exponents of a harsh incivility. One of the most striking features of the life of the liberal democracies of the past half century is the abdication from the civil roles which were once played by a significant handful of members of these strata. To some extent, this may be attributed to the loss of self-confidence which has afflicted the older upper classes in the face of egalitarian propaganda; perhaps they think that there is so much egalitarian prejudice against them that any efforts they make in public life would be certain to fail.

The new wealthy class, frequently rich by financial rather than industrial activities, has not offered much to compensate for the withdrawal of the stratum of the hereditarily wealthy and older plutocracy. The mass of the new wealthy class presents a spectacle of unrelenting pursuit of wealth and—unlike their earlier puritanical predecessors—great pleasure in spending it. Some of them go into politics and it is among these that some traces of civility are to be observed. Some of them engage in philanthropic activities; this too contributes to civil society.

The trade union movement, now that it has lost its socialist and communist *élan*, might be regarded as an alternative candidate to support civility. "Bread and butter" unionism has the civil merit of not being ideological. Yet the unyielding espousal of certain trade union demands in the decades following the Second World War has brought British and American industry into hazard. Latterly, they have shown a modest degree of conciliatoriness in industry.

The industrial working class which once had a marked sense of its own peripherality has in most liberal democratic countries come to regard itself as less remote from the center. Except for a small xenophobic and revolutionary margin, it has usually in the past half century in its relations with the center and with other peripheral groups been moderately civil. It is generally patriotic and in national crises even very patriotic. Although concerned with parochial benefits for itself, it has usually not shared in the extremes of doctrinaire class consciousness. It is probably even now the most civil of the major blocks of the population of present-day liberal democracies.

The intermittently uncivil attitude which was once present—not always salient—in the trade unions of the industrial working classes has latterly been taken over by trade unions of white collar workers, e.g., civil servants, postal workers, airport controllers, nurses and physicians and even university teachers. In most cases, their incivility is usually not ideological but it is uncivil nonetheless. Some of these occupations and professions were once markedly civil in the sense in which we have been using the term here.

The rural and small town population was often civil within its own restricted somewhat primordial radius. It was usually patriotic. The rural population has dwindled very much in its numerical position in present-day liberal democratic societies and it has also lost much of its high moral status. It is moreover very concerned to exploit what advantages still accrue to it from the mercantilist governmental tradition of being nationally self-sufficient in the production of food. In situations of damaged economic fortunes, the rural population has increased in incivility; but generally, these conditions are not the normal ones.

In a different sector of the population the prevailing pattern of conduct is almost wholly uncivil in its disruptive intrusions into domestic and economic private life. I speak of the rather large unemployed *Lumpenproletariat* and the criminal and delinquent class in the United States. All large urban societies have had *Lumpenproletarians*. Prolonged unemployment has added to their numbers so that there are many young persons in certain parts of the urban population in the United States and Great Britain who grow up without the expectation of earning their own livelihood by continuous work. Prominent in the criminal and delinquent classes in the United States are adolescents, largely black but by no means entirely so, who ravage whole areas of the large cities to an extent which makes their depredations statistically normal features of urban life. This incivility is not only to be found in the *Lumpenproletariat*. It is also found among fully and regularly employed young persons who find the routines of daily life too boring or too frustrating.

The activities of both these groups have become statistically normal and morally abnormal to such an extent that they have to be reckoned with in the daily life of the residents of large cities. On not infrequent occasions these groups, acting independently of each other—they are usually very hostile to each other—precipitate breakdowns of the civil order far beyond the powers of the police to confine and reduce them. This does not prevent the routines of life from being carried on but it requires adaptations which are constrictions of civil order and it weakens the motive of law abidingness which prevails in society and which is necessary for civil society. This phenomenon is not confined to the United States but it is more prominent there than in other countries of Western Europe.

The routine crimes of the criminal and delinquent class, on the scale on which they are carried on, are indeed not the only severe infringements on the order ostensibly guaranteed by law. There have been from time to time more extreme manifestations in riots, which are very gross infringements on the order of civil society.

The widespread consumption of narcotics which is characteristic of the young generation of criminals or delinquents is not confined to that generation. It is by now an enduring practice of a generation of mature years, whose immersion in the economy and culture of the consumption of narcotics brings them very close to the recurrent commission of criminal actions. There are many young and not so young persons who consume narcotics but who are not otherwise criminals; this may be true particularly of the consumers of "soft drugs." But unless they are employed with fairly good incomes, the costliness of narcotics drives them towards crime.

The consumption of narcotics, like the practice of homosexuality, is nowadays regarded by many persons as belonging in the private sphere and enjoying the prerogatives of private liberty, but in fact they are not confined to the private sphere. They encroach on the public or civil sphere and aggravate the agitation of civil society. The consumption of narcotics is linked with large-scale criminal activities which are also major economic enterprises with long-standing and highly organized criminal traditions.

Criminals and addicts to narcotics are nothing new in large urbanized societies. All large cities have had a large *Lumpenproletariat*, large enough to cause much civil disorder. I need only cite the Gordon Riots in London in 1780 or the riots in St. Louis and Chicago in 1919 or the riots in black quarters of New York, Los Angeles and other American cities in the 1960s to indicate that the *Lumpenproletariat* in a state of excitation is capable of disrupting and overpowering civil society, even if only transiently and locally. It is reasonable to think that the "successes" of the rioters, i.e., the fact that severe repressive measures were not taken against them, reduced the legitimacy of the indulgent and weak authority and encouraged further incivility subsequently. Where the authority is strong enough in will and force to put down these severe disruptions of the reign of legal order, its action often entails measures such as the declaration of "states of emergency" and curfews; these are acts which cripple, at least for a time, the institutions of civil society.

Against this background of incivility among the various classes and major institutions of present-day liberal democratic societies, the prospects of civility do not seem to be dazzlingly bright.

X

A thoroughgoing war of each against all is an utter impossibility. Violent conflicts, however, between various small parts of society, into which the *Lumpenproletariat* enters with enthusiasm, are certainly not unknown nor are civil wars for dominance and succession beyond the realm of possibility. Civility must be nurtured in order to prevent such degeneration into violent class conflicts which are usually conflicts only between rather small parts of each and any of the classes, and civil wars, which, like class conflicts, draw in only small parts of the population. Most of the members of the classes engaged in prolonged and violent conflicts between classes or of the warring regions of a civil war are relatively uninterested. They are severely afflicted bystanders who would prefer to live in a more civil society, or at least in a more quiet, i.e., law-abiding one.

Civility has become somewhat stronger in the United States after a low ebb during the war in South East Asia and in the decade which followed it, but it is still under siege. In Western Europe, civility has been surely helped by the diminution in the following and influence of the Communist parties. But there too there are areas of pronounced incivility: in Italy, the near paralysis of governmental capacity for decision because of the numerous parties which even in coalitions will allow practically nothing repugnant to them to be decided; in Germany, civility previous to unification was badly breached by radical terrorism and is now strained by the incorporation of the former states of the German Democratic Republic.

In the United States, where the rhetoric of partisanship has nearly always been more acrimonious than in other countries, the situation became worse over the 1960s and 1970s. The agitation about the war in South East Asia was a continuation and also revenge for the incivility of Senator McCarthy and his collaborators of the decade after the end of the Second World War. That decade was marked by the conspiratorial machinations of the devotees of the Soviet Union and the persecutory campaign represented in its most dramatic form by Senator McCarthy and similar investigative activities of the federal legislature. The press played an uncivil role in these events, amplifying them and disturbing unnecessarily the calm needed by a civil society. The institutions of civil society were disordered to some extent by these outbursts of incivility.

The partisanship of politicians has been aggravated by the very active participation of the press—including television—which has inherited the traditions of muckraking journalism and, more recently, the tradition of the literary and academic intellectuals, who are more deeply and pervasively hostile to American society than the muckrakers themselves. The rivalry of the leading figures of television programs and of networks, all eager for achievements in the derogation of political figures to whom they are antagonistic, has made this worse. Civility in American society has certainly been damaged by the press, both printed and broadcast. The press has not caused this incivility; it draws upon an old tradition of hyperbolic polemic. It has certainly aggravated it.

Nevertheless, it cannot be said that the processes of government and the institutions of civil society have been irremediably impeded by this incivility of journalists and their organs and the inquisitorial legislative determination to discredit the opponent political party. The machinery of bureaucracy has so much resistive power to any disruptive intrusion that it can scarcely be brought to a halt. A great number of the activities of the executive branch have so much momentum behind them that the tasks assigned to the executive branch or arrogated by it are in fact performed relatively effectively within the limits in which any very large organization can so act. There are embarrassments and hindrances in the conduct of affairs but there is never a breakdown. In short, American society is partly protected from the consequences of its own incivility by the momentum of its bureaucracy. This is true of other liberal democratic societies. There are from time to time zealots among civil servants, who, if they are powerful enough, can injure civil society by their wide departure from civility. By and large, however, unsatisfactory though they might be in other respects, the civil services of the liberal democracies do not harm the institutions of civil society.

But perhaps more important than the momentum of bureaucracy is the deep but not very subtle civility of ordinary people in most liberal democratic societies. First of all, by not allowing politics to become the be-all-and-end-all of their lives, they prevent the acridity of the public political scene from gaining a wide and persisting diffusion and from entering into the collective self-consciousness. This is a boon for the institutions of civil society because it keeps their burdens from becoming too heavy to bear. To make this point in more general terms, civility inhibits the extension of politics and the politicization of other spheres, e.g., the economic, the ecclesiastical, the academic and the domestic.

Being patriots, most practicing politicians in liberal democratic societies do not for long exile from their collective self-consciousness those who, whatever they have done in public or have been charged with doing, have not betrayed their country. I call attention here to the restoration of Mr. Richard Nixon to a marginally central position in American life—in contrast to the continued refusal to exculpate Mr. Alger Hiss. The failure of the efforts to damn Colonel Oliver North despite the prolonged agitation in the press and in Congress—the "Iran-Contra" case is a model of incivility by politicians and journalists against a Republican president—is evidence of the plain, uncomplicated civility of ordinary people in the United States. This is not just a manifestation of an inclination towards traditional patriotism and conservatism; it also contains a large element of civility. It indicates a certain degree of readiness to trust representative institutions and the government of society and a dislike of the extremes of partisanship.

There are almost always some politicians who can resist the ravages of extreme partisanship. They are sustained in their resistance by the knowledge that there are others in the broad and anonymous electorate who disapprove of the persecution of political rivals and antagonists. The defeat of Senator McCarthy was largely the achievement of civilly minded senators.

I will do no more than touch on the state of civility in Western European societies. The disillusionment of the intellectuals in France about the Soviet Union has reinforced the long beleaguered exponents of civility, scattered among the parties. Terrorism has diminished somewhat and sympathy with terrorists has also diminished in France. These are marks of increased civility.

In contrast with this, the enlarged following of the "Green party" in Central Europe has been a defeat for the progress of civility. Likewise, the increase in the following of the Le Pen in France and of the Republican Party in Germany and similar phenomena in other European countries are reverses of civility. The gradual increase in the German Federal Republic, prior to the utter collapse of the "peoples' democracies" in Eastern and Central Europe, of a combination of neutralism, anti-Western and pro-Soviet attitudes may reasonably be interpreted as an increase in incivility in the German Federal Republic. It has been a continuation of the "extra-parliamentary opposition" (the "APO") of two decades ago. Its "extra-parliamentary" character was the clearest evidence of the animosity of a strong, if small, minority against civil society in the Federal Republic. Nothing was more uncivil than that movement and the terrorism which it defended.

There are enough persons in liberal democratic societies whose sense of citizenship, i.e., civility, is strong enough for them to respect the law. Governments are sufficiently effective, despite the numerous inefficiencies of very large organizations, to be able to act against those who are at the outer margin of civility. They do not discover all the traitors in their societies. They are not quite capable of reaching those who are determinedly outside such as terrorists, gangsters and large drug dealers; the institutions of liberal democratic government and of the civil society in which it is embedded are not strong enough to deal with the more extreme kinds of incivility. Fortunately for the survival of those institutions, these extremists of incivility are not so very numerous.

No existing society in the West, except possibly for Switzerland, is a shining model of civil society. An entirely civil society is difficult to imagine but if one does succeed in forming some notion of what it would be like, it appears to be undesirable. A society in which no one thought of anything but the common good might be extremely boring, spiritually impoverished and intellectually infertile. Disagreement, individual self-seeking initiatives, saying things which might give offense, breaking away from the cover of the collective self-consciousness, are part of the spice of life. But there can be too much of a good thing. That is where civility has its proper place as a restraining power in the public sphere.

The situation of civility in liberal democratic societies is not wholly gratifying to persons who care about the survival and effectiveness of those societies. There are open breaches. There are large blocks of incivility at the peripheries with which the agents of the centers cannot cope. There are recurrent outbursts of incivility in the centers. Yet these societies remain liberal democratic; the institutions of civil society continue to function. They do endure and even, from time to time, improve; some of the improvements are long lasting. In view of the challenges to civility created by the pluralistic, liberal democratic nature of these societies, the achievement seems to be unique in world history. The institutions of civil society are sustained not only by civility but also by rational reflection on the benefits they confer on the pursuit of interests. But it is the ingredient of civility which makes the difference between their survival and their decay.

XI

It is interesting that the term "civil society" has recently attained a degree of popularity such as it has never had before. This has happened concurrently with the acknowledged failure and abdication of the tyrannical bureaucratic Communist regimes of Eastern and Central Europe. The Communist regimes had deliberately set out from the beginning to obliterate such fragments of civil society as had existed in the societies in which they seized power or in which they had it imposed on them by the armed forces of the Soviet Union. Marxist doctrine always spoke ill of "bourgeois" or "civil" society. (The two English words have a single German equivalent, "*bürgerlich*," and quite rightly too.) The Communist Party, the system of Soviets and the centrally planned economy are all recognized now as failures by those who controlled and profited by them. At one time they were proclaimed to be a "thousand times more democratic" than the corrupt liberal democracies which offered only "formal freedoms" through the institutions of civil society.

The resurgence of the demand for civil society in Eastern Europe in the past decade shows how false and even hypocritical were the ideas put forward after the Second World War to make it appear that the Soviet Union and the "peoples' democracies" were in fact civil societies in an unfamiliar form. The efforts to vindicate Jacobinism and Bolshevism under the name of "two kinds of freedom" have turned out to be just as false as they appeared to be forty and fifty years ago, to that minority of political theorists who were more interested in the truth than they were in disparaging the liberal democracies and in inflating the reputation of tyrannical Communist Party bureaucracies.

XII

There are some societies which have lived without widespread civility throughout their history. This was true of the ancient Middle Eastern empires which were not at all civil societies. Monarchies—including both empires and kingdoms—and all sorts of oligarchies have needed very small amounts of civility; in general they have not been conducive to the emergence, formation and maintenance of the institutions of civil society. Concentrations of authority in certain positions and institutions are antithetical to civil institutions and they inhibit or stunt in their incumbents the capacity for participation in an inclusive collective self-consciousness, such as is needed for civility. In aristocratic regimes, there has been a greater chance for the emergence and practice of civility within a narrow stratum, but there, too, the rulers have tended to cultivate a narrower and exclusive collective self-consciousness. Their collective self-consciousness has most often extended, where it existed at all, only to their own stratum and usually to the sovereign; it extended only very rarely or slightly to individuals and categories at the peripheries of their collectivity. Aristocracies, at the height of their powers, kept both royal or imperial centers and the peripheral populace in secondary positions in their collective self-consciousness—the latter more openly and harshly than the former.

These were, despite their large size and their central authority, largely primordial societies. Empires and kingdoms were composites of many primordial societies—village communities, clusters of village communities, clans and tribes. They were ruled by royal houses; the royal houses too were persisting remains of primordial societies, adapted to the exercise of power over lesser, weaker, primordial societies. Empires and kingdoms could go on for decades and centuries because the tasks of ruling were made easier by the fact that they ruled over numerously partially self-contained small primordial societies. Ruling consisted mainly of collecting taxes and tributes, raising levies of soldiers and compelling the intermittent provision of certain "services," i.e., labor on agricultural estates, road-building, etc. Most of the society consisted of numerous *Gemeinschaften* gripped intermittently by the central authority which could not control them continuously. (They were *Gemeinschaften* in a society which was not a *Gesellschaft* in Tönnies' terms but rather a patrimonial, bureaucratic, traditional, and tyrannical empire.[6])

The urgent necessity of civility became apparent when primordial ties were restricted and enfeebled, when exchange replaced economic self-sufficiency and when individual ambitions were set loose. Without the primordiality of kinship, lineage and locality, society would have turned into a war of each against all, had the market not been given an open charter and had civility not been aroused. Thus, these two great social inventions, civility and the market—two of the greatest in the history of humanity—made it possible for humans beings to live relatively peacefully and safely in large societies.

Civility was not invented by liberal or democratic social philosophers nor did the idea of civility emerge for the first time in the institutional practices of the more or less liberal societies of the nineteenth century and the more or less democratic institutions which joined them later. Civil society corresponds to liberal democratic society in its political aspects and to the pluralistic society of voluntary associations and private corporations on the other. Civil society entails the freedom of contract and the market economy; in this aspect, the idea of civility is also closely dependent on the fundamental feature of "civil society" as Hegel conceived it, namely, the private ownership of property in the market economy. The private ownership of property and the freedom of contract and the organization of the market economy around them, are necessary conditions for civility in society. Seen in the crudest

---

6. Shils is referring to the contrast between *Gemeinschaft* and *Gesellschaft* which Tönnies developed in 1887 in his book *Gemeinschaft und Gesellschaft*. *Gemeinschaft* and *Gesellschaft* are usually translated, respectively, as "community" and "society" *(ed.)*.

terms, civility and the market seem to be antithetical to each other—one altruistic, the other egoistic, the one inclusive, the other exclusive, but in fact, they are mutually dependent. The very anonymity of the market, its relative disregard for the primordial and personal, is a necessary condition of the extension of the collective self-consciousness to the inclusion of unknown and unseen persons. (The hierarchical system of self-alleged "planned economies" has turned out to be inimical to civility, as well as economically ruinous.)

Of course, some restrictions on the right of use and disposition of private property is, up to a difficultly determinable point, compatible with civility; but past that point, such restrictions have been damaging to civility. The abolition of private property in Communist countries was thought to be an indispensable condition of the full development of an inclusively civil society. It turned out to be diametrically the opposite. It made impossible the formation of independence of judgment, which was suppressed into secrecy or extirpated; it prevented entirely the free expression of independent judgment. It abolished the institutions of civil society which had existed in a very rudimentary form and with a narrow range of adherence in those societies before Communism was imposed on them. It rendered the rulers of Communist societies among the least civil in the history of the world, certainly since the beginning of modern times.

A liberal democratic society is a society of an inclusive collective self-consciousness. Of course, any society has some measure of collective self-consciousness, a minimum of civility which might be found from time to time in the circle of counsellors and scholars around the ruler in monarchies and empires, although the institutions of civil society have only a very rudimentary or practically no existence in such societies.

There is an inherent consensual element in collective self-consciousness—at least over the part of the population which participates in it. Collective self-consciousness becomes civil not only when it is shared or participated in by a large part of the population but when it assigns a minimum of dignity to the various sectors of the population which it comprehends. Beyond that minimum of moral dignity, there might be acknowledged differences in value; but, what is important is the inclusiveness of the referent in the collective consciousness.

Now this kind of comprehensive, even if unequal, awareness of nearly the whole population of the society is a crucial property of modern society. Centers in the past never thought much about peripheries except to keep them quiet, obedient and productive of foodstuffs, labor services and military manpower.

Modern liberal and then liberal democratic societies modified this markedly. The idea of equality of both center and periphery before the law, restriction of the powers of the central authority to imprison at will individuals, especially from the peripheries, the freedom of critics of the existing center to criticize it and to attempt to modify its patterns and practices, the development of institutions to represent, through the extended franchise and through consultation, the majority of the adult male population and, later, the entire adult male and female population, are a few of the indications of the extension of the collective self-consciousness of the center. There has been a simultaneous and corresponding extension of the society-wide collective self-consciousness to the peripheries leading to their partial amalgamation into their larger society. These developments have been the products of and the conditions for the growth of civility in modern liberal democratic societies.

Tradition and Liberty

ANTINOMY AND INTERDEPENDENCE

❦

I

ONE of the most deeply established traditions of liberal thought in East and West asserts that tradition is antagonistic toward liberty. Protestantism denied the validity of accumulated tradition in favor of the primacy of the revelation contained in Scripture. The process of emancipation of the mind from external determination went on, when revelation as well was rejected, to the point where the genuine source of valid knowledge and experience was found to reside in the powers of the individual spirit. Rationalistic liberalism, which ascribed validity only to what the individual himself had decided in the light of his own perceptions and reason, criticized tradition as the mindless repetition of inherited lines of thought and conduct into which individuality did not enter. Romantic liberalism was hostile to tradition because tradition cramped the spontaneity which constituted the essential nature of the individual. Tradition imposed barriers on man's conduct and restraints on his thought and sentiment; it prevented him from seeing with his own eyes and from feeling and valuing according to his own creative powers.

The inherent antinomy between *tradition* and *liberty* to which liberal belief correctly points has been underlined for the liberals by the fact

Previously published in *Ethics* 68 (April 1958): 153–65. Copyright 1957–1958 by The University of Chicago. Reprinted by permission.

that the antagonists of the movement of liberty—the defenders of oligarchical forms of government, the opponents of intellectual freedom and moral egalitarianism—have almost always claimed tradition for themselves. They have argued not only for the substantive traditions of particular institutional practices and beliefs but also for tradition as such as the right means of guiding conduct. The truths which conservatives put forward about the nature of tradition and its ineluctibility have been so intertwined with their support of arrangements which have become intolerable to the awakened sensibilities of the modern conscience that assertions about the value of tradition have come to be suspected as implicit arguments for the substance transmitted by tradition. A deforming, simplifying rigidity has been imposed on thought, and the proponents of liberty have become its victims. Just as the enhancement of individuality came to be thought of as inseparably associated with the restriction of the rights of property to the point of extinction, so the expansion of individual freedom has come to be regarded as incompatible with the maintenance of tradition. Political and social thought can no longer remain content with the inherited clusterings of liberal and conservative, of progressive and reactionary, and must discriminate the independent elements which have become hardened into apparently logically coherent wholes. Just as revolutionary deeds or state action are now seen to be by no means inevitably connected with individual liberty, creativity, or justice, so tradition too must be dissolved from its traditional associations. Both liberals and conservatives have misunderstood the nature of the antinomy and both have failed to dissociate the form of inheritance from the less admirable bequest.

II

Traditions are beliefs, standards, and rules, of varying but never exhaustive explicitness, which have been received from the preceding generation through a process of continuous transmission from generation to generation. They recommend themselves by their appropriateness to the present situation confronted by their recipients and especially by a certain measure of authoritativeness which they possess by virtue of their provenience from the past. Their authority is engendered by the sheer fact of their previous observance by those who have lived previously. Max Weber went too far when he declared that the legitimation of traditional authority rested on the belief that "it had always been that way." It is not essential that rules legitimized by tradition should be thought to have been observed or valid "from time immemorial." To appreciate the weight of the past, it is not necessary that the past be seen as an indefinitely backward-reaching span of time. Its backward time span is usually much more vague and indeterminate. All that is essential is that it should be "involved with the past," and not just as a historical fact. Traditions possess authority by virtue of the quality which they acquire in the minds of the persons of one generation when they believe these traditions were accepted by a succession of ancestors coming up to the immediate past.

The traditional rule possesses authority because its acceptance establishes an attachment to the past of a family, town, country, or corporate body to which an inherent value is attributed. Membership in a primordial and a civil body carries with it not merely attachment to the symbol of the body as it stands at a particular present moment in time but to symbols which evoke a sense of the body's past as well. Acceptance of tradition is the creation of a state of communion with past powers: It is of the same order as any act of communion with one's contemporary society, in a great ritual action or in the intimacies of daily intercourse or with a timelessly transcendent symbol such as divinity or truth or goodness. The affirmation of tradition, tacit or explicit, is an act which binds to the past. It might be an attachment to a particular person, older but still living. It might be an attachment to a dead person. It might be an attachment to events or assertions which occurred in the past and which have the "quality of the past" in them. It might be an attachment to symbols which refer to the past as such, so that anything which has had a long and continuous past existence evokes the attachment.

The traditional transmission of beliefs and knowledge is not one that is sought. The active searching for a past object to which to attach one's self—"the search for a usable past"—is something different. Traditional attachment implies receptive affirmation, neither reception without affirmation nor affirmation without reception. The drumming up of tradition, in the style of "les maîtres de la contre-révolution," of Charles Maurras and Maurice Barrès, or the efforts of American writers like Van Wyck Brooks and Irving Babbitt, who recommended the observance of traditions which were no longer being generally received, represents an ideological transfiguration of tradition. It is certainly quite remote from the process of traditional transmission. On the other hand, the stability through generations of a belief or practice does not constitute tradition either. Reception must be accompanied by affirmative attachment to the past, however vague, unconscious, and unspoken. The performance of an action which is presented from the past by authority but which is performed only because no other alternative mode of action can be imagined is at the margin of tradition.

The feeling for the "pastness" of traditional rules or beliefs can be very attenuated. There are surely persons who have practically no sense of affinity with the past, who live as if it had never existed. These must, however, make up only a very small section of any society. Extreme sensitivity to the "pastness" of traditional beliefs is also rather uncommon, even in "traditional" societies, and this small proportion includes the rebels who reject anything simply because it was once observed and the traditionalists for whom anything which once existed is entirely sacred by its very connection with the long past. Rather, it would seem that the mass of the race which lives in the grip of the past is marginally and not acutely aware of the pastness of the rules and beliefs it receives and accepts as its own. What is felt is that one way is binding and that it is because it is somehow connected with what has been before.

The unreflective reception of tradition is not an amoral, vegetative acceptance. There is an active, outgoing, positive tendency in the reception of tradition. The availability of a traditional rule or standard of judgment guides and stimulates a spontaneous moral tendency in man, a need to be in contact with the ultimately true and right, a sensitivity to the sacred, which reach out and seek the guidance and discipline of tradition. Most human beings are not creative enough to give birth to a wholly original experience of the sacred, to create their own individual image of justice and truth. Tradition makes available a set of judgments which command respect by their origin and by the plausibility which derives in part from their appropriateness to experience and in part from their origin. In doing this, tradition arouses man's rudimentary spontaneous sensitivity and helps it to take form. Although in personal relations our respect for the rights of the other person grows spontaneously from the process of interaction, in the political sphere the sense of obligation to the community and respect for the rights of others, which constitute the civil sense, can grow from their embryonic condition only with the aid and encouragement of tradition.

Tradition is not the dead hand of the past but rather the hand of the gardener, which nourishes and elicits tendencies of judgment which would otherwise not be strong enough to emerge on their own. In this respect tradition is an encouragement to incipient individuality rather than its enemy. It is a stimulant to moral judgment and self-discipline rather than an opiate. It establishes contact between the recipient and the sacred values of his life in society. Man has a need for being in right relations with the sacred. Most men do not need a continuous and intense contact with the sacred. A low level of intensity with intermittent surges serves their needs. But should they be entirely deprived of that contact for too long a time, their needs will flare up into a passionate irrationality. What was a stimulant to individuality becomes an intoxication which overwhelms it.

The traditional transmission of beliefs about the sacred things of a society curbs the intensity with which such beliefs are received and espoused. The traditional transmission prevents all of the need for contact with the sacred from becoming rigidly and explosively attached to a particular substantive belief by drawing some of the need for contact with the sacred onto itself. The simple reception of traditional transmission is itself a form of contact with the sacred past; and this reduces the need, occasioned in crisis, for individual search. Of course, the past as such can become the object of intense and continuous attachment, thus reinforcing the attachment to those substantive symbols transmitted by tradition—such as a particular form of property ownership or a particular pattern of governmental authority. But in the main, traditional transmission mollifies the needs for attachment to the sacred. Attachment to loose tradition is a substitute, within limits, for fervent devotion to intensely charismatic objects.

The attachment to the sacred cannot be evaded in any society. All societies regard as *sacred* certain standards of judgment, certain rules of conduct and thought, and certain arrangements of action. They vary only in the intensity and self-consciousness of their acknowledgment, the scope which they allow to the sacred, and the extent of participation in them. In varying degrees, deviations from these standards arouse anxiety and generate needs for expiation and repression. At its highest level of intensity, the belief in the sacredness of an institution or a system of institutions is inimical to liberty because it is hostile, in substance and in form, to innovation, which is an inevitable consequence of a system of liberty.

There is an element of the sacred in so-called secular and irreligious societies, like the great countries of the West, as well as in those, like India, where the sacredness of certain actions and symbols is open for all to see. The belief in the *sacred* finds expression not only in the acts of religious communion through ritual, prayer, or contemplation. These are merely the modes of communion with that category of the sacred called divinity. It need not be the conventionally conceived sacred, i.e., the divine, to which man is attached; it can appear to be entirely "secular." It might be nothing more "otherworldly" than "justice," "human dignity," "public order," "individual liberty," or "nationality." It might not have attached to it, in any obvious way, the cosmological myths or divine intentions which the conventional conception of the sacred carries with it. But as the final and ultimate ground of social existence, which evokes the *tremendum numinosem,* the sacred must be acknowledged to exist in "secular" societies. It finds expression, together with other beliefs, in the laws and customs of a society, in the written constitution, and, above all, in the unwritten expectations which govern conduct. It permeates the market place as well as the family, the church as well as the university. The values of truth, of individuality, of blood ties, of certain states of mind, even of professional achievement, can become endowed in varying degrees with the property of sacredness or *charisma.*

The sacred appears to be untouchable and unchallengeable and is as such repugnant to the idea of a free society. It means that the powers of individuals, alone or jointly, to modify and to tamper with institutions and beliefs are limited. Quite rightly, liberals have believed that the progress of liberty has in part consisted in the narrowing of the sphere of the sacred, in the "secularization of politics." When the sacred sensibilities are aroused, they generate intolerance and exclusiveness. When they die down, they allow some measure of intellectual detachment and independent action. A major task of liberal policy is to respect the sacred while keeping it at low ebb. This is one of the chief functions of the transmission of sacred beliefs through a loose tradition.

III

It is beyond human powers to conduct an elaborate system of free institutions—comprising a parliament, a system of parties, a free system of public opinion, the rule of law, voluntary associations for civic and private purposes—simply on the basis of rational calculation. Nor can such systems be stable if they are balanced on the razor edge of an equilibrium of the powers of the different sectors of society. That rational decision, calculations of interest, and the equilibrium of powers have a substantial and a crucial value in the institutional system of liberty is undeniable, but they are inadequate alone.

The political system of freedom must, for the most part, be accepted by its members, at any particular moment, as *given*. It must be the product of a free acceptance in which a belief in the *sacredness* of the order as a whole is latent. The intrinsic and autonomous value of the other man, of the other party, and of the institutions within which they meet, be they the parliamentary body or the university or the system of industrial negotiations, must be accepted as *given*. The "givenness" is not, however, a mere factual determinateness, an unquestioned inevitability. It must be something which elicits reverence and awe. The legal system and even specific laws must be regarded as possessing at least an element of intrinsic justice. In all of these acts of reception, then, there must be some infusion of a belief in the *ultimate rightfulness*—the *sacredness*—of the order.

Our appreciation of the value of the individual human being and of the value of his self-expression and self-protection is fundamentally an appreciation of the sacredness of his existence. That we call this appreciation self-evident is itself a product of a long tradition. The system of freedom—with its self-restraint of the powerful, its acknowledgment of the worth of other persons, its reluctance to submit to authority, and, above all, its aspiration to rational self-determination—can flourish only if it is permeated with a largely unreflective acceptance of these rules of the game of the free society. This acceptance, if it is not the product of ratiocination or of individual genius in the direct apprehension of the sacred, must, at least to some extent, be based on the affirmation of what in the present is involved in the past—of what *is* and *has been* existent and what is and has been accepted by others for this reason. The free society must rest, once it comes into existence, on tradition.

There is something paradoxical in this proposition. The free society is a society in movement. Tradition incorporates and transmits sacred beliefs, it entails self-reproduction, stability between generations and across centuries. The rules of the game, in which the sacred is incorporated, are the precipitates of this tradition working on current thought and experience. The free society entails a critical independent attitude toward authority; tradition entails the acknowledgment of authority inherent in a belief or mode of action by virtue of its having been performed or observed in the past. Nonetheless, the traditional legitimization of the framework of free action is compatible with, and even necessary for, rational criticism and creative innovation. The traditional legitimization of the framework of free society requires, however, that the rational criticism and improvement of any institution at any given time be carried on in a context which is set by tradition—by a tradition sustained by laws and rules which themselves derive their efficacy from the support they gain from this tradition. In this wise, any and every particular institution might in its turn be subjected to a far-reaching rational criticism and be amended and improved—but it can be done without harm to society only if, at any given time, much of the rest of the institutional system is accepted as legitimate. The legitimacy must flow from a general disposition to respect the order as a whole. Thus, at the moment when any component is subjected to the most thoroughgoing criticism and renovation, the legitimacy of the order of which it is a part must be affirmed. The paradox of liberty and tradition can thus be partially resolved by the maintenance of a delicately poised and labile segregation of the individual's traditionally received sphere of action and his free sphere.

The tradition of self-restraint, so essential to the free society, resolves the paradox through a segregation which honors a tradition restrictive of the freedom of one's own action, while leaving a free sphere for others. Tradition is self-restraining, it is in important respects restrictive on individuality, and it is no accident that freedom first emerged as a modern political system in Protestant countries where a powerful sense of individuality was curbed by passionate conflict with a Puritanical ethos. By virtue of its tradition, self-restraint makes possible—even though it does not create—the freedom of others.

The antithesis of tradition and liberty is also resolved by the shift in the locus of the sacred. Instead of being found only in institutions, it is found in the soul of the individual. Respect for the sacred then becomes respect for individuality and is reinforced by the force of its own tradition.

Despite these resolutions of the paradox of segregation, by self-restraint and by the displacement of the locus of *charisma* from institutions into the individual, the central feature of the paradox remains. The reception of tradition is a submission to anonymous authority; the exercise of freedom is supported by distrust of authority. The tradition of liberty—this *contradictio in adjectio* which is indispensable to the continuance of liberty—is greatly aided by the ambivalence of man's nature that rejects and accepts authority. Man is, as Professor Knight has said, a rule-making and rule-breaking animal.[1] His submissiveness must alternate with resistance to authority; and each supports the other and involves it. The reception of tradition is aided by resistance to it.

Finally, the coexistence of tradition and liberty is made easier when the pressures of tradition and individuality are light. The sacred resides both in the past and in individuality, and any exacerbation of either is disruptive. In personalities in whom the sensitivity to old and anonymous authority is very pronounced, that balance between reception and rejection cannot be maintained—any more than it can in one in which impulse toward a highly differentiated and immediately expressed individuality is both very intense and very comprehensive in scope.

---

1. See, for example, Frank H. Knight, "Science, Philosophy, and Social Procedure" (1942) and "Human Nature and World Democracy" (1944), both of which appear in Frank H. Knight, *Freedom and Reform* (Indianapolis, Ind.: Liberty Fund, 1982) *(ed.)*.

IV

The problem becomes more complicated when we leave the traditions of liberty and move beyond them to the traditions which govern religion, family life, the hierarchy of social status, and economic institutions. Liberalism has been more silent than condemnatory where the traditions of liberty have been concerned. But where it has been a matter of traditional attachment to institutions other than those of political liberalism, the attitude of classical liberalism has been suspicious to the point of hostility. It has been all in favor of the critical emancipation of the individual from the dominion of traditional institutions. The ideal society has been conceived as rationally self-determining, equally free from the pressure of irrational impulse on the one side and from dogmatic constraint on the other. The very existence of liberty has been alleged to be dependent on the erosion of tradition—above all, the iniquitous substantive traditions which restrict individual liberty by imposing dogmatic beliefs, by reinforcing parental authority within the family, and by maintaining inequities in the distribution of income and status.

Yet even there, where the incompatibility of tradition and liberty seems to be so obvious, the relationship is far from simple. A free political system does require a matrix of stable non-political institutions in which its citizens can live, and the best guaranty of stability is an effective reception of tradition. Many of these institutions are, however, governed by traditions which repress individual liberty within the boundaries of the institution and which extend this inimicality into the public sphere. Thus, for example, a strong tradition of kinship obligation is injurious to the rule of law and to equality of opportunity. Extremely hierarchical ecclesiastical institutions are permeated by traditions which extend their illiberal influences into the political sphere. Powerful traditions of the superiority and inferiority of certain qualities, such as kinship or color, inhibit the growth of the sentiments of esteem for the self and others that are necessary for political liberty. Such traditions prevent the expansion of the sense of affinity which is essential to a free society. Substantive beliefs which insist on the vast superiority of saintly, religious, or prophetic authority to ordinary civil authority derive much of their vitality from tradition and render more difficult the working of democratic political institutions. The traditions of caste and the fourth *ashram* in India, the traditions of ecclesiastical, national, ethnic, and class exclusiveness in the West, are injurious to political freedom because they enfeeble the sense of civility, interfere with equality before the law, and deny the equal rights derived from citizenship. Here the liberal repugnance for tradition seems amply justified.

V

The illiberal potentiality of tradition as such is accentuated when the attachment to tradition is transformed into *traditionalism*. Traditionalism is the self-conscious, deliberate affirmation of traditional norms, in full awareness of their traditional nature and alleging that their merit derives from that traditional transmission from a sacred origin. This is a revivalist, enthusiastic attitude. It is always dogmatic and doctrinaire and insists on uniformity. It insists on thoroughgoing adherence; it does not discriminate between the workable and the unworkable and it regards all elements of the tradition it praises as equally essential. Traditionalism, which is a form of heightened sensitivity to the sacred, demands exclusiveness. It is content with nothing less than totality. Traditionalism is not content with the observance of a tradition in a particular sphere, e.g., in family or religious life. It is satisfied only if the traditionalist outlook permeates all spheres—political, economic, cultural, and religious—and unifies them in a common subordination to the sacred as it is received from the past.

Sentiments of the sacred, when they are aroused to a high pitch of intensity, when men are extremely preoccupied with them, are harmful to liberty. At the height of their intensity, they render rigid the social structures which they regulate. Sentiments of the sacred, in their purity, are insistent on exact and thorough conformity. Variations are not tolerated. Those who regard themselves as their properly qualified bearers cannot stand rival claimants and they cannot stand deviations in conduct from the lines of conduct stipulated by *sacred* norms. Traditionalism, whether it takes the form of national patriotism or ethnic solidarity, is like political and religious enthusiasm. Both feel themselves to be responsible for the custody and propagation of something ultimately valuable, something entirely sacred. At the extreme point of excitation of sentiments of the sacred, such as arise in situations of crisis or under conditions of attack, attachment to the sacred can do mortal harm both to normal tradition and to liberty.

Those who self-consciously regard themselves as the custodians of sacred, traditional, or enthusiastic values in all their purity aggressively attack the ordinary traditions and practices of the society—or, by an inversion of aggressiveness, they seek complete withdrawal. Their alienation from normal tradition and the order in which it is involved spreads to others whose spontaneous attachment to the sacred values of tribe or sect is not strong enough of itself to make them into initiators of traditionalist radicalism but who, when they have the model and source presented to them, become ideological fanatics. The civil order, in which the traditions which transmit the sacred are more diffuse and less rigid, must either gather its forces to control the extremist reaction or succumb to it. In either case liberty suffers.

Traditionalism is almost always ideological and extremist. It insists passionately on the full and knowing adherence to tradition with a form and elaboration unknown in the ordinary observance of tradition. Exceptions, qualifications, deviations, are all regarded as wickedness itself, and only the pristine tradition in all its fulness is regarded as an adequate guide to conduct. Because the received tradition always has an element of authority in it and because it usually legitimizes existing authority, traditionalism alone, as an elaboration of tradition, would naturally tend to be hostile to liberty. But in its *extremism*, traditionalism finds another even more powerful impetus to illiberalism.

Traditionalism is not only hostile to liberty, it is also radically hostile to *tradition*, the vague, flexible tradition which even when it does not include the tradition of liberty at least allows liberty to live on its margins of ambiguity, to grow gradually, and to take deeper root. In oligarchical societies, traditionalism prevents the further growth of the elements which can give rise to freedom. In societies in which liberty is already established, traditionalism—despite its cant about community and continuity—is the greatest enemy of the tradition of civility which is essential to its life.

There is another type of traditionalist orientation which, in its aspiration to complete control over conduct, resembles ideological traditionalism, but which lacks its revivalist doctrinaire fervor. This is *primordial traditionalism,* in which the sacred tradition has not become differentiated and in which what is traditionally sacred in one sphere penetrates and dominates all the other spheres of life. Formalistic traditionalism which imposes the traditional rules of kinship obligation on every situation, or saintly traditionalism in which the tradition of the holy man renders activity in most other spheres of secondary value, are both restrictive of liberty. Primordial traditionalism, too, is hostile to freedom, because it inhibits the partial autonomy of the spheres of social life that is constitutive of a free society. Primordial traditionalism is, however, scarcely a problem in Western societies. It is a genuine problem, however, for the politics of liberty in peasant societies and in the newer democracies of Asia and Africa.

If ideological and primordial traditionalism were the only patterns of the working of tradition, then the classical antithesis of tradition and liberty would be correct. It is clear, however, that they are not. The normal condition of substantive traditional life is much looser and much more flexible. In most societies, even in highly traditional societies, deviations are many and unnoticed, because the traditional prescriptions of conduct are vague and because a certain range of

variation is allowed in many spheres. It is only intermittently in specialized ceremonials that they take on precise and specific form, and their
specificity is confined to a narrow range of events, and to restricted
spans of time. In daily life, the tradition is not so rigid that it does
not permit adaptations to individual idiosyncrasy and external pressure.

In large-scale, civil societies, the normal pattern of tradition is loose.
Gradual modifications in action are possible without arousing hostility
from others or guilt feelings within the actor. Normal tradition permits
diverse interpretations which, although they might be criticized as
incorrect, retain sufficient legitimacy to render them tolerable. It is,
indeed, within the framework of such a commonly shared tradition,
with its capacity for multiple interpretations and diverse emphasis, that
the system of political liberty can arise and flourish. Individual variation
and group diversity are both the fruit of normal tradition. They are
products of the loose amorphous character of normal tradition, and
the security of their existence is guaranteed by the single tradition from
which they are acknowledged to derive.

The regime of liberty is possible only as long as liberty is limited
and as long as the aspirations which can be freely expressed are limited.
Unrestrained appetites, ambitions for power, wealth, security, dignity,
and honor precipitate severe conflicts, insofar as they do not directly
subvert the institutions which provide the framework of order in which
liberty can exist.

The pursuit of interests unrestrained by standards common in society
arouses an aggressive response. In this approximation to the state of
nature, the institutions which have the task of adjudicating conflicts
and keeping them within peaceful limits undergo a heavy strain. Their
authority is diminished and formal justice moves toward self-help or
lynch law. Governing institutions lose their authority when they show
themselves unable to exercise it by coping with disorderly tendencies.
This in turn fortifies the existing tendencies to break out of the limits
imposed by traditional and legal norms. The perception and the fear
of chaos drives those who are sensitive and dependent to take refuge

in new symbols of order, usually of an intensely sacred and traditionalist nature. Social disorder awakens sacred sensitivity while normal tradition holds it in check; it holds it in a comatose condition, alive but not alert, vaguely responsive but not sensitive. Normal tradition, with its ambiguity and approximateness, muffles the sacred and reduces the intensity with which it is experienced by those who come into contact with it. General and reasonable conformity with the norms of a society, such as the normal traditional orientation brings about, makes less likely affronts to what is regarded as sacred. Traditions are not so demanding of precise observance as are freshly and directly experienced sacred rules. Tradition reduces both the motives for infringement and the sensitivity to infringements. The less likely are affronts, the less likely is the reactive, revivalistic insistence on complete and exclusive adherence to sacred rules. Threats to the interest of the other groups often engender a rigid adherence, an obstinate refusal to yield all that is demanded—or, more frequently, unwilling concession is accompanied by a slowly forming counterattack of equal intensity. Thus the breaking away from tradition arouses a reactive traditionalism, while a moderate respect for tradition does not give occasion for its desperate defense.

Even in non-liberal societies, a certain measure of liberty comes into existence in the interstices of society, thanks to the ambiguity of traditions. This meager liberty may be extinguished where there is an intensification of sensitivity to the sacred. Liberal societies move in the same direction when sensitivity to the sacred becomes more intense. Hobbes pointed out, and the twentieth century has shown, that the counterattack takes the form of an oligarchical order which expels freedom from the civil and intellectual spheres and leaves it to carry on a furtive existence in private relations which, for their own part, are soon dominated by the stringencies of a harsh political temper.

Order is preserved by the integration of conflicting interests, by the authority of tradition and law, and by leaving a certain area for the conflict of interests and individual tastes to work itself out freely. The integration is never wholly stable and an exacerbation of one of the component elements can cost so much in terms of the interests of other groups that the reaction of the loser is likely to be extreme. Insofar as traditions, which always have some communal and restrictive aspect, are effective, they aid in the confinement of individual impulse and ambition, and in the definition of interests in such a way that conflict can be kept down. They reduce the extent of loss and render the actually experienced loss acceptable by legitimizing the action by which it was inflicted. Not all traditions have this limiting function, but many do, and to that extent they aid in the support of the system of liberty.

Thus tradition reduces the rate of change in a society but, insofar as it allows a moderate amount of change, it enhances the orderliness of change and permits a free development in the direction of greater justice. All change infringes on some established rights, and there is nothing inherently wrong about this. It is important, however, that the expectations which are frustrated by redistributions of wealth and power should not be so severe as to alienate substantial sections of the population and to turn them into enemies of the free society. The more rigid and precise a tradition, the more it is incorporated in ritual and in law, the more it alienates those who suffer from it.

The losers in the social game, the lower castes and classes, are more likely to turn against a rigid and precise tradition than they are to turn against a flexible and ambiguous one. The latter gives them grounds for self-legitimization; it does not so completely exclude them from beneficent relations with the sacred. Hence the lower castes and classes will not spring so readily into attachment to new, sacred symbols of order when the authority of the hitherto prevailing order becomes enfeebled.

VI

The practice of respect for substantive traditions, even when they are neither liberal nor democratic, maintains the traditional receptiveness which sustains the tradition of liberty. The reception of the traditions of liberty, like the reception of any tradition, rests in fundamental part on the affirmation of the sacred authority of the past. The traditional affirmation of liberty resembles any other traditional affirmation. As such, it draws strength from the traditional outlook in other spheres, e.g., the respect for family traditions and for religious traditions, however widely these might differ in content from the tradition of liberty. The disruption of non-liberal traditions in a free society might well have a disruptive effect on the traditions of freedom in that society. Their maintenance in a labile state might well be very helpful to the prosperity of freedom, even though their existence might give umbrage to rationalism and liberalism.

While obtaining reinforcement from non-liberal traditions outside the political sphere, the traditions of liberty in the political sphere are by no means free of danger from them. Not only do the illiberal traditions have a potential expansiveness which can make inroads into the traditions of liberty but there is also a danger that the receptive affirmation of substantive, illiberal tradition can be so pronounced that, within the tradition of liberty, the independent and critical spirit toward authority can be excessively repressed.

The maintenance of a traditional receptiveness which facilitates the transmission of the traditions of liberty with their peculiar antinomies depends to a considerable extent, then, on the state of traditionality of the value system of the society outside the political sphere. If it is too dilapidated, it can cause the traditions of liberty to dissolve or can prevent them from ever being formed. If it is too strong, too comprehensive and precise, and too pressingly expansive, then it can prevent them from being formed or from gaining sufficient strength to maintain a free society.

VII

We see then that the relations between liberty and tradition are diverse. Liberty is sustained by traditions, both the traditions of liberty and traditions which flourish outside the sphere of political liberty. Liberty lives in a context of order; and order, beneficial to liberty, is maintained by traditions of many sorts, some quite illiberal in their content. Liberty is constricted by traditions which suppress the development of individuality and selfhood, and which obstruct the functioning of the sense of civility. It is menaced by traditions of political and religious enthusiasm which claim to possess the means and knowledge for the direct achievement of the most sacred values. It is endangered by the traditional outlook when it is pushed, by reaction against the disruption of tradition, into an extremist traditionalism.

The traditional receptiveness which is one of the ultimate pillars of freedom in society can never be supplanted by either calculation, reason, or power. It can and must be attenuated, it can and must be retracted, and it can and must be diminished in intensity; but it cannot be dispensed with, even though that is repugnant to our basic liberal conception of the dignity of man as a rational self-governing being. The art of the politics of liberty consists, in part, in the attenuation, retraction, and diminution of the intensity of sacred tradition to the point where liberty is at an optimum, but in which the matrix of the traditional outlook is left unimpaired. The fundamental impairment of the traditional outlook and damage to the individual's receptiveness to tradition can only lead to an indiscipline which is momentarily mistaken for an enhancement of liberty and which in the longer run gives rise to ideological traditionalism and to enthusiasm—in neither of which is there any place for the free man.

The right relations between liberty and tradition are not to be asserted in a single comprehensive proposition. The tentative guesses presented here are not fully in accordance with the traditions of liberal thought, although the standpoint from which this paper is written is that of pluralist individualistic liberalism. Much of what this paper asserts explicitly and in its overtones might be repugnant to the sentiments associated with the tradition of rationalist utilitarian liberalism. But nothing will be gained from a denial of the facts of life or from the determination of political affinities and affiliations by the compatibility or incompatibility of definitions and a few substantive historical coincidences.

The intellectuals of the West are now but slowly recovering from the disillusionments consequent on their alliances with movements which seemed to share certain of the values of classical humanitarian liberalism. It would be a pity if this misadventure, and a lingering sympathy for the prejudices of their quondam allies, were to result in a refusal to traffic with viewpoints which have been *historically* and *conventionally* alien to liberalism. Correspondingly, it would be an equal misfortune if, in order to overcome their own past errors or to avoid the errors of their contemporaries, they took refuge in an uncritical adulation of tradition, in which the past is always regarded as better than the present, and in which the wisdom of our ancestors is always regarded as better than our own. And all this allegedly on behalf of liberty.

The reconciliation of pluralist individualist liberalism with the affirmation of the claims of normal tradition may not be an appetizing task and is certainly not an easy one. It is in its achievement, however, that the responsibilities of liberals lie.

The Antinomies of Liberalism

§

I

I T IS very difficult to assess the merits of liberalism because it is
so ambiguous in its major concepts and so vague in its boundaries.
It is difficult to say what liberals believe not only because all beliefs
are difficult to study, but also because it is so difficult to define and
locate "the liberals." Roman Catholicism was relatively easy to define
because there was an orthodox doctrine, institutionally promulgated
and available in papal declarations. It was possible for a long time to
define and assess Communist policies and beliefs because they too were
promulgated by an authoritative, officially constituted group which
claimed the right to define the orthodoxy.

Liberalism in the United States has been a quite different matter,
since it did not express itself through any one institution. It is true
that since the Wilsonian "new liberalism," one major current of liberalism has been loosely connected with the Democratic party. There has
been another current of liberalism in the United States which has in
some points of its belief been inclined toward the Republican party.
Nonetheless, it has been one of the features of American liberalism of
the past fifty years that it has been free of strict organizational loyalties.

There is in addition a very deep cleavage within liberalism which
also makes it difficult to define any single liberal doctrine and to
locate its proponents. Liberalism has evolved from being critical of the

Previously published in Zbigniew Brzezinski, ed., *The Relevance of Liberalism* (Boul-
der, Colo.: Westview, 1978), pp. 135–200. Reprinted by permission.

authority of the state and recommending private and voluntary action into a set of beliefs which remains critical of authority in nearly all forms but which at the same time supports an extremely comprehensive and penetrating extension of governmental action. The adherents of these more recently emerged beliefs have become the chief bearers of the name of liberalism but they too are very heterogeneous in their composition and they share many beliefs with the liberalism from which they have departed.

The task of locating the object of our reflections would be easier if there were a comprehensive and well-defined conservative position in the United States acknowledged by its adversaries to be more than a justification of the prerogatives of the very wealthy. The liberals who are critical of the extension of governmental action are not conservatives, although in this rejection of the prevailing type of liberalism they have become mixed up with the tiny numbers of intellectual conservatives. Conservatism in the United States—patriotic appreciation of one's own country, respect for familial obligations, an expectation of religious piety and observance, a high regard for the virtues of manliness and womanliness, an attachment to locality, a belief that the burden of proof lies on those who seek innovation, and a corresponding respect for traditional ways of thinking and acting, the acceptance of a hierarchy of deference and authority, and a certain inclination toward pessimism regarding the abatement of man's earthly troubles by large-scale rational contrivances—has hardly any defenders among intellectuals and not many more among politicians. This type of conservatism in any inarticulate form is probably relatively common in what used to be called the working and lower-middle classes but it does not have many spokesmen among those who address larger audiences. There also used to be a type of conservatism which put forth "Darwinian" arguments in defense of private business enterprise; this scarcely exists anymore.

This being so, the prevalent collectivistic type of liberalism shades off into a neighboring liberalism which sometimes and wrongly calls itself "conservatism"—and which is in fact a root and branch sort of liberalism. The result is that it has been difficult to see what the various strands of liberalism have in common, and to recognize that there are respectable viewpoints in social and political outlooks that are not liberal. The situation is different on the perimeter of liberalism. The collectivistic liberalism now prevailing in the United States has socialistic revolutionary radicalism as another neighbor. There is substantive affinity between collectivistic liberalism and the socialistic and revolutionary radicalism but it is not as great as the sympathy of sentiment which inclines the former toward the latter.

The two types of liberalism have common traditions but their common traditions do not exhaustively describe either of them. They share a common individualism, but their traditions of individualism branch off from each other; one emphasizes more the rationally acting individual and the other more the affectively sensitive and expressive individual; but even this latter type of individualism also allows a considerable place for rational decision. Both set their faces against traditional religious beliefs and institutions although autonomist[1] liberalism does so less than the other; both set themselves against hierarchies of wealth, power, and deference which are inherited and transmitted within families. Both attribute high importance to formal education for the emancipation of the mind from superstition and for the cultivation of rational or the release of affective powers; both also regard formal education as a means of self-improvement and necessary for economic and social progress. Both, since the latter part of the eighteenth century and at least until very recently, appreciated the value of scientific knowledge

---

1. I am aware of the unsatisfactoriness of this mode of designating that current of liberalism which continues the older liberal tradition. But to call it traditional liberalism would be misleading since collectivistic liberalism too has a venerable and effective tradition. To call it "anti-statist" would be negative as well as inelegant. The liberalism which I wish to designate is individualistic but also is attached to the free action, under law, of corporate bodies. "Pluralistic" liberalism has too many other overtones. Hence "autonomist liberalism," unattractive though the term sounds, corresponds most closely to the kind of liberalism I wish to designate.

as a liberation of the mind from illusions and a replacement of the illusions, including traditional religious beliefs, by a truthful understanding of the world; they also both regarded science as closely allied to technology whereby greater material well-being could be attained.

Both types of liberalism are against tradition and inclined toward rationalism. Autonomist liberalism is less antagonistic toward traditional beliefs—although it is certainly not very sympathetic to them. Collectivistic liberalism has not only been less sympathetic to traditional beliefs and institutions; it has also been even more rationalistic and scientific. It is confident that the prospective accomplishments of an aggregation of rational and scientific intelligence has scarcely any limits. It is convinced that a government which draws on the resources of scientific knowledge could improve its performance and thus make itself more useful in the promotion of the common welfare. Both affirm the possibility of improving social institutions through rational action; they have both tended to believe in the desirability of gradual and piecemeal improvement rather than in a total and drastic resolution of all problems. Both affirm the desirability and possibility of improving the material standard of living and the working conditions of the mass of the population. Both are concerned about the public good, the good of the entire society. In consequence of their distrustful attitude toward the authority of tradition and of government, both have argued for the toleration of diverse beliefs. Both are rather indifferent and secularist in their attitude toward religion; they require the separation of church and state and the toleration of all religions. Both believed in the rightness of equality before the law and of equality of opportunity. Both believed in the rightness of individual autonomy and collective self-government. Both were pluralistic, believing in the organization of interests and in the legitimacy of the cultivation of diverse ends and values. Both accepted the ineluctibility of conflict in society, and proposed and effected institutional means for their restraint and compromise; neither believed in a natural harmony of interests. Autonomist liberalism became democratic through the extension of the franchise into universal suffrage; with collectivistic liberalism it shared an attachment to representative institutions, to the freedom of expression of political opinion and of political association and the separation of powers. Both acknowledged that restraints on the power of majorities to suppress minorities of religious and political belief and of eccentric private conduct were desirable. These are some beliefs postulated by both "autonomistic" and "collectivistic" liberalism. In the course of the latter part of the nineteenth and through the twentieth century, collectivistic liberalism emerged through a fusion with the authoritarian and philanthropic traditions which were alien to earlier liberalism, and by the consequent shift in the interpretation of the traditions which they had in common.

Liberalism has been a unique phenomenon in the history of mankind. It has drawn on much older traditions which arose in classical antiquity but, as a more or less coherent view about man and society and as a functioning pattern of the organization of society, it is a novel feature of the modern age. In one or another of its forms and in varying degrees it has dominated the thought and policy of Western societies and has almost obliterated conservatism as a realistic alternative. In its latter-day evolution in the form of collectivistic liberalism it is in danger of obliterating itself through an unseen modification of its postulates. In recent years there has been a gradual and unannounced slipping over of collectivistic liberalism toward radicalism. This has been made easier in the United States by the absence of significant large socialist and revolutionary radical organizations with clearly marked organizational and doctrinal boundaries. Unlike the radicalism of fifty or seventy-five years ago, this newer radicalism has become pervasive in the educated classes and in the governing and influential groups which are now dominated by the educated classes.

II

Autonomistic and collectivistic liberalism still have much in common, but the differences have now become rather considerable and the tension between them acute. The set of beliefs which now constitutes the dominant collectivistic liberalism in the United States is itself a heterogeneous complex which has become something quite different from what it was and even inimical to those original ideas. Its main present constituents are: first, a demand for far-reaching freedom of expression of opinion, particularly of opinion critical of authority and of established institutional arrangements; second, a demand for control over executive authority by "the people" and by a popularly elected representative legislature and, increasingly, by the judiciary operating with wide discretionary power—that is to say, "participatory" democracy has now become highly prized; third, a concern for the individual's freedom of affective expression from control by authority, private and public; fourth, a desire for a vigorous, comprehensive and far-reaching exercise of authority by the executive branch of government—above all, the central government—for the advancement of the "common welfare"; fifth, a belief in the urgency of realizing these various ends and in the wickedness of those who disagree with this from other than a radical standpoint.

The first constituents derive from a different tradition than the fourth and fifth; in earlier times and in different contexts, these traditions had been generally regarded as antagonistic to each other. Indeed, they are in many ways antithetical to each other. The desire for the freedom of the individual to express himself as the spirit moves him, implies a repugnance toward authority which goes so far as to place in doubt and even to deny the legitimacy of authority, private and public. The affirmation of the desirability of central governmental action on a large scale does not square well with hostility toward authority. The desire to control and restrain authority is not consistent with the demand that governmental authority be extended in order to protect and provide. The desire for substantive benefits through the action of government requires for its realization the enhanced power of the state to assemble and reallocate resources, to regulate and control their distribution and to enforce numerous laws which govern the use of resources; it has entailed also numerous laws and huge staffs for the regulation of productive actions and for the verification of conformity with these regulations. It has implied the exercise of governmental authority to impose patterns of associations which had previously been left to private choice. This has entailed an increase in the size and specialization of the bureaucracy and an attendant increase in the powers exercised by it on a scale beyond the powers of the legislature to control. The implicit reluctance to acknowledge the legitimacy of authority is not congenial to this vast expansion of the powers of government.

In the course of these latter developments, the principle of voluntary private action and organization for self-provision, which was associated with the freedom of action of individuals, has fallen by the wayside. This is so not just because the power of government has itself been so expansive—that is certainly one factor—but also because the demand to annul some of the consequences or to correct some of the insufficiencies of private action has become so clamant, and because federal government has seemed to be the only body capable of providing this annulment and correction. The demand has risen for goods and services not obtainable through the mechanisms of the market and obtainable in the past only through voluntary association and private initiative or, on a small scale, through the state. Welfare services and payments which were once intended for the needy classes have now been extended to the classes once regarded as capable of "paying their way" and under obligation to do so. The powers of the family have been increasingly limited on behalf of the freedom of the individual member and the power of the government. Testamentary freedom and succession, the power of parents over children and the responsibility of parents for children have all been restricted for various reasons which all involve the greater activity of the government.

Private associations abound but they function less to provide gratifications, services, and goods for their members than to urge and threaten the government into their provision. Private business enterprises still exist on a scale not equaled anywhere in the world but these enterprises also have come to demand and to depend on governmental subsidies, guarantees, contracts, and regulations; their legitimacy is not taken for granted or even acknowledged by some tendencies in collectivistic liberalism. In the justification of the "mixed economy," the governmental element enjoys a higher evaluation than the private one. The privately practiced professions exist but, once almost wholly self-regulatory, they too are now increasingly subject to the surveillance and regulation of the government, and this too is widely accepted by collectivistic liberalism. This combination of heightened and multiplied demands, the falling away of voluntarily and privately undertaken provision, and increased reliance on government's providence have engendered a great concentration of power in the state. The bureaucracy has become an organ enjoying a degree of initiative and autonomous action not previously anticipated by any one except persons of Cassandric disposition. Relatively little attention is paid by collectivistic liberals to the control of the bureaucracy. In the United States, there was recently an outburst of collectivistic liberal demand for control over the executive branch by the legislative. The control which was sought, however, was not over the executive as a whole, but over the staff of the president which had come into existence largely because of the difficulty of controlling the civil service. The intellectual and political prosperity of governmentalistic liberalism has left in the shadows the liberalism which distrusted governmental action.

III

Liberalism in the United States has always had greater sympathy for socialism than it had in Europe. Perhaps the absence of large social-democratic parties in the United States meant that persons who would otherwise have supported the socialistic cause found a home in liberal circles. They joined with the humanitarian social reformers, with the improvers of governmental machinery, and with "civil libertarians" to form a coalition such as has not quite existed elsewhere.

The United States did not have a tradition of "statism," the tradition of a strong state, of an intrusively arbitrary central authority such as the countries of continental Europe inherited from the *ancien régime.* Nearly everyone in the United States at one time was opposed in varying measure to the authority and majesty of the state. When the justifications for slavery ceased and when socialism was the ideal only of lower-class immigrants, nearly everyone was a liberal although the name itself was not invoked. Those who would have liked to respect the authority of the state were deterred by its corruption and vulgarity, and thus became critics of the existing system of politics and government. By virtue of this they were regarded sympathetically by philanthropic reformers and those who did not want the power of the state to expand. The effort to improve the probity and efficiency of government proceeded from a distrust of government as it was; those who disliked the existing personnel and machinery of government came to be considered by some to be liberals because they were critical of what existed. The desire to make government more efficient and less costly was indeed one tradition of liberalism when it was coupled with the intention to restrict the radius of governmental inquisitiveness and intrusiveness. Although support for the increased efficiency of government did not necessarily make its proponents into liberals, these reformers were moulded into a loose coalition with liberals who opposed the government on other, more fundamental grounds; they were all critics of existing practices and institutions, they were all reformers in one way or another, and hence they counted as "liberals."

There were also those "philanthropic" reformers who wanted government to do more for the welfare of the mass of the poor, the immigrants, the weak and unprotected. These persons were not liberals in the same sense as those who were critical of the expanded action of the state;

they were not opposed to state action but they were in favor of the improvement of the moral and effective quality of governments. They were also usually friendly toward civil liberties because it was the critics of existing social conditions whose civil liberties were being restricted. Among these critics fell moderate socialists and trade unionists with a large "social" perspective. The latter were certainly not liberals in the traditional sense, but since they were in favor of the civil liberties, they too came into the loose fold of the liberal coalition.

This coalition had been in process of formation since late in the nineteenth century but it became animated in the 1920s. Under the stress of the great depression in the 1930s it became consolidated. The philanthropic, reformatory element was brought into prominence by the visible distress of the unemployed. The civil libertarian element had already grown large in the 1920s in response to the "Palmer raids," the publicity of the Lusk Committee of the New York State legislature, and the Sacco and Vanzetti case, all coming after the suppression of *The Masses* and the trial of its editors during the First World War. The chief protégés of the civil libertarians tended to be radicals of socialistic inclinations. The protectors acquired the tincture of the protected.

The Russian revolutions of 1905 and 1917 were significant factors in this collectivistic turn of American liberalism. The sympathies of many educated Americans had been drawn to Russian opposition to the tsarist regime ever since Tolstoy, Turgenev, and Chekhov had aroused their appreciation. The revolution of 1905 seemed to be an outcropping of this movement and the two revolutions of 1917 even more so. Not many American liberals were critical of the Bolshevik phase of the revolution. Only "reactionaries," fearful of Bolshevist determination to abolish capitalism, argued that it would destroy political liberty as well as private property, family life, and Christianity. Their arguments were so crudely put that they deepened the suspicions of Americans toward the autonomist liberalism which supported private business enterprise; in fact, these arguments had the contrary effect of reinforcing the appreciation of the Bolshevik revolution as the fulfillment of the aspirations of a philanthropic liberalism concerned for intellectual and artistic freedom of expression. The gap between the two main types of liberalism was widened and autonomist liberalism became narrow in its explicit concerns. It became preoccupied with the protection of the autonomy of the economic order.

On the other side of the gap, the Soviet Union in its reality and its transfigured and derivative versions became a touchstone for American collectivist liberalism. That is why a repressive regime which called itself socialist usually had the support of American collectivistic liberals. It is also the reason for the persistence and pervasiveness of the simple-minded distinction between "Left" and "Right" and the disposition to think that the "Left" is always right and the "Right" is always wrong.

The movement toward collectivistic liberalism in the United States was influenced, too, by quite similar developments in Great Britain in the course of which Benthamism—which aimed at the greatest happiness of the greatest number—turned from individual freedom to the use of an efficient government as a means of increasing the general happiness. If the proper and chief end of man was happiness, then the means by which happiness was attained was only of instrumental and hence of secondary significance. From this standpoint, freedom of initiative and action in the political, economic, and cultural spheres became less important, once it was thought that the end of happiness could be effectively attained by the action of the government. Fabian socialism did not pretend to be liberal—it acknowledged that it was utilitarian. Nonetheless, it was widely esteemed by American collectivist liberals in the 1920s; the writings of the Webbs and R. H. Tawney's *The Acquisitive Society* were among the favorite books of liberal intellectuals of the 1920s. The more preponderant the socialistic philanthropic element in liberalism became, the more its bearers turned against individual initiative and enterprise, and toward the expanded action of a more efficient government. Nonetheless they did not swerve in their devotion to civil liberties, particularly those of radicals and literary men whose works were under ban for moral improprieties.

In the time of the administration of Franklin Roosevelt the liberal outlook moved toward an unqualified affirmation of far-reaching regulatory and initiatory actions by the central government. There was a growing confidence in the capacity of the central government to accomplish not only most of what had previously been accomplished by private and voluntary action, but to accomplish much more than private and voluntary action had ever attempted. In their eagerness to bring about increased material well-being, which had been one of the concerns of the older types of liberalism, liberals turned away from the precepts of that type of liberalism which asserted that government should do only those things that could not be done by private and voluntary action, as well as from the wide-ranging distrust of authority which had been common to all types of liberalism.

This modification of belief became more pronounced when the mechanism of the market and the ethic of individual initiative, self-help, saving, and ambition were shown to be of no avail for many persons. The depression of the 1930s brought collectivist liberalism nearer to its full flowering. Keynesian economics, which was disparaged by many socialistic and radical critics of the capitalist system as a means of saving capitalism, strengthened the foundation of collectivistic liberalism which was very critical of capitalism but not ready to replace it by socialism. Keynesianism raised the standing of government; it showed the dependence of the market on governmental action.

The Second World War increased the confidence in the capacity of government to accomplish things on a scale not conceived in earlier times. The successes of the American government in production, in organizing supplies, and in moving soldiers over a worldwide front of military operations, and in its organization of scientific and technological research for the development of the atomic bomb and radar, raised the credit of government to new heights. There was no turning back from this point. The collectivist liberals saw their faith in government tested and vindicated; they became confident of government and did not fear it. It seemed entirely possible to combine an omnicompetent government with public liberties without endangering the latter.[2]

The "discovery of poverty" at the end of the 1950s led further along the same path. The source of this was both humanitarian compassion and the resurgence of the temporarily suppressed animosity of the literary wing of the collectivistic liberal intellectuals against American society. The compassion but not the animosity had been latent in liberalism; the latter had been nourished by a long-existent tradition of bohemian literary culture admixed with a general sympathy for socialism. This had little to do with liberalism in its earlier form, but as liberalism moved toward collectivistic liberalism, its adherents found a congenial companionship there. In the United States for most of the 1950s, the combination of fear of McCarthyism, the discredit of the Soviet Union, the prosperity of American society, and the full employment of intellectuals had led to a pronounced recession of radicalism. The release of radicals from the burden of admiration of the Soviet Union occurred as a result of the events of 1956 in Poland and Hungary. The Anglo-French military action in Suez aroused the slumbering radicalism of French and British intellectuals. These events induced the birth of the "New Left." The tradition of radicalism was thus resuscitated. In the United States the first result of this rebirth of radicalism was the "rediscovery of poverty." Shortly after the rediscovery of "the poor" came a new awareness of the unhappy plight of the Negro part of American society.

In the United States, liberals were usually opposed to discrimination before the law and to the allocation of opportunities on the basis of religion and race. They were sympathetic with immigrants when these

2. It may be mentioned in passing that before the Second World War, when the universities had been severely constricted by the depression, heads of universities were adamant in refusing to seek the financial support of the federal government. They feared that it would lead to governmental intrusion into the affairs of the universities. After the war the universities accepted and then became dependent on the financial support of the federal government. They have since learned that the fears of their predecessors of the 1930s were far from groundless.

were inequitably treated; they disliked the maltreatment of Negroes. Nonetheless, except for the few who were involved in the National Association for the Advancement of Colored People and the National Urban League, white liberals, including the collectivist liberals, were not greatly exercised about the discriminatory activities against Negroes. Until the 1950s they disapproved of the disfranchisement of Negroes in the southern United States but did not become very concerned about gaining the franchise for them; they opposed restrictive covenants in northern cities but this was a minor and not a nationally prominent issue.

The situation changed in the course of the 1960s, and this change had important consequences for the subsequent evolution of the beliefs of American liberals during this period. In a way the white liberal experience of "the black experience" became as important as the liberals' interpretation of the Bolshevik revolution.

The movement of blacks for civil rights was, of course, a movement to realize the liberal ideals of equality of opportunity, of equality before the law, of the operation of the market mechanism without regard to ethnic qualities and the right of the citizen to affect the exercise of authority through representative institutions. It was liberal to demand equality before the law, it was liberal to demand equality of opportunity to take one's chances in the market, it was liberal to demand the right to vote and to hold office, to demand the freedom to political opinion, assembly, association, and petition. The civil rights movement was a movement to realize the traditional ideals of liberalism. The civil rights movement sought to establish the Negro as a citizen by virtue of his existence within the civil community. The idea of citizenship is one of the major ideas of liberalism; its extension to the entire adult population is one of the areas where the liberalism of privacy and autonomy and collectivistic liberalism are identical and it is crucial to both.

Liberalism, even collectivistic liberalism, lost credit on the intellectual plane when the riots of blacks in black districts engaged public attention. Black intellectuals and black political agitators denounced the insufficiency and the "failure" of liberalism. They counseled violence or at least praised it with overtones of recommendation; in this they were eagerly joined by white intellectuals who ordinarily passed as "liberals" but who now took to fancying themselves as "revolutionaries." The demand was no longer for freedom and rights within a preponderantly white society but for withdrawal from that society. Nothing could have been less like liberalism, which postulated the value of civility. The demand for secession was associated with the equally illiberal praise of violence and the explicit denunciation of many of the institutional arrangements that were basic to liberalism.

Collectivistic liberalism lurched further toward radicalism in its next phase. This was the war in Indochina. For various reasons and causes which cannot be entered into here, authority in the United States in the second half of the 1960s experienced an unprecedented buffeting. The vulnerability of authority disclosed by the assassination of President Kennedy and his brother and Martin Luther King, the incapacity to prevent the riots in the Negro districts of the large cities, the inability to bring the war in Indochina to a successful conclusion, the feebleness of university and college administrators and teachers in the face of the student agitation—all these showed authority to be inept and indecisive and even cowardly. In fact authority was collectivistic liberal in most cases, and it was dominated and paralyzed by its own convictions. The result was a desertion of liberalism, a going over to radicalism which was in point of fact only collectivistic liberalism writ large. The major transformation from liberty to libertinism and perversity, from civility to emancipation, from the welfare state to the omnicompetent and ubiquitous state, from equality of opportunity to equality of rewards, from "careers open to talent" to vehemence against "elitism" were products of these years.

The blacks and "the poor" were amalgamated to provide the justification for a vehement attack on the liberal traditions of American society. The attack was carried out mainly by collectivistic liberals, some of whom became more radical in their censure of the limited capacities of traditional liberalism, above all for its failure to bring about a degree of equality which neither liberalism had previously sought. This alliance of collectivistic liberalism and radicalism cast "elitism" and traditional liberalism in the role of the enemy.

IV

What was there in that loose constellation of beliefs called "liberalism" which permitted such transformations? Whenever American liberalism has confined itself to political concerns, it has for the most part placed the freedom of the individual and the values cultivated privately by individuals above the claims and standing of government. But when "the economic problem" and the "social problem" became the dominant concerns of liberals, a fissure occurred. When the "economic" and "social" problems came to the forefront of the field of liberal attention, the appreciation of individual freedom suffered and the state which had been distrusted was given the vital tasks of curbing the power of individuals and making up for their inadequacies.

The split in the ranks of liberals, which had been visible since the last decades of the nineteenth century, became more marked after the First World War. One section had remained faithful to the older liberal tradition that emphasized political freedom, individual initiative, and the rule of law, and to the belief that the market was the most efficient and beneficent mechanism through which individual initiative and decision could work. Adherents to this strand of liberalism also believed in the efficacy of hard work as a moral virtue and thought that professional politicians were by and large a meddlesome and shoddy lot. These liberals came to be called "conservatives" or "reactionaries" or at best and derisively "Adam Smith liberals" or "laissez-faire liberals" by other liberals. No distinction was made between liberals who had a vision of social order and of the human mind in which reason and liberty were central, and those persons who were preoccupied almost exclusively by their attachment to private property and private enterprise and who wanted not only an unintrusive government which acted as a "night watchman" but one which would also stand guard against the importation of goods of foreign manufacture and against radical criticism and subversive activities. The numbers of the autonomist liberals did not increase proportionately to the increase in the size and prominence of the educated class. As the latter grew, it provided fewer recruits for an articulate autonomist liberalism. Engineers, chemists, accountants tended to be silent adherents of autonomist liberalism. The social sciences, the fundamental natural sciences, and humanistic studies produced a more articulate body of collectivistic liberals. They pressed forward the ideas of collectivistic liberalism; they also gave currency to the identification of autonomist liberalism with narrowly self-serving capitalistic arguments.

The collectivistic liberals took an instrumental attitude toward government to compensate for the deficiencies of the market, defined from a philanthropic point of view. The intervention of government into the operation of the market was not thought by collectivistic liberals to be dangerous to political freedom in any respect as long as it was initiated and controlled by the politically qualified public. Some of the intervention supported by liberals was in fact intended to restore the competitiveness of the market by action against "trusts and combinations." This was another point where autonomist and collectivist liberals remained at one with each other. This action against monopolies was also intended to reinforce the representativeness of representative institutions by impeding the concentration of power in the economic sphere. Some of the philanthropic intervention by government was intended to aid individuals and families which would otherwise fall out of the circle of "respectability"; it was intended to "tide them over" until they could take their place in the market again. As citizens, the "needy" were entitled to support for the period of "neediness"; it was not thought to be a permanent condition. Unemployment insurance was the main instance of this type of philanthropic intervention and it too was a measure on which both kinds of liberals could agree. In these and other respects, collectivistic liberalism remained liberal. Nonetheless it was already launched on a new path with a compelling direction of its own.

There was another type of philanthropic intervention which was not liberal since it was not intended to restore the competitiveness of the market or the capacity of individuals to return to the market. It was directly Christian in inspiration and exclusively philanthropic in intention. It was directed to the care of those incapable of caring for themselves, such as the derelict aged, the parentless child, the deserted mother, the mentally defective, the severely deformed. They were persons who had to be protected in a regime which left so much to private initiative and self-maintenance. This current of philanthropic liberalism was also not intended to be broadened to the point where it would flood the sphere of autonomy; it was intended only to compensate marginally for the limited efficacy of autonomous action in making possible the attainment of earthly happiness. Nevertheless, when Christian philanthropic liberalism became governmental policy, it broke out of these earlier constraints and it lost its visible connection with Christianity.

To the major traditions which have entered into American liberalism from Great Britain there should be added that which came from a different source. American liberalism of British inspiration, embracing devotion to individual liberty, responsibility and initiative, rationalism, belief in the efficacy of the market, and Christian philanthropy, had eschewed recourse to the state except for the maintenance of public order and defense and for treating marginal situations. Private initiative, whether in business or philanthropy, was to prevail in all except marginal situations. But in the period after the Civil War many young Americans went to Germany to study the social sciences, history, and philosophy, and brought back with them some ideas and assumptions about the state that were quite different. The American students of the *Staatswissenschaften* saw the state as something superior to the individuals who constituted it. It was seen to have a value of its own, quite apart from its instrumental uses. For them the state was not to be distrusted; it was to be admired. It was not a supplement or corrective to individual actions that had gone astray or fallen short; it existed in its own right, an initiating creative power.

The situation in the United States at the time seemed to call for such ideas. The state was in disarray; it was corrupt and inefficient. There was no governor to restrain the excesses of successful economic individualism. The message brought back from Germany seemed to provide the ideal solution, especially in combination with American populistic postulates. Populism, which regarded "the people" as the locus of virtue and was in some respects the very antithesis of "statolatry," was very ready to avail itself of a very active state in order to control its adversaries, the banks and railways. The corruption of government which the muckrakers exposed was interpreted in the circles influenced by their German mentors as evidence of the need to repair and elevate the state and to animate it for high purposes. The action of the state, directed by this high calling, would thus serve the interests of "the people." Neither "statolatry" nor populism was liberal but, in the United States, they became amalgamated into liberalism.

Scientism was another tributary tradition which flowed into the making of collectivistic liberalism. American liberalism, with its dislike of traditional authorities, had always been strongly disposed toward science, both as a replacement of religion and for its practical utility. What was new, however, was the belief that scientific methods and scientific knowledge could provide the basis for social engineering on a massive scale.

This belief—that the application of science could "solve" social problems—affected a wide range of academic disciplines, and turned them into fortresses and arsenals of reform. The emerging discipline of political science, with its strong Germanic imprint, was thought of as the science which could purify, elevate, and strengthen the state, thereby permitting it to do what its own nature and the condition of American society required. Institutional economics, similarly nurtured from a German seed, also contributed mightily to the shift from autonomist to collectivistic liberalism. Sociologists were also eager to contribute to the progress of their society; they were reformers to a man—except Sumner. They were concerned with "social conditions," meaning poverty and demoralization. Even W. I. Thomas, the most profound sociologist of his time, moved in that direction. The natural sciences were less involved with the state; their beneficences went to industry, agriculture and medicine, and for a long time they expected little from government other than a modest contribution. (As a matter of fact, the contribution of the government to the development of science in agriculture was great.) Anthropology and psychology also tended to remain outside the circle; they persisted in the line of the natural scientists and the technologists. Still, the scientistic view that science should and could contribute to social well-being was strong, and flowed smoothly into the notion that government should become the chief instrument for ensuring the social welfare.

The reforming sociologists and the political scientists shared many liberal attitudes. In particular, both grounded their hopes for effectiveness on a pillar of traditional liberalism, namely the freedom of an enquiring and critical press. The organs of opinion would report on "social problems" and disclose "social conditions" in need of reform; they were not expected to examine those conditions which were not so deplorable and which were neither so newsworthy nor so demanding of academic and journalistic attention. Free inquiry would illuminate public opinion; legislators would be impelled to act on the basis of meticulously gathered facts. It was the journalists and social scientists who were to bring the issues before the public and thence to the politicians.

This is indeed what happened. From sociology and political science, the involvement spread into the teaching of law, and from there exerted a penetrating influence on educated public opinion and then on the judiciary and on the legislation of social policy. Roscoe Pound significantly called his doctrine "sociological jurisprudence." Institutional economics also entered into jurisprudence and, supported by what these learned lawyers thought to be social science, turned the law into an organ of collectivistic liberalism.

V

As events outside the boundaries of the United States achieved prominence in liberal attention, the foreign policy of the government became increasingly important as an object of contention. The attitude and action of the government toward the Soviet Union, toward "socialism" in other countries, toward the colonial policies of Western European countries, and toward the regimes of the Third World has become a primary interest of collectivistic liberalism. In consequence of this, the divergence between autonomistic liberalism and collectivistic liberalism has become wider.

By its traditions, liberalism has been universalistic in the direction of its attention. It was not fortuitous that Bentham was ready to write constitutions for countries everywhere. Liberalism has always been concerned with what has been happening in other parts of the world; the improvements in means of transportation and communication and the growth of scholarly and journalistic knowledge about all corners of the earth have fostered this disposition. Autonomist liberalism, especially during its period of formation, had a profound sense of the affinity of European humanity and the other parts of the human race. The moral relativism and the concomitant disparagement of Christianity which characterized some currents of European liberalism, particularly in France and Great Britain, were closely related to this readiness to see all of humanity as one. The growth of anthropological and oriental studies further opened the awareness of European liberalism of the rest of mankind.

However, liberalism has not only been universalist in its range of attention; it has also been "internationalist"—the word itself seems to have been coined by Bentham. There have been isolationist currents and moments in American collectivistic liberalism but they have never been dominant. For the past four decades, American liberalism has been internationalist. Liberalism generally has sought peace between states, it has disparaged the martial virtues—in its autonomist liberal phase, it also praised the mercantile virtues that were contrasted with the martial ones. For a long time liberalism was against tariffs and in favor of free trade. In its more collectivistic phase, especially in its alliance with trade unions, its attitude toward free trade has been somewhat more ambiguous. But it is against war, except when the war is on behalf of principles and especially when it is veiled as a civil war fought on behalf of a collectivistic liberal principle. It is certainly against nationalism in its own society; it wishes the foreign policy of its own government to be internationalist, and moreover to be internationalist in accordance with moral principles such as national self-determination, democracy, and populism.

Opposed though it has been to "chauvinism," "jingoism," and nationalism under whatever name at home, liberalism, and especially collectivistic liberalism, has been greatly exercised on behalf of the right of national self-determination in other countries. At one time, its proponents thought that the realization of the right of collective self-determination brought with it the advancement of the rights of individuals to education, enlightenment, and public liberties. Liberalism, especially in its collectivistic variant, has been consistently sympathetic with the nationalism of colonized peoples and of newly established states, even where this was accompanied by the suppression of public liberties.

Liberals—persons who desired freedom in their own societies—were once critical of tyranny abroad as well as in their own countries. So it was in the nineteenth century and the beginning of the twentieth century. A great change occurred after the Bolshevik revolution of 1917. Throughout the 1920s, collectivist liberals in the United States accepted the Soviet Union as a country in which their ideals of individual freedom and welfare were being realized. This was probably less true of liberals in Europe, including the United Kingdom. There, liberals were more concerned with political freedom and less with humanitarian ends; and the social democrats, who incorporated a considerable measure of political liberalism into their outlook, were reinforced in their dislike of Bolshevism by their awareness of the fate of social democrats under the Soviet regime and of the vehemence with which Communists denounced social democracy.

Why did the American liberals come to the support of the Soviet Union in the 1920s, even though they were not Communists? (I am thinking here largely of the contributors and sympathetic readers of *The Nation* and *The New Republic* although there were many more sympathizers than these.) They supported the Soviet Union because they associated "revolution" with the improvement of the conditions of "the poor" and with freedom of the arts and freedom of opinion. They supported it, too, because "reactionaries"—the supporters of private business—opposed it. The Soviet Union was after all the one place where capitalism had been abolished; the attachment of the collectivistic liberals in the United States to the Soviet Union for such a long time shows how hostile to capitalism they have been—even though within the United States they have reconciled themselves to its hobbled existence. They refused to believe about the USSR what more detached students of the subject told them, because they distrusted the "reactionary" press and found it nearly impossible to believe that revolution and freedom were not identical.

As many collectivistic liberals came under Communist influence in the 1930s, they also began explicitly to relegate political freedom to a secondary position. Fascism and National Socialism became their main enemies; and they were, of course, hostile to imperialism, an attitude consistent with their traditional views. With respect to the Soviet Union, however, they fell into a more self-contradictory position. On the one hand they opposed imperialism and tyranny in the name of democratic or collective self-determination and of individual freedom in politics, in the arts, and in intellectual activities. On the other, they were attached

145

to the Soviet Union. They reconciled these contradictory attitudes by denying the evidence of Soviet tyranny, or by explaining it away as a temporary measure, or by asserting that the Soviet Union was genuinely democratic but in a new way which was unappreciated in liberal-democratic countries.

There was another aspect of the Soviet Union which attracted American collectivistic liberals. The Soviet Union was a "planned economy," indeed even a "planned society." At a time when the United States was suffering from unemployment, the Soviet Union was portrayed as "the land without unemployment." This great accomplishment was alleged to be a result of central planning; this was contrasted with the chaos of "a laissez-faire economic system," with all its unhappy accompaniments. The New Deal was seen as a step, faltering and insufficient, in the right direction. "Planning" was held forth as an ideal toward which the United States should move. After the Second World War, the idea of comprehensive planning diminished in the publicly expressed affection of collectivistic liberals, but a strong subterranean attachment remained. There is still a clandestine love of planning. It is after all a logical necessity. If one believes in the powers of reason and of scientific knowledge, in progress toward ever higher targets or "goals," in collective self-determination, as well as in the limitless competence of government which proceeds in accordance with rationality and scientific knowledge, then one must be in favor of planning. However tarnished the image of the Soviet Union has become, it still retains the credit of being "planned."

For these very diverse reasons, the Soviet Union in its foreign policy was credited by a substantial fraction of collectivistic liberals with being generally on the right side. Liberals were temporarily swept loose from this position during the period of the Molotov-Ribbentrop agreement, and again after the Second World War. The assumption of Soviet virtue was eroded for a time during the cold war, when patriotism became stronger than usual among American liberals. The Americans for Democratic Action supported the policy of the Democratic administration which followed the war, although many collectivistic liberals also supported the Progressive Party of Henry Wallace and the fellow travelers who espoused the traditional pro-Soviet policy of so many American collectivistic liberals during most of the period after the Russian revolution.

The tendency of American liberals to view foreign policy from a moral standpoint, to combine a high evaluation of freedom with the demand for the material well-being of the mass of the population by means of governmental action in all countries, gave a particularly favored position to the Soviet Union. The tangible evidence of the brutality of Soviet domestic policies in the 1930s—in connection with the collectivization of agriculture and the "purge" of Stalin's opponents and his real and potential rivals—was often denied; and even when it was acknowledged it was, in the main, acknowledged unwillingly, and did not affect the attitudes of many collectivistic liberal intellectuals. Even today some liberals who have acknowledged the brutality of the Soviet regime—partly because of the publication of the works of Solzhenitsyn—still seem to waver in condemning the Soviet Union outright. Some write off Solzhenitsyn as a talented crank in political matters; others accept his evidence, but tend to discount it as the report of an aberration whose repressiveness does not affect the claim to inherent superiority of a "truly" socialistic regime. And of course they are passionate in their denunciation of the cold war. They denounce the cold war not because it was conducted in a doctrinaire fashion by John Foster Dulles but fundamentally because it was distrustful of the Soviet Union. They seem to think that socialistic regimes must by their nature realize the ambitions of collectivistic liberalism. The reports of the brutal repressiveness of socialistic regimes they interpret as exaggerated or as referring to transient conditions necessitated by the "needs" of development or of the threat of inimical "capitalist powers." They have added to the traditional liberal view of the larger world an image inexpungibly impressed on the recollection of liberals more than a half-century ago by the Allied intervention in Russia in 1919.

It is a paradox that the Soviet Union, which is one of the most illiberal of all the regimes of modern times, should hold the lingering affections of many American collectivistic liberals who are so devoted to civil, artistic, and intellectual liberties. When affection for the Soviet Union is renounced, then it is redirected to some other regime like it. When attachment to all these regimes is renounced or qualified, the attitude of the collectivistic liberals toward American foreign policy which underlay their affection for these regimes still endures.

This same attitude finds expression domestically in the animosity of most collectivistic liberals toward the Federal Bureau of Investigation and the Central Intelligence Agency, which they see to a large extent as being directed primarily against the Soviet Union and its American and foreign sympathizers. Trotskyites, Maoists, and all the various combinations come under the protection of this attitude, which has at its heart the unextinguishable memory of the Soviet Union as the bearer of the best hopes of humanity. The emptied ideal still guides their outlook; they might have renounced their old love but they retain their old enemies.

VI

The radicalism which asserts the failure of liberalism—it does not generally distinguish the autonomist liberalism from collectivistic liberalism—considers itself to have broken out of the confines of liberalism. But it has done so only in the way in which a neurotic exaggerates and distorts the dispositions of a person of normal conduct. Radicalism claims to offer something to mankind which liberalism has failed to offer. It is in fact only an extension, to the point of corruption, of the principles contained in liberalism. Radicalism extends the ends of liberalism to points beyond the intentions of those who promulgated it and beyond the traditions that have sustained it. Contrary to the beliefs of radicals that their program is disjunctively different from that of collectivistic liberalism, there has been a movement toward a loose approximation between them. A process of transformation has swept collectivistic liberalism toward radicalism. The transformation has not been announced. It is not even noticed because—since contemporary radicalism is no longer dominated by a dogmatic Marxian orthodoxy—it has become easier to pass from liberalism to radicalism. Nonetheless the central ideas of liberty of expression, equality of opportunity, and individuality have been subjected to reinterpretations which have moved them away from liberalism. Collectivistic liberalism has become thereby radically different from what it was.

Liberty of expression has until relatively recently meant the liberty of expression, in an intellectual form, of a substantive belief. It meant the liberty of expression of an argument that was intended to justify the belief and to convince others. It meant the liberty of expression of scientific ideas, moral ideals, political ideals and programs, and religious ideas; it meant the liberty of publishing literary works. The argument for the liberty of expression has always presupposed the seriousness of intention, and the intellectual and aesthetic character, of the works and activities to be protected. Liberty of expression was not intended simply to be the expression of an affective state, unless it was given an intellectual or literary form. Liberty of expression did not mean the liberty of expression as such, without regard to content; the content was expected to be something *serious* in the Durkheimian sense. The content was expected to be a belief regarding a problem of society, a problem of the proper conduct of authority, or of the church, or of the individual; it was expected to be a belief about the earth or the cosmos. These were the matters which the right to freedom of expression was intended to open to public view.

Traditional liberalism tended to be puritanical regarding affective expression and particularly regarding erotic matters. At various points, its principles contained implications of freedom of affective expression, but these were not developed. What is specifically collectivistic in collectivistic liberalism does not logically require the extension of the freedom of expression into the sphere of affective and erotic expression. But in the course of the nineteenth century, philanthropy and idealistic individualism became fused with the romantic idea of individuality as the cultivation and development of the emotions. Autonomist individualism spurned this alliance. The entry of bohemian radicalism accentuated this tendency in collectivistic liberalism.

Still, in the nineteenth century and in the early twentieth century literary works which would now be called pornographic were not at issue for either of the currents of liberalism, even though they were already becoming quite widely separated from each other. The writing and publication of pornography and blasphemy and the public performances of sexual actions for purposes of public entertainment or for the sheer pleasure of performing them in public were not regarded by the liberal political theorists of the eighteenth and nineteenth centuries as falling within the class of the actions whose freedom they were attempting to establish. The arguments on behalf of works that were soon recognized as literary classics, such as *Madame Bovary, Fleurs du Mal,* and *Leaves of Grass,* which were prosecuted for offense to public morals, did not extend to the justification of pornography nor to the performance of sexual acts in public. The idea that avowedly pornographic works should be protected by the right to freedom of expression apparently did not occur to the political philosophers who argued for a regime of intellectual freedom. They lived in a tradition which simply did not acknowledge the legitimacy of such works; they accepted that tradition. It is only recently, when the tradition of literary and artistic seriousness has faded and when any sort of posturing and self-exhibition has come to be regarded as art, that pornography has been placed under the protection of the right to the freedom of expression. The protection of the liberty of authors like James Joyce and D. H. Lawrence has been extended to works of pornography and acts of public indecency.

The liberal defenders of pornography have extended liberalism to justify actions and works that were not intended to enjoy the benefits of a liberal regime. They have done so effectively, to the extent that any proposal for the censorship of pornographic works and of acts of public indecency is avoided by liberals for fear that they would thereby show themselves to be illiberal. After all, should not any affective states and erotic impulses be as expressible as scientific or religious or moral beliefs or as political aspirations? According to this radicalized liberalism, whatever can be expressed must be provided with the guaranteed liberty of its expression. Liberty of expression has become distorted into a doctrine of emancipation from the restraints of social institutions, cultural traditions, and interior inhibitions. The criticism of the repression exercised by public and ecclesiastical authority over the expression of beliefs and opinions in an intellectual or artistic form has been extended to the rejection of restraints of any kind.

A similar process has occurred when the argument for equality of opportunity was jostled and forced aside by the ideal of the equality of rewards. Classical liberalism in its autonomist branch was at first egalitarian in two very specific senses: it insisted on equality before the law and on equality of opportunity. It was ambivalent about equality of the franchise and it moved very cautiously in that direction. It accepted that there were inequalities of nature, propensities and talents among individuals, and it was concerned for *la carrière ouverte aux talents*. Abilities should be rewarded commensurately to their magnitude and application.

Liberals of both major types have in principle always been opposed to the privilege of unearned, superior rewards and opportunities; they have disapproved of competitive advantages which have not been won by achievement and talent but acquired through birth. They had therefore to regard educational qualification and educational achievement as better criteria for occupational appointment and promotion than familial and ethnic connections. They both regarded the education of the natural talents as the best means of undoing the injustice of the familial transmission of wealth and status.

Liberals were concerned to see that the cultivation and training of these natural talents were not impeded by inherited wealth or any other institutionally sustained privilege based on affiliation or biological descent. Yet liberalism in the nineteenth and even through much of the twentieth centuries accepted that human beings within any particular society, however successfully that society had realized the program of liberalism, would be inegalitarian in the distribution of deference. It would be less inegalitarian than the societies of the *ancien régime,* and it would maintain a floor of dignity below which human beings would not be degraded. Nonetheless, since there would be differences in excellence of achievement and differences in excellence of moral character, there would inevitably be differences in deference.

It has not appeared to be a great step to pass from equality of opportunity to equality of results—after all, both were about equality! What good is an equality which ends up in inequality? Equality is a term sufficiently ambiguous to allow diverse constructions to be laid upon it without a sense of inconsistency or of departure from its "true" meaning. To pass from disapproval of differences in deference derived from differences in the status of ancestors, to the disapproval of differences in status derived from differences in achievement or in moral merit, is not a great step either. Might it not be argued that the qualities which foster achievement or moral merit are not themselves the product of the individual's achievement or moral merit? They might be inherited genetically, although few equalitarians would argue that; or, they might be results of luck or chance, or they might be the results of hidden privileges. Hence, equality of opportunity is only another way of guaranteeing the continued existence of inequality. As a result, it has not appeared to be a great step to pass from the removal of present and actual inferiorities to compensation for inferiorities inherited from the past. If past ancestral advantages were to be obliterated, it has not seemed inconsistent to argue that past ancestral disadvantages should be compensated. Nor has it been any more of a strain to pass from the disapprobation of unearned or inherited superiority of position to the denunciation of earned superiority, of superiority of accomplishment, together with the institutions which make superior accomplishment possible.

Insisting on the desirability of equality of opportunity, liberals have insisted particularly on the opportunity to become educated. This was regarded as of the first importance because it was the way in which abilities were trained and tested. This is why liberals pressed for the extension of educational provision and for universal and free primary and secondary education; in the United States they also supported the provision of higher education by the states so that the offspring of poorer families could attend. This high evaluation of education has, in an increasingly bureaucratic and governmentally dominated society, become adulterated by an excess of confidence in educational certification, as a precondition of admission to a widening range of occupations. There have been two by-products of this. One is the deprecation of the development of talents through experience, and the other is the willingness to accept the simulacrum of education represented by a diploma or a degree and an increased indifference toward the intellectual substance of education. Both of these unwholesome occurrences may be attributed to liberalism and above all to collectivistic liberalism. They are the price that has been paid for the elimination of familial descent and affiliations as qualifications for deference and opportunity.

Education has become the chosen instrument of the radical equalitarianism that has been insinuated into collectivistic liberalism. There were many reasons for the liberal reformers' desire to widen access to education. Through it, economic and cultural benefits would accrue to the individual as well as to society by incorporating new generations into a common national culture and a common civilization, and by promoting a sense of civility. It was also regarded as just that those who were especially talented should have the opportunity to develop the talents with which they were endowed; this was integral to the belief that if these especially talented young persons were successful in the use of those talents they should be rewarded correspondingly and more amply than those with poorer talents, less developed talents, or less fruitfully applied talents. This was thought to be beneficial not only to the talented individual but also to the society that would be improved by superior accomplishments, whether in the economic, artistic, intellectual, or civil spheres.

Some liberal writers occasionally referred to the injustice of the unequal distribution of native endowment. They did not make anything of it, in contrast with early socialist writers who regarded it as an argument against remuneration in accordance with performance and who argued that "needs" should be the criterion for remuneration. Liberals have been opposed in principle to the inheritance of advantages such as titles, ranks, offices, and powers, but they did nonetheless admit the existence of differences in genetic endowment, and they accepted them.

There was however a significant difference between these two types of hereditary transmission. In the one, which classical liberalism allowed and which autonomist liberalism still allows, the superior reward was conferred in acknowledgement of an actual achievement, presumably made possible by superior endowment and by corresponding effort. In the other, there was no achievement. There was thus a rationale in the liberal acceptance of differences in the quality of genetic endowment. Nonetheless, this difference has not been tolerated by the radical criticism, and it has been increasingly rejected by collectivistic liberalism. Beginning with the denial of genetic differences between class, ethnic, or racial aggregates, the denial has now been extended to a reluctance to acknowledge the existence of individual differences within such aggregates. Where such differences between individuals are admitted, it is argued that they should not be provided with correspondingly different opportunities, for example, different kinds of schools in which superior endowment could be cultivated so as to lead to superior achievement. The result is a shift of collectivistic liberalism from acknowledgement of superior achievement made possible by superior hereditary endowment, to the radical stress on the injustice of any superiority of genetic endowment and any prospective advantages which might be conferred by it. Achievement has come thus to be disregarded and disparaged as an important criterion by which human beings are to be assessed.

THE ANTINOMIES OF LIBERALISM

One of the most striking manifestations of this self-transformation of collectivistic liberalism is the allocation of opportunities by "quotas" for particular ethnic groups—by "targets," as it is sometimes evasively put. It sets aside the accomplishments in the prior utilization of opportunity which have resulted in differences in standing and begins the race again. It is as if in a one mile race, the differences between the runners are cancelled after a quarter mile, after a half mile, and after three-quarters of a mile, and all the runners are forced to begin again from the same starting line. Even those runners who fell out of the race earlier are enticed into returning to the race and their past failures are cancelled. At the end, according to this policy, the prizes are equally distributed to all the runners, the poor ones receiving prizes as good as the superior ones. This is, of course, never done in athletics, but this is the policy which collectivistic liberalism recommends in the allocation of opportunities for higher education. American collectivistic liberalism in its latter-day desire for substantive equality has replaced one primordial qualification by another. Kinship descent and affiliation are replaced by ethnic descent and affiliation. And yet, collectivistic liberalism remains specifically liberal in spirit, in that it persists in treating educational certification as the qualification for reward. In doing so, however, it has ceased to treat educational certification as having any necessary correspondence with the application of talent.

Traditional liberalism was not in favor of equality of income. It was against inequalities of income which arose from contrived, organized, or traditionally or legally protected monopolies. It was in favor of equality of opportunity. But equality of opportunity did not mean that outcomes would be equal any more than the requirement that all competitors in a foot race begin at the same line and moment meant that all must be treated as having run with equal speed and arrived at the finish line at the same moment. Traditional liberalism never doubted that in any society there would be different tasks which were differently assessed, that they would be performed with different degrees of proficiency, and that these differences would and should be differently rewarded in deference and income. Most socialists did not think this way but liberals did. Accordingly, the progressive income tax was first conceived as a means of raising revenue for governmental purposes; these purposes did not include the equalization of income. The progressive income tax was intended only to make the tax burdens commensurate to the ability to pay, which was a way of equalizing responsibilities for the maintenance of government. The introduction of estate or death duties again was not at first intended to equalize income, although it moved in that direction by its attack on the ethical validity of familial continuity over generations and on the freedom of testamentary disposition. Gradually, fiscal policies came to be viewed as appropriate instruments for influencing the distribution of income; those which did not diminish the inequality of the distribution of income were censured. Recently, collectivistic liberal economists have established the equalization of income as a desideratum of public policy. Of course, like the liberal political philosophers of a century and a half ago, who did not mean to assert a justification of pornography, the liberal economists do not really mean a complete equality of income. Nonetheless a path has been taken and a direction has been set. It is everywhere noticeable in the policies of collectivistic liberalism.

Collectivistic liberalism in its newest, radical phase has coined the term "elitism," an ugly coinage to express an ugly attitude. "Elitism" is employed to denounce any institutional arrangement which allows some human beings to perform in a manner more excellent than others. Any belief which asserts the desirability or inevitability or differences in excellence of achievement is similarly denounced. Institutions which offer a superior, more exigent education are denounced as "elitist." Acknowledgement of superiority in science or in business is denounced as "elitist." Training and education which aspire to maintain, inculcate, and demand a high standard of achievement are denounced as "elitist." Praise of and aspiration to observe a tradition of moral excellence are also denounced as "elitist." Collectivistic liberalism seems to be veering toward an apotheosis of mediocrity and even failure; the very term "failure" is regarded as reprehensible. Few indeed have been the collectivistic liberals who stood out against this stampede toward radicalism.

This many-sided transformation of collectivistic liberalism into radicalism has been eased by the complex ambivalence of the foundation of liberalism. In one tendency within the traditional liberal conception of man, liberal ideas were joined to a secularized conception of original sin which took the form of a belief in the egocentric character of human conduct. In the thought of Adam Smith, this egoism was balanced by the operations of the moral sentiments; in Mandeville's, by the transformation of private vices into public benefits; in Bentham's, by the various arrangements for the artificial identification of interests. (All of these views were put forward with the understanding that human actions took place in a realm of scarcity.) On the other side, there was the idea of a natural benevolence and sympathy in human beings which makes them "other-regarding" rather than "self-regarding." This latter idea, coupled with associational psychology, made it possible to conceive of a humanity which, if subjected to proper educative influences, would not sink into the morass of egoism. The addition of an expectation of a state of plenitude, which was alien to liberalism, fortified attachment to this idea of natural benevolence.

Although autonomist liberalism was not attracted to the idea of natural benevolence, the idea was increasingly assimilated into collectivistic liberalism. Education was thought to be a means of cultivating man's rational faculties so that egoism, enlightened by the informed consideration of the consequences of action, would be disciplined and constrained; but it was also thought of as the nurturing of the essential benevolence of the human being. In the right environment, man's natural benevolence and intelligence would come into realization.

The belief in the decisive influence of environment on the development of the mind and character acquired an additional ingredient from a populistic romanticism which saw in ordinary human beings capacities for creativity reserved by a more restrictive, "aristocratic" romanticism for rare geniuses. This has led to the view, which is now widespread among educators, that every human being possesses not the spark of divinity in which radical Protestants believed but the secular equivalent, a spark of genius. Every person has a creative power which the cessation of an artificially maintained scarcity and the right kind of emancipatory education would bring into flower.

VII

The rationalism that was characteristic of autonomist liberalism, and the combination of radicalism and expressiveness which became characteristic of collectivistic liberalism, have both been uncongenial to the coherence and continuity of the family and to traditional things. Liberalism has always been distrustful of the family largely because it has represented such a fusion of authority and traditionalism. Liberalism would not accept traditionalism. It offered alternative paths to freedom from the "cake of custom." In autonomist liberalism with its characteristically narrow, puritanical hardheadedness, the path was set by the "genius of hard work"; more sentimentally, collectivistic liberalism has chosen the realization of "creative" or "true individuality," of the "vital self" as the path to its ideal.

Such a "true individuality" can, it was thought, be attained only after the emancipation of the individual from the traditions in which he was born and raised. "Society," "tradition," "culture," suffocate human beings. A person who possesses such true individuality, who is really alive will see the world through his own eyes, experience it with his own senses, not through the senses of those who have gone before him. A person who possesses true individuality will assimilate into himself the fruits of his own experience, which he elaborates into something distinctive and therefore valuable.

This ideal of the vital self has undergone a transformation. Originally the ideal was both disciplined and aesthetically aristocratic; it envisioned a life made whole by complete devotion to "work"—whether literary or artistic work, or one's own "life as a work of art." Now, however, the ideal has become more discontinuous and momentary, and the attainment of states of sensation has become the end. Being creative is not an accumulative process, but a series of creations and states of mind. It does not require the development of a "unique life-style," as much as it involves trying out all sorts of "life-styles" in succession. Thus a radical syllabus of religious education for state schools, prepared by a commission of the Church of England, calls for each pupil to "examine alternative life-stances," none of them to be dogmatically recommended by the teacher; the child would presumably try them all and adopt them as and when he saw fit.

In contrast with major currents of autonomist liberalism, collectivistic liberalism—especially in its educational program and in its increasingly radicalized outlook—thinks that the discovery of our true identity, the creation of a "satisfying life-style," is open equally to everyone. According to this view, individuality entails the exercise of powers of feeling and imagination, which every human being could, under the right circumstances, attain. To be a true individual is to be "alive," to be in contact with and to experience what is vital. "Everyman a king!" "Everyone burning with his own hard gem-like flame!"

This particular extension and self-annulment of collectivistic liberalism into radicalism is even more unsympathetic toward tradition than collectivistic liberalism was in its unextended form. Whereas the latter stressed the value of the rational and reflective assimilation of immediate experience, in its radical variant it has laid the accent more emphatically on the affective side of experience. It has emphasized the need to create and discover the self rather than to develop it through sensation and experience, through discipline and rational reflection on experience, training, etc. The idea of a "search for identity" is something which did not occur in the theories of autonomist and collectivistic liberalism through most of their history. The idea is still alien to autonomist liberalism, which assumed that most normal human beings "know who they are," and thus require no long and arduous search to "discover themselves." The self was formed from what it received from an unacknowledged tradition and from experience, and the superior individual could enrich it by disciplined and discriminatingly assessed experience and by rational reflection. The "self" did not have to be created: it was there and it had to be and could be improved.

In the liberalism of the eighteenth and nineteenth centuries, there was no idea of a "search for identity" in order to fill the "awful sense of emptiness." Critical though it was of the "dead hand of the past," it was not so much in revolt against the past as to think that every human being should "make himself" *de novo*. Even collectivistic liberalism was not so thoroughgoing in its rejection of tradition as to refuse completely the inheritance with which the self begins; it only emphasized the need to go ahead and build on it. Only when it moves toward radicalism and opens itself to the aestheticism of vital expression and sensation which the long alliance of revolution and bohemia brought before it, does it become sympathetic to the belief that the only life worth living is life wholly and freely chosen and created. The notion of choosing one's' "life-style" in complete freedom is, of course, an unrealistic fantasy; it does nonetheless form a part of the newer radicalism.

Fragments of this outlook have been taken into American educational doctrine and in some distorted way into educational practice as well. It attributes little importance to the assimilation of the past achievements of the human race, and in this regard it is not much different from the traditional progressive education that has been part of the collectivistic liberal program. It has now become an egocentric irrationalism, destructive of learning and art, and inimical to individuality which builds on tradition and goes forward through the disciplined accumulation of experience and imaginative reflection of it. Not many persons attempt to realize this ideal in an unqualified manner; those who do end in disaster and disillusionment. Nonetheless, the ideal has inserted itself into the idiom of one strand of contemporary radicalism.

The "new sensibility" which underlies the desire for complete freedom and a voice which "shares in every decision which affects itself" has produced a new turning toward plebiscitary democracy. Autonomist liberals had been aware of the noxious inconveniences of plebiscitary democracy ever since the end of the eighteenth century, and consequently had noted a tension between democracy and liberalism. Representative institutions were thought to resolve this tension. However, with the passage of time and the emergence of monstrous totalitarianism, the tension has receded as a subject of concern. After the end of the Second World War, criticism was silenced; repairs were suggested here and there but generally democracy—representative democracy—seemed to have reestablished its good name in the West and not least in the United States.

A new turn was taken however with the resurgence of the new brand of radicalism. The universities and related institutions of science have been the loci of this radicalism. "Participatory democracy," "people's science" are its demands, although what it usually comes down to are places on governing bodies for radical intellectuals who proclaim the imperative of giving a voice to "people" who will look after the interests of "people." Participatory democracy is the companion piece of "anti-elitism." Prior to the coming together of the New Left and the student agitation, participatory democracy had never been a part of the program of collectivistic liberalism. Guild socialism was indulged from afar with a marginal sympathy. Despite the great prestige of the Soviet Union, the idea of *soviets* as mechanism of collective self-determination never caught on among collectivistic liberals who were otherwise ready to swallow a great deal of the Soviet mythology. "Industrial democracy" never moved into the center of the concern of collectivistic liberals in the 1920s, when it had a faint and flickering existence as an aspiration but not as a practice. The New Deal, and the National Labor Relations Act which was one of its monuments, did nothing more than offer legal protection for the organization of workers into trade unions for the purpose of collective bargaining.

Since the universities and colleges were the first institutions affected by the movement of the New Left in the United States it was there that the demand for participatory democracy made its first insistent appearance. Once made, it was often readily agreed to. To some extent the alacrity of accommodation to it was simply the result of cowardice and cynicism. But like many of the seepages of the radical outlook into collectivistic liberalism, participatory democracy seemed obviously correct. After all, if democracy was right, then its extension was right. Teachers and administrators were overpowered by the patent truth that if universities and colleges were "communities of scholars," the case for participatory democracy was unanswerable. Democracy had moved forward through the extension of the franchise from property owners to citizens, from adult males to adult females, and from those over twenty-one to those over eighteen. What could be more reasonable therefore than participatory democracy, which was after all nothing more than the more thoroughgoing application of a generally acknowledged principle? (The special claims of youth gave further impetus to the acceptance, but "juvenolatry" is not a phenomenon unique to collectivistic liberalism; Nazis and Fascists also reserved a special place of prominence for youth.)

There has been no pronounced renascence of the older instruments of direct democracy—neither of the initiative, nor the referendum nor the recall, which were the three favorite recipes of populist reformers of the early part of the present century. Nor have the trade unions in the United States been very demanding for "codetermination." On the other side, tenants associations, welfare-rights associations, public access to the meetings and records of regulatory bodies have been taken into the repertoire of collectivistic liberalism. There is a widespread belief in "responsiveness," which is understood to mean more than the responsibility of elected and appointed officials. The demand for continuous institutional "responsiveness" is another manifestation of the pattern whose dominant theme is the primacy of "feelings"— the belief that desire establishes a right to the desideratum.

Liberalism, both in its autonomistic and its collectivistic variants and especially in the latter, has always had a strong cast of progressivism; it has been especially prone to a belief in the perfectibility of human existence. The education of the rational and the expressive powers of the "person" unencumbered by the baggage of literary and cultural tradition came to be regarded as the indispensable means to this attainment of perfection. Reason in the form of scientific knowledge and the scientific approach would give human beings the knowledge they needed to organize and govern themselves toward this end; the release of the expressive powers, in themselves creative, would itself be an installment or movement toward the ultimate condition of perfection.

With this intellectual tradition, which insisted on the perniciousness of tradition, collectivistic liberalism acquired the basis for further movement into an ultimately anarchistic radicalism. The contradictory combination of unrestricted individual expression, a denial of all authority over the individual, plebiscitary self-government, and rational central planning by an omnicompetent government provided both the ends and the means of progress.

Malthusianism has for a long time been a term of accusation and abuse in the vocabulary of collectivistic liberalism. It has suggested the idea of an ineluctible scarcity and of the inevitable hardness of life. It denied that all human problems are definitively soluble. Collectivistic liberalism, with its belief in the powers of scientific rationality and in the benignly "creative" powers inherent in emotional expression, with its belief in the efficacy of the education of the sentiments and in the exercise of governmental authority as a means of developing and harnessing these for the highest ends of man, was antithetical to the Malthusian conception of man's existence here below. Plenitude such as has been imagined to prevail only in heaven came to be thought of as a realizable condition, under the stimulus to the imagination given by the modern economy and the technology and science on which it increasingly depended.

In its "social gospel," liberal Protestantism had preached the striving for the attainment of the kingdom of God, the kingdom of plenitude, justice and peace on earth; but what it sought in practice were small, piecemeal reforms of particular institutions and practices. The voice of collectivistic liberalism in the early part of the present century was muffled in the traditions of a Christian bourgeois society, the structure and leadership of which seemed almost irrefragable. Although increasingly subject to scrutiny and criticism, the authority of governments and of property owners—like that of military officers, policemen, clergymen, and professors—was still accorded a high degree of legitimacy. Nobody expected them to provide a clear road to the kingdom of God.

As long as collectivistic liberalism was to a large extent dominated directly by practicing politicians or was very dependent on them, it was hampered by the restraints of tradition and the necessity of compromise. However, once the academic intellectual culture of collectivistic liberalism became more influential, the utopian potentiality began to appear more clearly in the lineaments of the collectivistic liberal program. Utopia came within the realm of earthly possibility. Government would be its deliverer.

Traditional radicalism has held itself aloof from government. It did not expect to be invited to join governments as cabinet members nor did it anticipate a large-scale entry of radicals into the civil service. It accepted that governments would rule, would use all the powers to keep the existing social order intact, and would keep secret those matters which concerned them most vitally. Secretiveness was regarded as one of the constitutive vices of existing governments, and radicals showed no interest in obtaining the secrets. Radicals were much more concerned to keep their own secrets from the police under whose scrutiny they knew themselves to be. Radicals benefited by the "exposures" of governmental misdeed by energetic journalists, but they regarded themselves as so far outside the central circle of society that they could not obtain such guarded information themselves.

Liberals, on the other hand, have from the beginning been against the secretiveness of governments. From the Benthamite maxim that "the eye of the public is the virtue of the statesman," through the struggles for the freedom of the press not only to express opinion but also to scrutinize publicly the actions of government, to Woodrow Wilson's declaration for "open covenants, openly arrived at," liberalism has always been in favor of publicity. How else could the iniquitous propensities of government be restrained and its beneficent potential promoted? Liberalism was not, however, thoroughgoing, and it left many traditions intact; one of these was the secrecy of governmental activities having to do with "intelligence." It was ready to accept that the gathering of "intelligence" was essential to the effectiveness of the military and the police, and that the value of such intelligence would be negated by its public disclosure.

After the Second World War, another phenomenon emerged. This was the scientists' movement—mainly those who had worked on the Manhattan Project—which denounced secrecy regarding nuclear weapons. They desired the abolition of secrecy on the grounds that "nature has no secrets" and that the knowledge kept secret would sooner or later come into the possession of rival and potentially inimical states. They said that disclosure of information about the construction of nuclear weapons would have beneficial effects in international politics. The persecutions set loose by Senator McCarthy and like-minded politicians only increased the enmity toward secrecy. The efforts by governmental intelligence services purporting to deal with subversive activities and the development of a new electronic technology of surveillance only raised the opposition of collectivistic liberals against secrecy.

Radicals of the newer dispensation played only a small part in this movement toward the universal transparency of authoritative institutions. It was only partly to protect radicals, and partly to extend the liberal tradition of publicity, that liberals pressed for a legislative guarantee for access to hitherto withheld governmental documents. Radicals themselves contributed very little to it. The Freedom of Information Act was passed in 1966 before the student agitation began to concern itself with the confidentiality of university records, "secret dossiers," etc. By the beginning of the next decade, however, a common front was formed between collectivistic liberalism and radicalism. There was an accumulating insistence on public participation in governing investments, the demand that universities disclose their investments, that students have access to the files of the universities which refer to them, that governmental files be made available to radicals engaged in litigation against the government, that the records of private corporations likewise be made available to litigants and thus, as part of the public record, become accessible to competitors and opponents. The disclosure of the "Pentagon papers" by Dr. Ellsberg and the universal acclamation of his action was greatly aided, of course, by the press with its liberal tradition and with its professional interest. It was, however, more than that. It was accepted as evidence that authority could not be trusted, least of all when it could keep its deliberations secret.

The radical view, which carries further the liberal postulate of man as his own creator, demands that all institutions and all of society become transparent, that all become visible, that walls be torn down, that boundaries be washed away. Man can become his own creator, completely self-determining only in a completely transparent society. A collectivistic liberalism that has slipped its moorings and a new self-confident radicalism form a common front here.

Together with this insistence on transparency or publicity, there has been a marked but ambivalent concern about privacy in the past two decades. On the one hand, the enhancement of the powers of observation through electronic technological inventions, and the promulgation of techniques for the study of behavior, have fostered a new desire to protect the privacy of individuals. But this desire is largely a concern for privacy from the authorities of established institutions in government, business, and universities who have become more curious about their citizens, employees, customers, and pupils. It is a desire for privacy from institutions that have grown so large because so much has been demanded from them. It is a demand for privacy that is at the same time a denial of the legitimacy of established authorities.

On the other hand, however, there has been very much less interest in the private sphere as an area of seclusion from perception by others. This has for many decades been an object of invasion by the press, the popular press at first and later the "quality" press, and this intrusiveness has been justified by appeals to the liberal principle of the freedom of the press. Yet, one of the saints of collectivist liberalism, Louis Brandeis, was also the author of what, for a very long time, was the most elaborate argument for respect for the private sphere and its protection from the invasion of malignant or idle curiosity. His concern in this regard has almost been forgotten.

The romantic bohemian strand in collectivistic liberalism was never very attentive to privacy and particularly the privacy of the erotic sphere. Radicalism of the newer sort, unlike Marxism which was rather Victorian in this respect, has been indifferent to the value of personal privacy, except in the face of institutional authority. The commune has given institutional form to this indifference toward personal privacy. Collectivist liberalism in its latest phase has assimilated this indifference. The rule of publicity has been extended.

The strains of governing a society of indescribable complexity in which multitudinous voices, hitherto silent, have become clamorously demanding, have been very trying. Wants rise faster than resources and capacities to satisfy them. On top of this, scientific knowledge—ranging from scientific knowledge about the structure of the atom to scientific knowledge provided by experts in the surveying of public opinion—has made politicians even more than ever aware of their insufficiencies. Continuous exposure to publicity has the same effect as moral relativism. Neither keeps the center of gravity low enough to keep judgment steady. This misleading appearance of steadiness in policy is the result of the constant pressure of collectivistic liberal opinion.

Moral relativism, at least as a polemical device to weaken the ascendancy of church and state, has long been a device of liberalism. It was never a wholehearted thing adopted without qualifications. It was sort of a moral luxury which did not completely supplant the self-confidence rooted in the acceptance of a secularized variant of Christian belief. Nonetheless it was always there in liberalism and in the increasingly antinomian and antiwestern attitudes of many intellectuals. It has taken a prominent place in collectivistic liberalism. Hence, when faced with the furious criticism which radicalism directed against them, collectivistic liberal intellectuals and politicians had no answer with which they could confidently rebut their critics. Indeed since the radicals were only extending many of the collectivistic liberal arguments, it was difficult for liberals to resist the pressure to move from equality of opportunity toward substantive equality, from the emancipation from tradition by the exercise of reason toward the emancipation from tradition by the expression of emotion and the attainment of "genuine" selfhood, from the prizing of expression of belief toward the freedom of expression of affect, from self-government through representation toward continuous and direct participation, and from the support of the needy toward universal subsidy by government. Collectivist liberals, unsteadily attached to the balance of their values through their commitment to moral relativism, and at the same time facing charges of inconsistency with their own principles and of being "elitist" and self-interested, could not withstand the force of the radical criticism.

Under the fire of radical criticism, collectivistic liberalism also became prone to the loose praise of revolution. Ever since the beginning of the present century it had had a *faiblesse* for revolutions in other countries; revolution was a way for backward countries suffering from aristocracy or foreign rule to enter on the road of progress. The crisis of the late 1960s made the adherents of revolution abroad think sympathetically of revolution in their own country. They found themselves in a position in which the burden of proof lay on them to show that their own "system" could achieve the ends sought by revolutionaries, and they were not confident that they could supply that proof. "Radical chic" was one trivial manifestation of their going over to belief in the rightfulness of revolution. For some time, any public disturbance, any unconstitutional violence which designated itself as "leftist" was accredited by collectivistic liberals. "Revolutionaries" were accorded the sanction of "history"; they came to be regarded as the authentic instrument of the purposes of history. Those who set themselves against this were classified as "rightists." It became fashionable among intellectuals who had, for all they knew, been liberals, to espouse the illiberal revolutionary ideas of radicalism. After all, were not these ideas an extension, a logical and consistent application of liberal ideals which held out the desirability of extending to all members of society the goods and conditions of self-discovery and fulfillment that hitherto only some had possessed? If liberals had been critical of authority, was it not right to go further and to deny its legitimacy? If equality of opportunity was liberal, was it not right for those who did not possess it to commit crimes "in protest" against the society which denied them such opportunities? All these activities coalesced into an image of an anticipated revolution.

For the present, the exhilarated anticipation of a "revolution" in the United States has passed. The affection remains.

For much of the nineteenth century and a part of the twentieth century liberalism could be contrasted with fanaticism. Its belief in progress by small and steady increments and its devotion to rational discussion moderated its demands and its way of expressing them. Its rationalism and its unsympathetic attitude toward tradition did, it is true, make it prone to a doctinaire, schematic application of its principles but fanaticism was in general avoided. This cannot be said equally for the more recent rhetoric of collectivistic liberalism; it has acquired some of the rhetorical decoration as well as the substance of radicalism. Political discourse under conditions of modern democracy and mass communication tends in any case toward hyperbole and the melodramatic. Collectivistic liberal speeches now are well-embellished with ill-defined but no less bitter words of accusation: "racism," "elitism," "fascism," "genocide," "cold warriors," and the like. Such words derive from a Manichaean distinction between the "children of light" and the "children of darkness." They inject an air of commotion into political discourse that is not conducive to the moderation of conflict or to the maintenance of a sense of affinity which reaches across the lines of partisanship.

Collectivistic liberalism in its noisy decline toward radicalism has lost much of its civility. It bespeaks a lack of concern for the whole of society. It has become a crusade on behalf of the "poor" and "minorities" and of its own moral outlook on a scale and a manner which offends the larger interests of society and other sections of the population as much as did the references to "bloated capitalists" of an earlier generation of radicalism. It has become disregardful of the moral outlook of the working and lower-middle classes, which it regards as plainly reactionary for their dislike of the emancipationist views of the collectivistic liberal intellectuals. It has forgotten that liberty of opinion and liberty of organization were intended to serve the common good, and not just the good of individuals or the groups into which they formed themselves.

Contemporary radicalism has absorbed enough of Marxism to retain the peculiar sectional partisanship of that doctrine. It speaks of "the workers" rarely, of "the poor" or "the people" far more. Its aim is to change society so that "the poor" will no longer have to suffer inferiority of status or remuneration; incidentally it is to see to it also that the protectors of the poor also benefit by ample opportunities, remuneration, and power. The former is a worthy goal; the latter a repugnant self-seeking. But even the former goal is worthy only in a constellation of other goals, and not as the sole or determining one.

The assimilation of elements of radicalism into collectivistic liberalism has been rendered easier by changes in radicalism itself. The cracking of Marxist orthodoxy after 1956 and the crystallization of the New Left released radicals from their fixation on the "working class" as the destined agent of revolutionary possibilities. The "working class" had obviously been heedless of this mission which "history" had assigned to it. Most radicals had had enough of it. The "poor" became the stick with which the dog of bourgeois society could be beaten; they replaced the working class as the favorite of revolutionary hopes. Collectivistic liberalism—with its inheritance of the old concern with the "debtor and dependent classes," with the weak, poor, and friendless—found

THE ANTINOMIES OF LIBERALISM

the "poor" a more congenial category to which "to devote its solicitude" than the "working class." The latter was a term with Marxist overtones and hence was implicitly hostile toward the philanthropic strand of collectivistic liberalism; the real working class was moreover made up of persons who on the whole looked after themselves—except when unemployed—and who were independent in spirit and did not offer so many opportunities for the services of the welfare-providing state. Among others, this change reduced a barrier which had hitherto separated collectivistic liberalism from radicalism.

Another change which has aided radical influence is the common intellectual culture. Contemporary radicalism, although drawing much from Marxism, has also absorbed a lot of contemporary academic social science. The theme of "bureaucratization" as a main feature of contemporary society is of course drawn from Max Weber; words like "life-style" come from the same source. The New Left in the United States has been an academic matter. It was supported and given its doctrine by teachers and students and its main activities have occurred in universities and colleges. Collectivistic liberals are to be found mainly among the highly educated; "middle America" might accept the subsidies offered by collectivistic liberalism in power but it does not like its outlook. Furthermore, radicalism no longer has a "special relationship" to aesthetic bohemianism. Liberalism, even collectivistic liberalism, was always more puritanical and traditional in its erotic and aesthetic dispositions than radicalism, which early formed an alliance with aesthetic bohemianism. However, it could be said that Greenwich Village now embraces a large part of the educated class throughout the United States. As a result of these changes, to a far greater extent than was the case a half century ago, collectivistic liberals and radicals share a common culture. The shift from collectivistic liberalism to radicalism was not a drastic conversion; that is why so few of those liberals perceive the change in themselves. If they do call themselves radicals—some do—they think that they are still faithful to their old convictions. They are probably correct.

The instances which I have given of certain ideals of radical ethos—such as free undisciplined expression, of equality of reward, of individuality, and of the attainment of perfection and plenitude—are alien to liberalism as well as hostile to it. So is the idea of a universally active and omnicompetent government. These ideas will destroy liberalism, even collectivistic liberalism, if their temptations are not resisted. Yet it would be incorrect historically and a disservice to the rehabilitation of liberalism to refuse to see the lines of affinity which link both kinds of liberalism, at least in their points of departure, to radicalism. They show the dangers of utopian self-transfiguration which lie in wait for all social and political outlooks when they turn into doctrines and cast off traditional inhibitions.

VIII

Collectivistic liberalism in the United States has triumphed. Much of its program has been realized; even administrations which purport to be conservative have accepted its accomplishments or have been unable to undo them. It has also triumphed intellectually; those who disagree are thought at best to be eccentrics, at worst, misanthropes—and misogynists. Its demand for the freedom of the individual has been realized far more extensively and intensively than was anticipated or even initially sought. Its demand for governmental regulation and provision has been gratified to a far greater extent than had been believed possible by its earlier proponents. Yet it has recurrently been said by radical intellectuals that liberalism has failed. Many persons who had always regarded themselves as liberals—in the collectivistic, American sense—have agreed. Some did not go so far; they said it was "on trial"—obviously, in a trial in which radicals were judges and prosecutors. It was conceded by collectivistic liberals that if the "system" were found wanting, then it was to be jettisoned and rightly so.

In the 1960s, liberalism was charged with having failed to satisfy the demands of the poor, and the public disorders of that period were, it was said, protests against these failures to eliminate poverty. It was also charged with failure to renounce a foreign policy which entailed the support of reactionary governments against those which were popular, democratic, and socialist.

The radicalization of collectivistic liberalism had reached the point where the liberals regarded it as fashionable to say that liberalism has failed. They seemed to think that they would stand condemned by right-thinking persons if they did not stress the horrible failures of their society. It could hardly have been otherwise when "poverty" was recurrently being redefined by social scientists and social workers so that it was necessary to run faster and faster to remain in the same place.

Can it, however, be said in good faith that liberalism has "failed"? On the contrary, it seems to have succeeded better than its chief competitors.

The late John Plamenatz once enumerated the "rights to which liberals in the West attach great importance." These were "the right to an education which enables you to assess the opportunities (occupations and ways of life) that society offers to its members; the right to choose your occupation provided you have the requisite skills; the right to get the special training needed to acquire these skills, provided you are capable of profiting by it; the right to choose your partner in marriage; the right to be gainfully employed; the right to a minimal standard of living, whether or not you are so employed; the right to privacy, especially in your own home; the right to express and publish your opinions; the right to form or join associations for any purpose that appeals to you and does not invade the rights of others; the right to be tried for alleged offenses, and to have your disputes settled by courts not subject to political pressures; the right to take part in choosing at free elections the persons who make policy at least at the highest level, in the communities or associations you belong to."[3]

---

3. John Plamenatz, "Liberalism," in *Dictionary of the History of Ideas*, ed. Phillip Paul Wiener (New York: Scribner's, 1973), vol. 3, p. 52.

If we look at the societies of Western Europe and North America at the beginning of the nineteenth century before liberalism became the belief of those who were active in politics, and the present situation after more than a century and a half of autonomist and collectivistic liberalism as it was incorporated into the programs of various political parties, we will see that much has been achieved in the realization of this "program." If we compare the situation in these countries of Western Europe and North America with the countries like those of Eastern Europe, Asia, and Africa where liberalism is denounced as a bourgeois deception and where socialism is offered as a vast improvement, we will see how successful liberalism has been in contrast with its adversaries and self-proclaimed competitors. In some respects liberalism has been more successful than its great nineteenth century proponents intended.

Nonetheless, the success of liberalism—the realization of the ideas of liberalism in the practice of contemporary Western societies—leaves much to be desired from the standpoint of collectivistic liberalism. Some of these deficiencies are indeed indirect results of autonomistic liberalism. Others are results of the excesses of collectivistic liberalism.

There is too much unemployment of persons who seriously attempt to find jobs and fail to do so. There is still discrimination against blacks simply on grounds of their being black. The large cities of the United States have become an eyesore and a menace. The housing conditions of some parts of the semiskilled and unskilled sections of the working classes are unsatisfactory. The costs of medical care are higher than genuinely ill persons with low incomes can pay. Inflation is a curse to all. Criminality has increased. Some of these defects are the results of collectivistic liberalism; for instance, unemployment is partly a result of minimum wage laws and of government fiscal policies which hamper investment. Inflation is partly a product of the determination to use the powers and resources of government to control the economy and to provide for the poor and weak; the condition of the cities is largely a result of governmental policies promoted by collectivistic liberalism; criminality is in part a function of the liberal restraint on the repressive powers of the police; etc. There are many other features of our society that are unsatisfactory from conservative and autonomist liberal standpoints, but these are not relevant when we are considering the successes of the collectivistic liberal movement of ideas and policies.

All these notwithstanding, the civil, intellectual, and artistic liberty and the material conditions of life for the vast majority of the population are far superior to what they are in regimes which allege that they have gone far beyond collectivistic liberalism. Some of the critics of liberalism are not radicals; they are social democrats. Although they take no pleasure in the actual accomplishments of existing regimes that have been thoroughgoing in their socialism, namely, the regimes of Eastern Europe, they persist nonetheless in holding out socialism as superior to liberalism.

The myth of the universally curative powers of socialism seems almost unexpungible from the human mind in our country. Socialism has certainly not been a success in any country. In the existing socialist-Communist, totalitarian societies, the economies are failures even from their own standpoint, and politically they are, of course, destructive of even the degree of freedom which the mass of the population was able to acquire under the regimes that preceded communism. In the democratic-socialist countries—which remain largely capitalistic in their economies and which are governed by socialist parties, alone or in coalition, like the Federal German Republic, the Netherlands, and the Scandinavian countries—the alleged socialism is in fact collectivistic liberalism and it is supported by capitalistic enterprise. The successful democratic-socialist countries are what they are largely because of the success of autonomistic and collectivistic liberalism and not because of the successes of socialism. The freedom they enjoy is an autonomistic-liberal inheritance; their high standard of living and their elaborate and pervasive welfare services are made possible by the productivity of their capitalist economies.

There is no question that liberalism—both autonomist and collectivist—has succeeded, that communism has failed, and that democratic socialism has not itself been responsible for the successes it enjoys.

The absence of public liberties in Communist countries and their amplitude in liberal and democratic-socialist countries is surely evidence of that. The condition of intellectual life in science, scholarship, and literature is evidence of it. The condition of economic well-being of the mass of the population is evidence of it. So real is the success of the liberal societies that those which are as diametrically different from them as the authoritarian and oligarchical societies of Asia, Eastern Europe, and Africa, insist that they too provide for the liberty and material well-being of their peoples, or that they will do so as soon as it is feasible. Thoughtful democratic socialists admit that their socialist forerunners went much too far in disparaging the achievements of liberalism as a transient, historical phenomenon, or as the by-product of a class interest. In Eastern Europe, courageous persons testify to the value of liberty at great risk to themselves. Even the most extreme terrorists allege that they are committing their desperate deeds in order to establish regimes that will provide the freedom and material well-being possessed by liberal societies. This is evidence that despite the denunciations of liberalism, its accomplishments are so great and impressive that even its enemies claim its merits for themselves. Their hypocrisy is the compliment which vice pays to virtue.

Nonetheless, the achievements of collectivistic liberalism are not generally esteemed in countries where they have been most marked. They are disparaged or denied. The deficiencies of their liberal societies preoccupy the minds of many intellectuals. Autonomist liberals who call themselves "conservatives" (which they are not) naturally are very critical of the methods and accomplishments of collectivistic liberalism; collectivistic liberals who do not call themselves radicals heap abuse on their own position in the idiom of radicalism. Even where they have not yielded to the temptations of the fashionable radicalism, they see nothing but the flaws of their own society and complain that their program is not being realized. They are so concerned with innovation and the correction of shortcomings that the positive achievements of the institutions of a liberal society pass unnoticed and unacknowledged.

The achievements are there but they are so taken for granted that they are not recognized. What has been accomplished, even if admitted, is thought to be insufficient.

The failures of Communist regimes are failures to live up to the vague promises of "genuine freedom," of "workers' rule," of greater material well-being which are contained implicitly and explicitly in the writings of Marx and Engels and their epigoni. They are the failures of Communist regimes to live up to the ideals of liberalism which they appropriated without acknowledgement. They are failures of "Soviet democracy" to be "a thousand times more democratic than bourgeois democracy." Communism was alleged to realize the ideals of liberalism, which could not be realized under capitalism. It has certainly not done so. The standpoint from which communism is criticized within the Communist regimes testifies to the vitality of liberal traditions, to the urge to discover them anew, and to the desire to reinstate them under conditions of harsh and brutal adversity.

The criticisms of liberalism that are made within liberal-democratic countries also testify to the vitality of liberal traditions. On the one side, collectivistic liberalism is criticized by a more austere autonomist liberalism which holds firmly to its central belief in the value of the private sphere of individual freedom and initiative, and which would confine the power of governments. There is practically no criticism of liberalism from a conservative position which would replace the rule of law by laws that deal differently with individuals in accordance with their lineage, that would establish a hierarchy of status and privilege in accordance with differences in lineage and affinity, that would make inheritance and prescription the decisive rule of society. There is no conservative criticism of liberalism which asserts as self-evident the rightness of tradition and authority. The critics of liberalism who call themselves conservatives and who are called "reactionaries" by radicals and collectivistic liberals are in fact liberals, more stringent and more faithful to the tradition of liberalism than the collectivistic liberals whom they criticize and who criticize them. For better or for worse, much that was valid in the conservative tradition has been put aside, together with what was ethically intolerable to the progressivist and individualistic attitudes of liberalism.

Collectivistic liberalism sees only autonomist liberalism as its enemy nowadays. It sees nothing inimical to its ideals in radicalism. It might disapprove lightly of the tactics of radicalism; it might say at times that radicalism goes a little too far. Insofar as it is uneasy in the presence of radicalism, it is because it regards radicalism as the keeper of its conscience and as the purer embodiment of those values which it most esteems.

IX

Liberal politicians and theorists in the past assumed the moral rightness of a liberal regime. They seemed to believe that once it became established its merits would appear to be so great to all its beneficiaries that there would be no danger of its subversion from within. Locke was more realistic: he thought that there was a danger of subversion by atheists who did not feel bound by their sworn undertakings, although he did not seem to believe that they had an alternative regime which they would, in their infidelity, attempt to establish. Liberal politicians and theorists were negligent about the dangers to the liberal regime from subversion by those who would benefit from its toleration. Furthermore, contending as they did against mercantilist and absolutist regimes which resisted their replacement, liberals assumed that those who were responsible for governing a society would, as a matter of course, believe in its rightness and would not freely and voluntarily yield when pressed to change their fundamental arrangements.

But this is not wholly characteristic of the governing contemporary liberal regimes, and even less true is it of the intellectuals devoted to the collectivistic liberalism their regimes practice. In the United States, collectivistic liberals have become so devoted to the liberties integral to liberalism that they are apprehensive of any actions which might be needed to save it, particularly if those actions would involve disadvantages for radicals; they are indeed sympathetic with the carriers of ideas that are subversive of the liberal order and think that there is much that is right in their arguments. Partly, too, they are fearful of regressing into the tyrannical attitudes and practices of "McCarthyism."

The dangers to liberalism posed by the transformation of collectivistic liberalism into radicalism are not the same as the dangers which the Communists constituted in the liberal-democratic regime in Czechoslovakia in 1948 or as the Bolsheviks did in October 1917, or the armed *putschists* in any black African or Middle Eastern country of the last few decades. There is no danger in the United States for the time being that a group of armed revolutionaries—led by *The New York Review of Books*—will "seize power" through the commandeering of arsenals and garrisons, railway yards and airports, centers of communication, etc., or that nests of civil servants and soldiers coordinated with a revolutionary armed force under the leadership of a new revolutionary clique outside the government will announce that they are henceforward in charge of affairs.

The domestic safety of collectivistic liberalism today is in a far different position. Its instability lies within its own standpoint; it lies in the tendency of those who are powerful in it to slide unwittingly and without any sense of contradiction or inappropriateness toward a regime governed by the radical outlook. It lies in their acceptance of elements of the radical view as self-evidently correct. It has been said repeatedly, ever since Joseph Schumpeter wrote it in *Capitalism, Socialism and Democracy,* that intellectuals are the grave-diggers of the liberal order. The intellectuals are not alone in this grave-digging action. Many politicians, civil servants, and businessmen have joined them; they accept the extension of collectivistic liberalism into radicalism. The transformation by extension is very patchy and uneven; far from all collectivistic liberals have been swept into it. Some resist the transformation. Its progress is undramatic and unannounced. This makes its progress that much easier.

X

In the United States today, the political terrain is almost entirely divided between autonomist liberalism and collectivistic liberalism. The autonomist liberalism is not unalloyed. In most of its varieties it contains a definite admixture of genuine conservatism; it has also incorporated a modest amount of collectivistic liberalism. Among the varieties of autonomist liberals, there are few simon-pure "Manchesterians." Collectivistic liberalism has been making the run since the great depression of the 1930s. In the last decade of its advance, it has begun to turn toward radicalism, for which its proponents used to have a protective sympathy and which now has become an imitative sympathy. The autonomist liberals have allowed the designation of "liberal" to become the possession, nearly exclusively so, of the collectivistic liberals.

As a result, when we think of the outlook that is now called liberal in the United States, we think of a person who is hostile to capitalism, a strong advocate of civil liberties especially for radicals and revolutionaries, and who is critical of "machine politicians." He is very critical of the government but he automatically turns to governmental action to remedy every wrong which he sees in abundance in American society. He is in favor of larger welfare programs and favors rigorous, extensive, and penetrating governmental regulation of private business enterprise. He is for the "poor" against the "rich." He is nominally and selectively an "egalitarian." He is against "respectability" and the idea that some persons are better than others—although in practice he departs widely from this belief. He is for trade unions, favoring unions against employers, although he is discomfited by "bread and butter unionism," by gangsterism in unions, and by the lack of a sufficiently progressive outlook in union leadership. He favors the right of public employees

THE ANTINOMIES OF LIBERALISM

to strike. He is critical of "law and order" which means the repression of criminals, and he favors penal arrangements only if they "rehabilitate" criminals. He is a "progressivist" who thinks that the new is better than the old and that scientific research is the proper instrument for continuous progress. He is a hedonist and, although critical of "materialistic values," is eager for the multiplied possession of material goods. He is strong for academic freedom including political agitation by academics within universities, favors "relevance" of academic studies but wants universities not to be "too involved with the present system"; he thinks that criticism of existing institutions should be one of the main functions of universities. He views with disdain the difference between "manliness" and "femininity" and would obliterate them and all differences between the sexes. He is against puritanism. He favors the free publication and sale of pornography. He is critical of advertising and favors public subsidy of television. He favors abortion on demand, free governmentally provided child-care centers and a national health service. He is critical of Communism but opposes others who are critical of Communists; he favors the Soviet Union and, even when critical of it, regards it as more often on the correct side in international politics than is the United States. He regards American foreign policy as unduly aggressive and as supporting reactionary regimes everywhere. He is critical of "patriotism," which he regards as "jingoism," but he is very sympathetic with the "nationalism" of the Third World.

The adherents of these beliefs have been so successful in establishing their hegemony in public opinion, particularly the opinion of the more educated classes of American society, that they have made the autonomist liberals think of themselves as "right-wing" or as conservatives. Collectivist liberals have become so ignorant of their own traditions that they think that they alone are "liberal" and that everyone else who does not share or enjoy their sympathies is a "reactionary" or "conservative." They are wrong in this belief, although they are right in seeing that there are significant differences between themselves and the autonomist liberals.

The autonomist liberal does indeed incorporate into his liberal out-look some important elements of conservatism. The Republican in the United States does indeed embody such a combination. He believes in the rightfulness of individual initiative and voluntary action and the abstention of the state from activity in the corresponding sphere. He is in favor of civil equality and of equality in the assessment of achievement and personal merit. He believes in the rightfulness of a commensurate relationship between achievement and reward. He believes in the desirability and necessity of progress through exertion and technology and the application of science. He is a hedonist in that he believes in the goodness of material possession, in the ownership of physical property, of ample supplies of food, physical conveniences, facilities in transportation, etc. He is what used to be called materialistic. He believes in the rightness of popular sovereignty through representative government and the separation of powers. He affirms the validity of the freedom of intellectual expression—although in the past he has occasionally supported the restriction of the freedom of intellectual expression by radicals. He accepts the rightfulness of the rule of law and hence, in the broader sense, the rightfulness of law and order and the obligation of government to maintain it and of citizens to observe it. He believes that there is a significant difference between criminality and lawfulness. He believes in the virtue of civility, although in historical fact, he has at times diverged in the direction of the protection and advancement of the interests of private business enterprises when these have been disadvantageous to the rest of society—for example, the privileges of tariffs and monopoly. He regards the Third World as backward rather than as the locus of major moral and political values.

The preponderantly autonomist liberal elements are combined with certain elements of conservatism such as patriotism and local loyalties, piety, appreciation of the family and of the virtues of manliness and femininity, an inclination toward traditionality. Certain elements of conservatism are excluded: deference of authority is greatly hedged about; the evaluation of lineage is restricted. Traditionalism is likewise given a limited place. Deference and traditionalism have tractive power but they are confined by the values of autonomist liberalism.

The puritanism which autonomist liberalism has carried with it has made this outlook less open aesthetically, less drawn toward the culture of Europe and other continents. Its old cultural Anglophilia has yielded to its patriotism.

It must be emphasized that liberalism—although it is in some respects conservative in the only sense which makes sense—is for better or for worse "progressive." It is certainly not "reactionary," unless that term is used in the radical sense of being opposed to violent revolutionary replacement of existing government and the establishment of what radicals understand as a reign of complete equality.

The world is a far more complex thing than modern radicalism, with its naive contrast of "right" and "left," has ever dreamed.

XI

Can collectivistic liberalism be saved from its degenerative potentialities? Can it renounce the sympathies—sometimes the sympathies of bad conscience, sometimes the sympathies which arise from the wish to be consistent and thoroughgoing, and sometimes the sympathies of a desire to be up-to-date—which have caused it to be extended and transformed into radicalism?

Every outlook can become an ideology, through the distortion of certain of its values toward extremes and through the neglect of others. In becoming such, it makes itself unwittingly into the protector and ally of movements of opinion, campaigns, and organizations which not only bring it into discredit but which deform it and endanger its continued existence. Conservatism and autonomist liberalism, too, have similar potentialities. There were European conservatives who thought, at least for a time, that Fascism and National Socialism were a form of conservatism appropriate to a time of crisis. Most of them were painfully disillusioned by the spuriousness of the conservatism of these movements once they attained state power. In the United States, there were conservative and liberal Republicans who tolerated and helped Senator Joseph McCarthy in his campaign of persecution in the decade that followed the Second World War. They had reservations about his vulgarity and harshness, they thought that he "overdid things"; nonetheless they thought that he and they were proper allies because they had the same cause at heart. They were patriots, they were against governmental dominance over economy and society, and they were therefore opposed to Communism and Soviet infiltration and expansion. Why, they might have asked themselves, should they not support a politician who by and large espoused the same values as themselves? It was true that they also were attached to the toleration of divergent opinions, to the separation of powers, to the rule of law and hence to the right to fair trial, and to the superiority of representative institutions over plebiscitary rule. For the time being, however, they were willing to suspend these other beliefs and to give greater weight to these values which McCarthy seemed to espouse. In the end the alliance was dissolved when they realized that McCarthy's procedures affronted their other values and were not necessary to attain the ends which they shared with him.

The attitude of one current of social-democratic opinion toward Communism and to the Soviet Union in the period between the wars, and even since then, has a certain similarity to this. These social democrats—usually not in the leadership of their parties, except in Italy—believed that fundamentally, in what is most important, they and the Communists held the same ends: the abolition of private ownership of the means of production as the indispensable precondition for realizing a reign of plenitude and freedom. The absence of political freedom in the Soviet Union they regarded as transient, necessitated by conditions of emergency and the "hostility of capitalist countries." The shortcomings of the Soviet economy, where they were perceived and admitted, they regarded as of the same transiency as the abrogation of political freedom, when they did not deny them altogether as a fabrication of anti-Communist scholars and journalists. They were so confident in the economic superiority and greater justice of a regime without private property in the means of production that they were willing, despite the destruction of the elements of liberalism to which they were attached, to place those elements in a secondary position. They were willing to suspend their concern for the liberal values which distinguished social democracy from Communism. Their unquestioning acceptance of traditional Marxian doctrine and the refusal of Marxists to acknowledge autonomist liberalism as one of their ancestors made them believe that there was a basic affinity between themselves and the Communists who declared themselves to be the sole heirs of true Marxism. They averted their minds from the affinities which bound them to liberalism.

So it is with many contemporary collectivistic liberals. They have slipped into a radical position because it seems to be only an extension of their liberal beliefs, and a more insistent demand for their more consistent application. Their long-standing prejudice in favor of the Russian revolution supports this complaisance.

Many of them, of the older generation which supported the New Deal, had been drawn into the fellow-traveling of the 1930s. Some are still under the impression that a country which has abolished private property in the means of production and established a "planned economy" to replace it must be on the right side of the movement of history. So it was with the older generation and those now in the fifth and sixth decades of their span of life. Those still younger found congeniality in the New Left bond and were spiritually formed by the student revolution of the 1960s. There is no sharp line separating them from radicalism.

Neither liberalism nor radicalism has been promulgated explicitly as a doctrine, and neither is advocated by a single organization such as a Communist party. Hence the boundaries are vague, and permeation of radicalism into collectivistic liberalism is easier. Many of the tenets

185

of radicalism seem only more thoroughgoing, less qualified extensions and applications of collectivistic liberalism, just as the Marxism-Leninism of the Communists seemed in the 1920s to be a more thoroughgoing and less inhibited extension and application of the social-democratic version of Marxism. Like Communism, which annuls the ideals of social democracy by its "thoroughgoingness" and "unqualifiedness," so radicalism annuls the ideals of liberalism.

Can collective liberalism stop its slide toward radicalism? To do so will require that it become critical of those elements in its own outlook which have brought it where it is. It will have to renounce its beliefs in the omnicompetence of government and in the solubility of all problems by governmental action. It will have to renounce its belief that if any institution or activity is worthwhile, it should be conducted or at least subsidized by government. It will have to renounce its belief that every important decision in life falls within the political sphere; it will have to give up its belief in the primacy of the "political kingdom." It will have to reanimate its skepticism about the necessary beneficence and dependability of government authority and its capacity for self-restraint. It will have to reconcile itself to the limited capacities of human beings, individually or collectively, to govern their own lives and the lives of others in a wholly rational and scientific manner. It will have to recognize the value of traditions and the foolhardiness of the belief that every innovation is in itself a good thing. It will have to detach itself from its dogmatically unthinking belief in moral relativism. It will have to show more respect for traditional moral standards and traditional standards of taste. It will have to acknowledge that the care of the common good is not exhausted by the care of "the poor" or of particular ethnic groups, designated as "minorities." It will have to acquire and exercise more common sense and free itself from the doctrinaire application of formulae, such as "quotas," "racial balance," and from salvation by any recipes, such as "busing." It will have to recognize its closer affinity with the autonomist liberalism that is now wrongly called "conservatism," than with the radicalism toward which it has been moving. It will in fact have to learn something from traditional conservatism regarding the value of social order, patriotism, and locality. It will have to remind itself of the value of civil, intellectual and artistic and literary liberties which it enjoys. It will have to give up its belief that any government, party, or movement which calls itself "socialist" is automatically a good thing. It should draw a moral lesson from the courageous efforts of a few hardy souls in Communist countries who take great risks by seeking to establish there the liberties which have for a long time been well established and are relatively secure in the liberal-democratic countries.

None of these changes will require it to renounce its traditions of humanitarianism and of political democracy, or its commitment to the improvement of social arrangements. It will have to become, however, more aware of the limits of human powers and that every human action and every undertaking has costs that are economic and more than economic.

Autonomist liberalism must also renew itself. For one, it must see that there is more to its tradition than the market, crucially important though it is. It must broaden its interests and reassert with greater force its ethical foundations and its cultural interests. It must go beyond scoring easily made points through calling attention to the enormities of collectivistic liberalism at work. It must be careful not to forget the virtue of compassion simply because collectivistic liberals have become incontinent in its espousal. It must heighten its awareness of the ties which bind it on the one side to collectivistic liberalism and on the other to traditional conservatism. Incidentally, it must also cease being on the defensive and regarding itself as somewhat eccentric. It must leave behind the perception of itself as "right" on a continuum of "right" and "left"; this is a construction of radicalism and collectivistic liberalism which confuses minds and darkens counsel.

The cause of liberalism is not a lost cause, but much reflection and many repairs are needed if it is not to become one.

Nation, Nationality, Nationalism and Civil Society

§

Nationalism, Nation and Nationality: Definitions

NATIONALISM arises out of nationality. It adds something to nationality. It adds emulative, combative, aggressive, bellicose elements to nationality. Hatred is not necessarily part of nationality; it frequently is so in nationalism.

Nation and nationality are less tangible than nationalism, which is embodied in movements and parties with visible leaders and with members and followers as well. Nationalism has programs and platforms. Of course, these tangible things do not exhaust nationalism. It often has doctrines, although its collective self-consciousnesses are poorly formulated in those doctrines.

Nationality is a more subtle thing but it is no less real. Nationality is a phenomenon fundamentally of collective self-consciousness. National self-consciousness is a state of mind, a state of belief, but it is also much more than that. The nation too is a collectivity with a structure, often amorphous. But it often has many closely associated structures such as clubs, athletic associations, cultural and educational associations and schools, and it is often linked with religious associations and churches. The nation attains its fullest realization institutionally in the national state; the two—nation and state—are seldom identical. The

Previously published in *Nations and Nationalism* 1 (March 1995): 93–118. Reprinted by permission.

most important of these relatively amorphous relationships of the nation is its relation to civil society. Whereas the other associations sustain the nation, the nation by contrast sustains civil society.

Nationality is a state of collective self-consciousness. It is not a collectivity—although it is often used interchangeably with nation which is a collectivity. Nationality, as used in this article, does not refer to the legal status of an individual, or to a status acquired by birth or by the naturalization of his parents or by his own naturalization in a particular national state. It is more approximate to "citizenship" in a national state which confers certain legal rights and obligations on residents of that state. It is usually taken for granted in the process of naturalization that the naturalized person will become a member of the dominant nationality and will acquire some share in the national collective self-consciousness and will become thereby a member of the nation as well as a citizen of the national state.

A nation is constituted by its collective self-consciousness, the referents of which are birth in a specifically bounded territory, residence in that bounded territory or descent from persons resident in that bounded territory. The members of a nation might have been born of parents who resided in a bounded territory which is not the one in which the particular individuals in question now reside. They might have been born in bounded territories different from the one in which they now reside. A person might once have been a member of a nation different from the nation of which he is currently a member. Individuals can change their nationality by taking up residence in a territory different from the one in which they were born and by participating in the collective self-consciousness of the new society. An individual may have several nationalities simultaneously, participating in the original national collective self-consciousness of the society residing in the territory of his previous residence and in his newly acquired national collective self-consciousness. This is different from the possession of several citizenships, which is a legal matter, depending on the laws of the national states.

One or some of the nations within a national state might be in a state of recession and attenuation, others might have a more salient and intense national collective self-consciousness. The various national attachments might be in conflict with each other or the individual might participate in all of them without strain or tension. Alternatively, he might experience such strain or tension only when they come into conflict with each other, i.e., when it is demanded that he be faithful to them, while the nationalities in which he participates are in conflict with each other, as with German-Americans during the First World War from the spring of 1917 until the end of the war.

Nations do not have differentiated structures like communities of religious believers who are members of a church which requires atten-dance at its services, participation in its rituals and in its liturgy. There is no corporate body which is completely congruous with any single nation. That is the desideratum of the numerically and politically dominant nation but it is a condition practically never attained. Nations do not have institutional arrangements such as parishes or dioceses or congregations which are distinct and peculiar to religious communities. Nations have a social structure of individuals who are mutually aware of one another as fellow members of the nation. They are members of numerous associations, nearly all of them voluntary, most of them containing only a small percentage of the membership of the nation residing in the particular country—whether it is their own national state or whether they are aliens in that state.

A society or state with a dominant nation is called a national state. The correspondence between nation and state is often expressed in the constitution of the state but that is not always or necessarily so. The educational institutions of the society attend to the cultivation of those objectivated symbolic configurations which are especially esteemed by the dominant nation. Each of the fields of culture, art, natural science and jurisprudence is affected by the national collective self-consciousness of its practitioners. Even though the criteria of truth and beauty are universal in their validity, the collective self-consciousness of the nation leaves an imprint which marks the product as distinctive.

The institutions of the state periodically celebrate nationality with the birthdays of famous national figures, national heroes, great national literary figures, etc. Military institutions are associated with the nation; the flag of the state is the flag of the nation; the holidays of the state are to a large extent holidays of the nation, celebrating national figures and great events in the history of the nation. Citizenship and nationality become conflated.

Where several nations live in states dominated by one nation and in which they themselves are less prominent and alien to the dominant nation, and where there are neither facilities nor inducements for assimilation into the collective self-consciousness of the dominant nation, the lesser or subordinate nations often tend to seek a national state or government of their own. They wish to have a state which is congruent with their own nationality and in a territory in which they form a majority or with which they have a distinctive traditional linkage. Minimally, under such conditions, they establish or seek to have provided for them institutions which will permit the continued existence of their particular nation. In the first instance, they seek schools in which their offspring can be educated in their national language. They seek equal opportunities to gain appointment to the civil service, the freedom to publish newspapers in their own language, and to form associations devoted to the maintenance of their national traditions, such as the celebration of anniversaries of important events in their national history, the celebration of the dates of births and deaths of great national heroes, the performance of traditional national spectacles, dramas and processions to affirm their appreciation of their nation. Not least they seek to advance their own collectivity within the national state in which they reside.

Being a nation in a subordinate status with a national state dominated by a major nation is one of the causes of nationalism. It is the cause most prominent at the present time.

The kind of nationalism manifested by the rulers of existing national states and their supporters is a different matter. There we have national hypersensitivity, a belief that their nation and their national state has been maltreated. They believe that they are not accorded the dignity to which they are entitled. They demand more territory, more praise for their cultural and political achievements and a greater share of the world's wealth. This nationalism is directed against the great powers of the world; the granting of benefits to them by those powers is either not acknowledged or regarded as insufficient.

In many of the national states, the intense nationalism is not equally shared. It is the ruling and educated classes among whom it is most intense and continuous, but occasionally it is manifested in the mass of the uneducated and poor sections of the population. Proponents of extreme nationalism are often very aggressive against their fellow nationals who are less fervent in their nationalistic aggressiveness.

Origins of Nations and Nationalism

Some writers have contended that nation and nationalism are products of the post-revolutionary epoch in Europe. If they are interpreted to mean that the nation and popular nationalism share closely related histories with the history of modern nations, there is some ground for their argument; otherwise not. The term nation in its contemporary sense reaches far back into the Middle Ages. It is perfectly reasonable to speak of nations in classical antiquity. As long as human beings regarded membership in a territorial collectivity, going beyond kinship and ethnicity, as a valid criterion for regarding themselves as members of a distinctive collective unity, there was rudimentary nationality. It is true that that belief was more pronounced among the educated and well-established classes. Could it not be said that Pericles' Funeral Oration was a moderate nationalist celebration of national achievements?

Classical rhetoric is filled with such references to national greatness. These declarations might not have been shared by all the residents of the area referred to but there certainly was a tradition of declarations of affinity and pride. And there was always an assertion that the national collectivity had a tradition. It might be agreed that the national collectivity existed and that it was not a kinship nor an ethnic group—although possessing pronounced elements of both—but it is indubitable that there was reference to it. But why did it exist at all? Why did nations, even if only in rudimentary form, come into existence before the growth of the large-scale societies which Europe has known since the beginning of modern times?

The answer seems to be partly a matter of demography. Growing populations spread beyond established political boundaries. The individuals who lived within those boundaries regarded themselves and were regarded by others who lived within the old boundaries as members of the same society. They seldom regarded them as kinsmen but they could regard themselves as coming from that same general ancestry without any specific tracing of kinship lines. But no less important, they regarded themselves as living in the same collective unity. Moreover, they regarded their children born in those new territories as members of the same collective unity.

The expansion beyond established political boundaries was a gradual process. The population grew gradually. There were times when the new boundaries had to be declared in a determinate and decisive manner, for or against, but that was usually after gradual extension of the society beyond its older boundaries to include residents of the adjacent territories.

An expanding society acquired new names for new categories of activity. As the number of categories of affinity increased, so the number of new names for those categories increased. The names of *patria* and *nation* appeared because they designated new and important things. The members of one's *patria* and *nation* became approximately equal with the other collective unities. New nations emerged.

But still the question may be asked: Was it of practical or rational value to form a new type of unity, to generate new referents or criteria to bring these additional residents of the adjacent territory into the collective unity?

Territorial proximity in small (primitive) societies has never been prominent as a criterion of inclusiveness. It appeared as less urgent than ties of blood. Do ties of blood become less forceful or less urgent as territorial affinities—no less primordial, no less connected with vitality, which is the underlying and fundamental property of primordiality—gain in sovereignty? As societies grew in size and territorial extent, they turned more to territoriality as the basis for their unity—which they had to have—in place of more biological primordial criteria.

Man cannot live without the primordial. Later in the individual life span, an individual can reduce its power in his / her current affairs. Before then, however, the primordial has formed his or her present. Why the primordial is so important in human life and society is an enigma still to be resolved.

Nationalism and Ideology

The nation in the course of the nineteenth century was regarded by British and French liberals as the proper matrix of a free society—as long as those societies were foreign. They did not however apply that insight to their own countries. They did not see their own countries as national societies; they did not apply the principle of nationality to themselves. They applied it to Ireland, the Balkans, the Middle East, and later to South Asia and then to Africa.

In Great Britain, they saw their legitimacy as established by tradition, through a series of great enactments or agreements such as Magna Charta and the political settlement of 1689. The national character of these events stood on the surface for all to see. It was probably too self-evident to be elevated into the form of a principle. In France, there was more conflict about legitimacy. The bearers of liberal and radical opinion thought that the principles of 1789 provided the legitimating propositions which declared liberty, fraternity and equality to be the values around which the collective self-consciousness of French society must be formed. The conservatives or reactionaries thought that dynastic legitimacy was the legitimating proposition. But neither thought of nationality as generated by the consciousness of a shared image of a bounded "French" territory as the basis of a legitimate regime.

The radical and liberal bloc thought of their values as being of universal validity without any special connections with French territory. They did not bring into their reflections the revolutionary wars or the battle cry of *la patrie en danger!*, which in fact brought into prominence the first national mass armies, the *levée en masse*. In fact, for French radicals and liberals, the principles of 1789 postulated the territory of France as the site for the realization of the principles of 1789. It was the territory of France and the principles of 1789 to be realized in that territory and then throughout the world that formed the objectivated symbolic configuration of the French national collective self-consciousness. French liberal and radical thought accepted them as postulates but it did not articulate the idea of territorial nationality into those postulates.

There was a powerful current of contrary thought in France. *Les maîtres de la contre-revolution* thought of *l'ancienne France* as the proper image in accordance with which French society should be rehabilitated. This idea was appreciated by French conservatives but they did not make the running among the French intellectual circles for much of the nineteenth century.

Similarly, British liberal utilitarians did not attribute much weight to the criteria of territorial location and descent from those resident in that territory. Utilitarian political thought had no place for patriotism or nationalism in their reflections about the right ordering of British political life.

Nevertheless utilitarians did think of territoriality as the basis of nationality and of national states in those parts of Eastern, Central and Southern Europe in which nations did not have their own national states. That is why they proposed traditional territoriality and the cultural nation to serve as the criteria for the establishment of the successor states to the two great empires, the Ottoman and the Habsburg Empires, which had lost their legitimacy. The Fourteen Points of President Woodrow Wilson in the last stage of the First World War gave great authority to the principle that states should be formed on the basis of circumscribed territories and the main nations resident in them.

The League of Nations, which was formed in response to the surge of pacifistic liberalism after the First World War, proceeded in two contrary directions. On the one side, it acknowledged the legitimacy of states formed on the basis of territorial nationhood. On the other side, it recognized the dangerous character of nationalism and the urgent need to curb its aspirations and ambitions.

Throughout the period between the two great wars, nationalism was severely criticized. Not only was it regarded as a disturber of the traditional international order but it was also associated with tyranny, the conquest of other countries and the suppression of the liberties of its own citizens and of those in the countries which it conquered. The developments in Italian politics following Mussolini's "March on Rome" and then, only about a decade later, the accession of the National Socialists to power in Germany, fixed the link between nationalism and tyranny. This view did not diminish after the Second World War.

The discussion of nationhood was much affected by these events. Nationality seemed to be indissolubly linked with nationalism. Liberals as well as conservatives and the fellow-travellers of communist totalitarianism abhorred both nationhood and nationalism as European phenomena. Liberals found benevolence in their hearts only for the insurgent nationalism of the indigenous peoples of the dissolving British, French, Dutch and Belgian empires. Signs of nationalism and even of nationhood in Europe or North America were roundly condemned. The nationalism which opposed the alleged imperialism of the United States and Great Britain was accepted as natural and worthy of approval. Nationalism, except as a reaction against imperialism, was coupled with imperialism. It was said by some to be the cause of imperialism, by others to be a propagandistic contrivance to legitimate imperialism and to deceive the populace so that it would support imperialistic policies which were contrary to its own interests.

In all of this, the phenomenon of nationhood—sometimes reduced to "patriotism" and exculpated—was reduced to inconsequentiality or disregarded. It was practically never analyzed. One of the consequences of this is that the phenomenon of nationhood has almost disappeared from the intellectual scene.

Nationhood and nationality do, it is true, sometimes reappear as "national identity" or "national character" but these terms mean something different. Sometimes they refer to the stable similarities of members of a nation as perceived by external observers. The other meaning which sometimes is stressed is the self-imagined self-designation of individuals who belong to a particular national or ethnic group; this is closer to what I have in mind when I speak of national collective self-consciousness.

Nations, Tradition and Territoriality

Traditionality is inherent in nationality. Nations could not exist without the reception and reenactment of traditions which convey images of significant past events and persons. A nation is as such a collectivity in which the past and the present exist simultaneously.

It is in the nature of a nation to be constituted by its past as well as by its present. Much of the effort to promote a nation is focused on the reaffirmation of the continuity of the present state of the nation with significant elements of its past.

A nation is never an affair of a single generation. It is not only that the process of formation of a national collective self-consciousness can only be gradual; but quite apart from this necessary precondition of formation, a nation always has a traditional legitimation. The connection with the past is effected through descent but what is transmitted is not blood and not physiological features, such as hair, pigmentation, physique, etc., but rather the relationship which ancestors had in and to the territory.

A nation is by its nature a transgenerational entity. It would be a contradiction in terms to conceive of a nation as a phenomenon of a single generation. A business firm may be conceived of or it might in fact be an entity which need not refer to its past. (That business firms do often refer to their past is a different matter—an important matter but not one of concern to us here.)

"Historical achievements," "heroic deeds," "immortal works" of literature or art enhance the dignity of a nation but they are attached to the nation by virtue of having been created by members of the nationality. Members of the nationality, i.e., persons who have stood in the line of descent of the nation, might become renowned as members of the nation if they have attributed to them such great works but it is not the authorship of the works which makes them members of the nation. Membership of the nation is prior and primary. It is true that in the course of time, membership in the nation becomes in part constituted by participation in the national cultural collective self-consciousness (which includes knowledge of the works of art), but, again, that is secondary. The primary criterion of membership is birth or prolonged residence in the bounded territory; when such knowledge of each other is shared or mutual, that is what is referred to as the national collective self-consciousness.

Territorial location and nativity in the territory is the fundamental referent of national collective self-consciousness.

Nations exist because of the sensitivity of human beings to the primordial facts of descent and territorial location. Unlike *Gemeinschaft* in Tönnies' account, the shared descent is not confined to "blood relatives" but it is a more inclusive categorical aggregation of all persons descended from persons who participate in the common territorial location. The common element is descent from persons who had a particular territorial location. Nativity and location are more important in nationhood than ties of blood among contemporaries and recent ancestors. Yet, descent is important in nationhood. But the descent entails the transmission of qualities derived from territorial location.

Biological descent cannot be eliminated entirely from nationhood because it is the mechanism of "genuine" connection with the past. It is sometimes adduced metaphorically but does not ordinarily extend far into the past.

In the inheritance of nationality what is transmitted is "territoriality," and not "blood," nor any physical qualities. There is a tendency for the non-biological quality which is transmitted by descent to be gradually transformed into a presumed biological quality so that a nationality becomes an ethnic group in the sense that the members of a nationality come to believe that, in addition to inherited residence, they share common blood or other physical or physiological features. There is a tendency for residence or territoriality to turn, in the mind, into "blood" or at least "blood-like" physical features.

Human beings do form themselves into nations when their members do not know each other. Why do they regard those who reside within the boundaries which they regard as "their" boundaries as different in important respects from those who reside outside those boundaries? Why should human beings care about the esteem or lack of esteem in which they are held by reason of the fact of their residence in a particular territory? Why does territory mean so much to them? Why should one be more in sympathy with one's fellow countrymen than with persons of other countries, other things being equal? It is not that they have calculated an economic advantage, although economic benefits do indeed accrue from residence in one particular place rather than another. No, it is the fact of residence and their feeling that one place of residence—on one side of a boundary or another—is of intrinsic value. If we free attachment to one's native village from its habitual encrustations, from recollections of happy personal associations, we will begin to understand what is meant by spatial or territorial primordiality.

A nation might also claim that it can be traced back to a common ancestor or to common ancestors, such as "founding fathers," or a particular individual or a few particular individuals as the creators of the nation, e.g., George Washington or Romulus and Remus, or the patriarchs, Abraham, Isaac and Jacob. On the whole, however, nationality is in principle distinct from ethnicity, although there are many instances of their partial fusion.

Ethnic groups believe that they are constituted as collectivities through the participation of their members in a certain common or shared inheritance of definite physical properties which they have from their biological ancestors; these include pigmentation, hair form, physiognomic features, etc. One of the reasons why there is an overlap of nationhood and ethnic collectivity is that the members of the latter tend to associate biological descent with long residence on a common territory.

Immigrants, persons born in an alien territory, often retain in their collective self-consciousness an image of a common territory in which they originated or from which they have descended. They have also in their collective self-consciousness images of common color, common physiological features, common hair type which distinguish them from others.

Where many persons of a particular nation immigrate to a society with a strong predominant nation, the members of which are self-confident and insistent on the preponderance of their nationality in that society, attachment to the earlier nation will become attenuated. The immigrants will become assimilated to the preponderant nation. They may retain traces of their former nation, e.g., celebrations of events in the history of the earlier nationality, retention for some time of newspapers in the language of the earlier nationality, but in the main they will come to participate in the national collective self-consciousness of the host society. This was the process which prevailed in the United States until recent decades; similarly in Great Britain with respect to immigrants from the English-speaking dominions and from European societies.

Nationality, Religion and Language

Thus far I have not mentioned religious beliefs. Spiritual religious beliefs are not primordial phenomena. Nonetheless, they, like science, art and literature become incorporated into nationhood. They become partly incorporated into the national collective self-consciousness. They are not exhausted by it. They acquire an existence outside their national collective self-consciousness or what Hegel called the "national spirit."

Common language, participation in a common vocabulary, a common grammar and common verbal usages are properties of collectivities. A language cannot exist without a collectivity. It is through communication in a common language that individuals are able to participate, i.e., acquire common knowledge of each other through participation in the body of knowledge shared through communication. But a common language is also a referent of collective self-consciousness. For many reasons, language and national collective self-consciousness are intertwined with each other. A language is integral to a nation, although the same language may be spoken by a plurality of nations. But this creates a particular common collective self-consciousness among the several nations which share the language.

A linguistic community is often congruent with a national community. This is not always the case. Indeed linguistic communities frequently extend beyond national territorial boundaries, just as they often fall short of them. There is however a general affinity between the two kinds of community. Within a national state, the dominant nation has its own distinctive language which it would like to see adopted by the other nations in the society. Nations which have no state but which aspire to be national states allege that they have originated in the antiquity and distinctiveness of their national language and from the greatness of the works produced in that language.

Participation in a common language has a solidarity-producing function. Why is participation in a common language productive of solidarity? Why is it taken into the collective self-consciousness as participation in the common substance in the same way that "blood" or territorial location or an ostensible common biological inheritance are taken into the collective self-consciousness? A particular sacrality attaches to language.

A national collectivity is in part constituted by having a common language and by the common participation in the objectivated symbolic configurations expressed in language. It is not inevitably so; Switzerland is the chief example of a national society in which there is not a common language—although the French-, Italian-, and Romansch-speakers do to some extent regard themselves as marginal to the linguistically dominant German-speakers in the nation. In Switzerland there is no serious question of separation. The examples of Belgium and Canada support the view that the sacral national unity may be endangered by the hostility of the linguistic communities towards each other. Nonetheless, in both cases, the hostile linguistic communities have hesitated when confronted with the real possibility of separation. National unity triumphed over linguistic and ethnic unity! The conflicts of linguistic communities in India have been almost unremitting since the middle of the 1950s, yet India remains intact in its national unity.

Will Dominant Nations and Nationality Survive?

Many people have, over the past seventy-five years, claimed that the national state has lost its justification and that the nation never had a rational justification. They argue that the world of sovereign states needs to be arranged into larger transnational functional groups. Such transnational groups need not be territorially congruent with each other. Various functional groups would have various territorial jurisdictions.

Nevertheless, despite the disappointments of the two decades between the great wars, the idea of overcoming nationality, nationalism and the national state has had great momentum. Some progress has been made in reducing the claims of nationhood and of the national state, for example, the European Community, NATO, the United Nations and its specialized organs and the European Defence Community.

The question is: Will dominant nations and nationality survive? At present they are under severe attack from lesser nations in France, Spain and the United Kingdom. The former Soviet Union is a scene of resurgent nations, likewise the former Yugoslavia, Iraq, Iran and Turkey are torn by the demands of a particular nation for a new national state. South and South East Asia also face such demands. Only a few major countries seem to be free of them. Japan, the United States, the Federal Republic of Germany are among those countries. But they too are subject to the demands of lesser nationalities for more rights and dignities. In short, the nineteenth century, long defined by historical writers as the "age of nationalism," can no longer enjoy a monopoly of that designation. The twentieth century and probably the twenty-first century—as far as can be foreseen—will share that distinction as well.

In a different way, Black Africa has also become a nationalist continent. It is not, in the sense that long-existing nationalities seek to escape from the dominion of long-established national states in which they live, but rather they are seeking to consolidate the national states which they formed following emancipation from the European imperial powers. They have states of their own, but they suffer severe impediments preventing them from being as orderly, prosperous and as respected in the world as they would like them to be. The most opulent nations have not been able to establish dominance over the smaller and less powerful ones.

Thus it is evident that those who would like to see nation, nationality and nationalism obliterated from the face of the earth can take little heart from the present situation, except for the developments in the European Community and the United Nations. And they are not all that heartening!

Yet, it may be asked: Is it possible that the nation as a human collectivity will fade away as a reality in human society? This is most unlikely. Primordial sensitivity to biological relatedness and attachment to locality were the first fundamental referents of collective self-consciousness. The expansion of populations rendered biological relatedness unfeasible when populations grew so far beyond the scale in which individuals could reasonably claim biological connections with very large populations. Even ethnic ties lost their plausibility and became dissolved between tribal and national ties.

Will not the tie of nationality become as attenuated as the ties of kinship and clanship? This is unlikely to happen because territoriality, with its boundaries underscored by the jurisdiction of the sovereign national state, cannot be expunged from the objects of human consciousness. Human beings cannot live without collective self-consciousness focused on boundary-generating referents. Perhaps we should say that human beings want to live in a state of enclosure. They need enclosure because they need community. Nationhood supplies both. This human sensitivity will never vanish.

Why Nationalism?

The great question, urgent for the understanding of our time, is why nationhood and nationality turn into nationalism? Nationality turns into nationalism when the nationals believe that their nationhood is affronted by a demand for "their territory," by a campaign of derogation, by the persecution of one's own nationals by members of other nations, particularly, but not only, within the boundaries of another national state. Persecution or an acute belief in being persecuted is one step from nationality to nationalism.

What is there about territoriality and common, presumably "biological," qualities which gives rise to such strong emotions and particularly to such strong emotions as repugnance towards persons outside one's collective territorial and biological boundaries? Surely, there is in nationalism little that is rational calculation about the financial costs of the loss of territory or of the financial benefits of the gain of territory.

Why is it then such a powerfully disturbing thing to experience a loss of territory or to be disjoined from part of the "natural territory" of a nation? Why is secession so abominated that civil wars, full of death and hatred, are fought to prevent it?

Scholars need to discover why territory, which is just a condition or a convenience for their routine activity when routines prevail, becomes sacred when territorial integrity is threatened and invasion is feared. Why does the Irish Republican Army wish to incorporate Northern Ireland into the Republic of Eire? Why does Spain care about Gibraltar? Why did and do many Germans think that it was of the greatest importance that Germany be unified?

The real task is to understand why human beings regard territory as "serious," in Durkheim's sense of the word. Why do they think that there is a "proper determinate," "necessary relationship" between the territory they live on and themselves or rather the "national community" that they form?

Nationality, Rights and Citizenship

Rights arise from membership in a collectivity despite the fact that they are ordinarily lumped under the heading of "human rights." They are claims upon other members of the collectivity. They are not rights which an individual human being possesses simply by the fact that he belongs to the species *homo sapiens;* he demands and acquires rights in consequence of being a member of a collectivity.

First, regarding citizenship: If by citizenship we mean the legal status of the possession of the rights and the obligations to which a person is entitled and which are required of him by virtue of the fact that he is resident on the territory which is under the jurisdiction of the national state, then citizenship in and of itself has little to do with nationality as we speak of it here. To say that a person is of British nationality, that he travels with a British passport, that he is entitled to vote in

British elections, is to say much less than what we mean by nationhood or nationality here. Nonetheless, the two things, citizenship in the narrow sense and nationality in the broad sense, are in some respects quite closely connected with each other.

Citizenship pertains to a particular national state. It is enjoyed within the boundaries of the national state; of a territory ruled by a state and by laws the powers of which run up to the boundaries of the territory in question. Citizenship is granted to persons born in the territory or born of parents born there, or who have themselves become "naturalized," i.e., been accorded citizenship after a period of extended residence and after taking an oath of allegiance to the existing system of institutions of the national state prevailing on the territory. Citizenship is not conferred for a limited term and it is not granted with the expectation that its recipient would renounce it. Citizenship is a permanent role. The process of naturalization purports, through the oath of allegiance, to imply the obligations inherent in citizenship, i.e., membership in the nation which is approximately coterminous with the civil community. It is the latter membership which is provided by citizenship; it is the former which is regarded as the ultimate outcome of citizenship.

Citizenship presumes that the citizen is or will become a member of the nation. It assumes the existence of a particular nationality which is intended to have precedence over all other nationalities within the boundaries of the national territory which is the territory over which the laws of the state are valid. Nationhood entails obligations which are much more informal, much less articulated than the obligations and rights of citizenship. Nationhood entails all sorts of emergent obligations to a fellow national, such as lending money if he is "stuck" in a foreign country without enough money to "get home"!

The rights enjoyed by an individual as a citizen are civil rights; they are not simply human rights. His citizenship in a particular national state governing a particular bounded territory entitles him to claim that his rights should be respected by his fellow citizens. These rights of the citizens are claims on the respect of citizens or subjects or rulers of the same society.

Civil rights have, however, their own distinctive medium or context and that is the particular national society which exists within specified territorial boundaries and which is ruled by laws valid within those boundaries and for the validity of which no effective claim can be made outside those boundaries. To the extent that effective claims to respect for human rights can be made, the boundaries of the national state and the national civil society have been suspended. A more comprehensive civil society would thereby be in the process of formation.

The fact that the rights and obligations of citizenship are valid and can be asserted and enforced within the territorial boundaries of the national state refers only to the coercive enforcement of those rights and obligations by the state. It says nothing about the readiness of the other members of society to acknowledge those rights and expectations of members of the society and to accept the obligation to honor those rights.

The readiness to acknowledge the rights of other individuals within one's own society and the disposition to fulfil obligations to other individuals, to the institutions and authorities of one's own society, are functions of the strength of the nationality and the national collective self-consciousness. To the extent that such a national collective self-consciousness exists, we may speak of the society as a nation. Such a national collective self-consciousness is a precondition for the effectiveness of the constitution and the laws of the national state. This national collective self-consciousness is the matrix of citizenship; it is the self-consciousness of the civil society. (It should be added that this society-wide nation is compatible with other, more parochial nations if they are not aggressively hostile to the dominant nation.)

National Consciousness

National collective self-consciousness is the shared image of the nation and the mutual awareness of its members who participate in that image. It entails at least a minimal perception of other collectivities beyond the territorial boundaries which delineate it, although in itself national collective self-consciousness is no more than the perception of the existence of the collectivity in question, as constituted by residence within the bounded territory or descent from persons resident in that territory.

Yet, the image of "the other collectivity" or collectivities need not be very prominent in the national collective self-consciousness. It must however exist. In the case of a nation, the national collective self-consciousness need not be focused primarily on "the other"; it may be focused mainly on itself, and on the referents by which that collective self-consciousness is constituted. In their scrutiny of the individuals they encounter, the individual participants in the national collective self-consciousness respond to them immediately with regard to their provenience from within or outside the significant territory. That very act of participation in the national collective self-consciousness entails at least a minimal awareness that there are other human beings whom the national collective self-consciousness does not comprise. They are "outsiders" but beyond that nothing else necessarily attaches to that category of the "outsider." It does not entail hostility to those outsiders; only awareness of their coexistence and not necessarily a very prominent awareness at that.

Self-classification—and the classification of "the others"—automatically entails at least minimal self-evaluation; that entails also the evaluation of others—individuals and collectivities. They may be regarded as more or less virtuous, brave, handsome, generous, intelligent, skilful, etc., according to any or all of the qualities or capacities which human beings possess.

Where, however, scarcity in the distribution of valued objects among nations exists, there is some likelihood that action to procure some of those scarce valued objects by a member of one nation might indeed be detrimental to the members of other nations. Thus in its relations with external collectivities, national collective self-consciousness can scarcely avoid some sensitivity to the latent competition between the individual's own national collectivity and the national collectivity of "the other." This competition might be primarily for material objects and the well-being they bring; it is at least as likely to be about matters of status, dignity and prestige. Concern about the latter are frequently reinterpreted so that they are regarded as concerns about the territorial integrity of the society and its prosperity. The concern about territorial integrity is often conceived in primordial terms, e.g., *Lebensraum,* access to "resources vital to national existence." Sometimes their claims are realistic, at other times fictitious. They are often a mixture of both, but their realism or their fictitiousness does not affect their intensity or aggressiveness towards "the other."

Nations and the Quest for Autonomy

The propensity of a nation towards autonomy is inherent in its nature as a nation. The propensity towards autonomy is manifested in the propensity towards self-maintenance. This entails the creation of cultural and educational institutions which are indispensable to the maintenance of its cultural traditions.

There is a profound necessity for a nation to develop and maintain educational institutions in which the national language is used as a medium of instruction or is taught, and in which the history and literary, artistic and musical culture of the nation is taught. Otherwise the language is lost, and with that loss the national self-consciousness of the nation is diminished.

Where a nation is coterminous with a religious community or a church, the actions required to maintain and carry out the religious and ethical obligations of the communicants of the religious institution became linked with the actions called for by the propensity to maintain the nation. There is always a tendency for a church to be "nationalized," i.e., for its self-image to include references to its territorial location and hence its primordial aspect.

Nations which exist in multinational societies and which do not accept the prospect of assimilation into the dominant nation have a pronounced disposition to acquire political autonomy, i.e., to become a sovereign national state. The fulfilment of political autonomy means a sovereign nation-state, with its own bounded territory, etc. It is not an invariable consequence of nationhood that it should seek to live under a government which is its own, shared by no other nation and having jurisdiction over the territory of no other nation. Nevertheless, in the nineteenth century many nationals in the Ottoman and Habsburg Empires claimed that they were being maltreated by a government the members of which were not of their own nation. They contended that they would be treated more justly if they were under rulers of the same nation or ethnic community as themselves. But it is not only such practical claims which are adduced by the argument that each nation should have its own government.

Hegel believed that the only satisfactory site of the universal spirit was the nation. The universal spirit did not need an organ beyond the nation and the national state. He regarded the nation-state as the proper culmination of the evolution of the spirit from particularity to universality. For Hegel this was self-evident; he did not provide any argument as to why there could not be a collectivity larger than the nation-state.

Explanations of the emergence or continued existence of nation, nationality and nationalism as a consequence of the pursuit of "interests" are not satisfactory. The term "interest" is extremely ambiguous but ordinarily, in its context, it refers to the benefits anticipated by particular groups, e.g., schoolteachers of the literature, language and history of the particular nation, who anticipate more opportunities for employment, higher and more assured incomes and enhanced prestige if the nation in question has schools in which the medium and some of the substance of instruction are consistent with the language and history of the nation in question. Another variant of the explanation in terms of interests is the anticipated benefits of office and of patronage—both giving and receiving—which enhance the pleasures flowing from deference and the exercise of power. Neither of these two explanations is completely wrong because they both postulate the prior existence of a nation. They are, however, no more than supplementary factors. They do not touch on the questions of "why does the nation and nationalism exist?"

Another unacceptable explanation of nationality and nationalism is that it is a contrivance by the ruling classes to deceive the lower classes into support for policies of profit and power which they would not otherwise support. This explanation fails to consider why "nation" is "useful" as a "cover." It fails to say that it would be "useful" only if the masses who are ostensibly to be deceived by the argument are already participants in the national collective self-consciousness and believe that the nation is a serious thing.

This invocation of "interest," like the others, treats interests as "real" and "objective" while the "nation" is treated as "ideological" and illusory, a variant form of "false consciousness." It is simply wrong.

Nationality: A Necessity of Human Existence

To summarize this section: Nationality is a necessity of human existence in society. It is a consequence of the necessity of the human mind to find sacrality not only in the spiritual transcendental sphere but in the primordial transcendental sphere as well. It has repeatedly happened in world history that the transcendental sphere has become largely free of primordial connections but it has never become completely separated, even in the case of the three spiritual world religions— Buddhism, Christianity and Islam. Even where in principle, i.e., in their theological construction, they have been made genuinely spiritual, in their concrete manifestations they have been less successful in freeing themselves entirely from their primordial connections. No spiritual religion with universal aspirations has ever been able to realize its transcendental aspirations. Each of them has penetrated extensively into certain territories but they have fallen far short of universality. They have come up against ethnic and national barriers. One of the reasons for their failure is the fusion of primordial and spiritual elements in the religions over which they would triumph. Spiritual and primordial resistances were too strong. Furthermore, the genuinely transcendental religions have never been able wholly to free themselves of their primordial religious environment.

Human beings cannot divest themselves of their primordiality. The need of the human mind to expand beyond the boundaries of the individual self, the need for communion not only with deities but with other human beings and the impossibility of completely sloughing off their primordial dispositions are jointly features of the persistent formation of the communion of human beings with each other.

Nationhood and nationality are not simply primordial. They have become entrenched by the growth of tradition which forms about them. The emergence of national languages from tribal and local languages reinforces nationhood—even though, as stated earlier, there is no rigorous fixation of one language to one nation. The development of a body of literature in poetry and prose, first oral and then mainly written, in what becomes the national language, the emergence of traditions of the images of great individuals who performed grandiose heroic deeds on behalf of the nation, the preponderance of marriages between spouses sharing the same locality and territory of a nation, all have a consolidating effect on the continuity and persistence of the traditions which transmit the national collective self-consciousness.

Any particular nation, especially if it is a small one, can disappear. But the disappearance of the particular nation occurs only with the assimilation of its bearers into another nation. The phenomenon of nationhood as such is not expungible. This was Hegel's view of the course of life of the national spirit; his view is very plausible.

It is however not uncommon for particular nations to change in their scope and intensity. Nations themselves are not likely to disappear even if nation-states disappear and even if they were replaced by a single world government or regional or continental governments larger than those they replace. If the nation-state does not disappear, the nation will persist as the collectivity formed around the territorial collective self-consciousness. The existence of boundaries and of a political authority, exercised from a center (or centers) up to the boundaries within which its laws and decrees are valid, maintains the nation-state and at least its dominant nation. Although deliberate action by the nation-state can influence the intensity of nationality, through its control over primary and secondary education and its influence on higher education, and through its intertwining with symbols of nationhood such as the flag, the national anthem, the celebration of national holidays and the use of the national language in the transaction of governmental business, the powers of the state to overcome or eliminate nationality and the nation are limited. Governments cannot directly affect the foundation of nationhood which is the sacrality of the national territory and descent from persons resident on it. Immigrants might change to some extent the content of national collective self-consciousness through the infusion into it of some of the content of their previous national collective self-consciousness. Changes in the content of education could change the intensity of the experience of nationhood, but no government, if it is at all representative of the society, i.e., if it participates in the national collective self-consciousness, is likely to undertake to extirpate the attachment to nationhood in the society which it rules. Not as a rule, though the federal government of the United States would on occasion appear to wish to do so. Efforts have been made by tyrannical governments in the past and in recent years to extirpate small nations. They have done great damage but they have not been successful.

Civil Society and Nationality

Civil society is a feature of modern national states. It is able to function, as it does, independently of the national state because of its integral role in relation to the dominant nation. Civil society is guided and oriented by nationhood. Civil society is one of the institutional manifestations of the nation.

Civil society, as the term is nowadays understood, is not a society constituted entirely by contractual relationships. Such relationships have an important role in civil society because of the large place accorded in it to private property and to commercial relationships but they are very far from the whole thing. The national collective self-consciousness of most of the members of a civil society is a precondition for the functioning of the larger society within which the contractual order is effective. The contractual order occasions damage and grievances; it causes ravages beyond the boundaries of those anticipated risks and losses which are accepted as part of the game. Civil society through the effectiveness of the national collective self-consciousness eases some of these damages and grievances.

There are many other aspects of life in civil society which are injurious to some of its participants. The scarcity of resources and of opportunities in relation to aspirations and the consequent inequality in the distribution of deference and monetary rewards, etc., all can give rise to grievances which question the justice of the existing institutions of civil society and the nation-state. These inequalities, especially frequent in modern societies where so much is visible, where grievances are legitimate and demands are interpreted by those who utter them as tantamount to natural rights, accentuate or precipitate conflicts. These conflicts, if they are uninhibited and self-accentuating—which is often the case—do much damage to society. On the other side, they can be held in check by the collective self-consciousness of civil society, which is dependent on its close relationship to the nation.

The civil collective self-consciousness, shared by various sectors of society, inhibits conflict between those sectors. It does not prevent the outbreak of conflict because important sources of conflict lie outside the process of formation of national or other less inclusive collective self-consciousnesses. The civil collective self-consciousness, drawing its support from the national collective self-consciousness, imposes the norm of the internal solidarity of the collectivity.

There are different interpretations of what is required by the norm of solidarity but the norm of solidarity as such is generated by participation in the image which is a more or less common possession of all those who are members of the collectivity.

Alongside of this normative image of the collectivity which imposes a degree of concern for its well-being and its freedom from acute conflict, there are conflicts of interpretation among individuals or blocs of individuals regarding what is required or permitted by participation in the normative image of the collectivity. Individuals frequently seek to frustrate the intentions of others and to promote their own policies and candidates. Yet, there is a point at which their readiness to engage in conflict becomes attenuated. They are inhibited by the rules of the collectivity which require that the majority in an election prevail or that a single authoritative power decide which policy or which candidate should be accepted.

Conflicts in societies—and within institutions—can be diminished or brought to a halt, with the triumph of one of the parties over its antagonists. The idea of triumph is defined by the criteria implied in or articulated from the collective self-consciousness. The defeated parties accept their defeat because they accept the fact that the rest of the institutions will invoke the rules of the society against them, should they seek to triumph or to avoid defeat by breaking the rules. The renunciation of membership in society—or in the institutions—is usually too costly an action to take. The loss of freedom, the loss of income and the loss of status are among the prices which ordinarily have to be paid for by renunciation of membership or severe and recurrent infringement of its rules. At the same time, it is difficult to form combinations or alliances which will permit the realization of the policies or appointments desired by individuals. They cannot act like revolutionary or *putschist* groups in a revolutionary situation in a larger society, which, having or believing that they have the military power to suppress violently or to intimidate any opposition, can disregard their adversaries. They are simply not in a position to assert: "We have the tanks and guns. We are the ruling power. We have abrogated the constitution." This holds especially for conflicts which do not bear visibly on the wider society or the nation-state. The conflicting parties have to bear in mind the obduracy of the civil society as a whole.

Within a society, short of the exercise of physical force or the threat of its exercise, no sector of a society can carry through its policies or appointments without the articulated and inarticulated consent of the other major sectors of the society. The discontented or aggrieved sector might not like the policy but they cannot successfully oppose it by the threat of violence or by the actual performance of violent actions. The rules of the society as a whole and of particular institutions forbid that.

Of course, things practically never go this far. Most groups within a society, even in quite acute conflicts, do not usually think of trying to bring off a *putsch;* they do try to manipulate the voting rules, and regulations about procedures of deliberations and decision-making. They know that they must observe legitimate rules, rules having the affirmation of most other members of the institution. The chances of detection and prosecution have a deterrent effect.

Only very small numbers of persons in any society actually engage in the violent actions entailed in revolutions or threaten to exercise violence in order to expel the incumbents of positions of legitimate authority from their posts. Even revolutionaries think that most persons will obey the laws and that they will therefore obey the laws and decrees of the usurping revolutionaries.

Whether or not a society has a written constitution, the national collective self-consciousness has the effect of a constitution through its imposition of a general acceptance of laws, conventions and beliefs about legitimacy and justice. The latter are inevitably vague but they have, nevertheless, a more or less determinate content and their adherence is also noted and adopted too by those who also think of infringing them.

We could say that the individual in any large national society "feels powerless" in the midst of this dense setting of individuals, offices, and rules which limit his powers and which he accepts as limiting his powers. He might rage against these limitations but he also accepts them. He accepts them because he thinks that it would be hopeless to attempt to disregard them or to overcome them when he wishes to acquire an object or to attain a goal which he desires. He also accepts them because he regards them as legitimate. They are the rules of his national society. This renders them acceptable.

There must be many individuals in any society and especially in a large modern national society whose view of society is like that of K in *The Trial* of Kafka, who are conscious of their impotence in the face of this mountain of offices, institutions and rules. There are also many others who are alert in seeking "loopholes," seeking ways to "get around" this mountain, who do not attempt to change it but who are imaginative enough, intelligent enough, to have their way without falling foul of the laws. Then there is a large number of people who do not even worry about whether they are "staying within the law" and who are determined to have what they desire without regard for what the laws permit. Many of these are successful. They break the law and do not "get caught." They are perhaps a larger group than those who do "get caught."

But all of these together in any single year are probably a minority of the population of any modern liberal democratic society. There are some areas—occupations and districts—within a country where a fairly large section of the inhabitants belong in the last two categories, i.e., the categories of those who knowingly break the law and escape detection or at least conviction, and those who knowingly break the law and are detected, convicted and imprisoned. They might be numerous in those particular quarters and even in the society as a whole, but they are only a minority, even if a substantial minority of the population. They damage the civil society but they are not a direct threat to its survival.

For the rest, there must be very many who would like the laws, as they are and as they bear on some prospective actions of their own, to be different from what they are. Nevertheless, they accept the laws as they are without enthusiasm or zeal and submit to them without attempting to evade them. Some of that acceptance or submission might be nothing more than resignation. Yet not all of it is. Much of this resignation is an acknowledgement of the legitimacy of the reigning authority of the national state.

Legitimacy is not a rational deduction from first principles of natural or divine law or of the sovereignty of the people. It is certainly not habit; it is not a mechanical or a conditioned reflex. The acknowledgement of legitimacy is an act of belief; it is an act of belief in sacred, i.e., charismatic, things. An individual who accepts the legitimacy of the law and of authority acknowledges the sacred by participation in its objectivated symbolic form which is an emanation from its source. The source is the highest authority in a collectivity constituted by residence in a bounded national territory. The sacred source is the national collective self-consciousness.

Legitimacy does not depend on enthusiasm. It is like any other phenomenon of national collective self-consciousness, intermittent in salience and various in intensity of affect.

Legitimacy of rule or authority, the legitimacy of any rule or authority, is not attributed specifically to single rules or laws; it is general in its attribution. It is attributed to what is perceived as a relatively undifferentiated mass of rules or laws, etc. The legitimacy of any specific rule or law derives from the legitimacy of the sacred institution or from a general sacred rule or in some cases from the amorphous and general rule of a charismatic leader.

Pluralism and Civil Society

Civil society requires a certain amount of spontaneous conformity. There is much "conformism" in "civility" as there is in the ethics of responsibility.

The question which I must deal with now is whether civility includes the acceptance of much of the existing institutional structure of society. The answer is that it does include it but that it is not wholly constituted by that acceptance. It would not be a civil society if it required complete acceptance of all existing institutions. Civil society is characterized by plurality of interests and ideals and hence with some freedom of choice according to one's interests or to one's idea of the common good but with an overriding respect for the "rules of the game."

An individual who in his sphere of freedom takes into account only what will affect his own interests or those of his family or his class or his ethnic group cannot be said to be acting civilly, even though he accepts most of the institutional structures of society both in its obligatory sector and in its free sector. It is uncivil to pursue one's individual or sectional or party interest in contravention to the constitutionally enacted laws or contrary to the stipulations of the national constitution. Law-breaking is uncivil.

The acceptance of the existing institutional structures is compatible with and is even required as a precondition of civility. It is uncivil to denounce or rail against or conspire to change comprehensively the existing institutional structure of society. Civility does not necessarily accept and it certainly does not actively affirm every feature of the existing institutional structure. A civil society certainly allows for the freedom to criticize any feature of that structure; the freedom of a civil society even permits the most comprehensive criticism of the fundamental or even the entire institutional structure. It might even permit the organization to seek to persuade public opinion to change the total structure in accordance with the prevailing laws which allow such activity but not to replace it by an uncivil society.

The idea of civil society excludes the right to organize for an illegal or unconstitutional transformation of the fundamental or the entire institutional structure. Such actions are uncivil.

Why are conspiratorial revolutionary actions uncivil? This is a question which has so many obvious answers. One answer is that it breaks the consensus of acceptance. Civility entails consensus about the value and necessity of the existing rationale and of the institutional structure of the nation-state. This sounds terribly platitudinous but the crucial point is worth making. There can be no civil society without a certain amount of order which assures stability, holds in check the demand for the expanded exercise of governmental authority, avoids placing severe strain on the capacities of the family and civil institutions (private and political) and upholds the symbols and values of the nation. When such institutions cannot perform, more or less effectively, their wonted functions, there is a call for more exercise of authority by the state or central government, and a readiness to heed the declarations of charismatic leaders, agitators and "prophets," etc.

Conspiracies are destructive of the nationhood which is bound up with civil society. Conspiracies are often the work of extreme nationalists who are inimical to normal nationhood. They usually desire arrangements which are much more authoritarian, if not totalitarian. They are enemies of nationhood.

Conspiracies encourage suspicion, fear of subversion and persecutory tendencies. They make for insecurity in the civil sphere—private and public or political—and in government. If they are successful, which they seldom are, under normal conditions of civil society, then of course they institute at once an abrogation of civil society. They are repressive of public liberties and representative institutions. They are enemies of the routine life of a nation which provides the sustenance of civil society.

Nations, Nationality and Civil Society

I may now return to the question of the relationships between nation and nationality on the one side and civil society on the other.

I will deal first with nationalism. I have no doubt that the aggressiveness of nationalism has no place in civil society. Not only is it contrary to the norms of a pluralistic society, but it is also in fact injurious to the maintenance of those norms.

Nationalism is not only aggressive against foreign societies; it is also aggressive against persons or groups in its own society. It is against those who disagree with their nationalistic programs and actions. I do not mean criticism in words—although a properly functioning civil society has, if it is to survive, to place some restraints on those who repeatedly and dramatically recommend the employment of violence against other groups within the society. But nationalist movements of an extreme sort do not merely recommend the use of violence against their fellow countrymen; they do in fact use violence against them, their institutions and their property. There is no need to elaborate this point here—the experience of Germany before 1933 and, on a much smaller scale, some of the experiences there since unification, and the experiences in Italy up to and after the "March on Rome," as well as some experiences since the end of the Second World War, show the incompatibility of nationalism and civil society.

The relation of nation to civil society is very different. The nation is necessary for civil society. It is one of its main supports. The crucial collectivity within the nation-state is the dominant nation. Nationality is a necessary ingredient, perhaps even precondition for civil society. It is the collective self-consciousness which sustains the civil society. Concern for one's nation reinforces the concern for the common good. Concern for one's nation is sustained by attachment to the traditions. Indeed, the nation would not exist without these traditions.

Nationality and "Constitutional Patriotism"

Jürgen Habermas has attempted recently to deny the existence, efficacy and legitimacy of the nation and nationality. He has declared that "constitutional patriotism"—*Verfassungspatriotismus*—is the proper political culture of German society, not nationality, not patriotism which has territory as one of its referents.

Now it is perfectly clear that a constitution, just like a government, can be a referent of the collective self-consciousness of a liberal society. There is nothing amiss there, but the territorial reference cannot be disregarded. After all, the constitution is the constitution of a territorially located society of a nation-state.

Indeed, the constitution (*Grundgesetz*) of the Federal Republic of Germany is the constitution of a territorially bounded society which houses a nation. It is not the constitution of the Federal Republic of the Earth or of Eastern or of Central Europe. It is the Federal Republic of Germany, a determinately bounded territory over which the constitution is valid. In short, the constitution of the Federal Republic of Germany is the constitution of a territorial and national society; it is a constitution which applies in principle to events occurring or originating in that territory, not beyond it. The collective self-consciousness of German society is a national collective self-consciousness of which the constitution is an important referent which refers simultaneously to the territory over which it is valid. German society is older than the *Grundgesetz,* it is older than the German Empire which was declared in 1871, and Germans of the present day share participation in that collective self-consciousness with Germans of earlier decades and centuries.

Habermas was one of the most vigorous critics of the failure of his fellow German historians for their resistance to face up to the responsibility of *Vergangenheitsbewältigung.* But the existence of a German nation with a long past and with a relatively long defined set of territorial boundaries is why the problem of *Vergangenheitsbewältigung* exists. If Germans of the present day had no sense that their own generation and the German generations of the past are equally members of German society, the twelve years of National Socialist tyranny and the Holocaust which it perpetrated would not be a moral problem for them. Some Germans would like to deny that these twelve years actually occurred but their denial of it recognizes it is something that they cannot deny because they participate in it as Germans. That is why Habermas censured them.

You cannot speak of *Vergangenheitsbewältigung* while denying the identity of the German society of 1919–33 or 1933–45 with the German society of the 1970s or the 1980s or 1990s. If all that is entailed in being German is to be loyal to and to have reverence for the present-day *Grundgesetz,* then the whole past would be wiped away. Now that might or might not be a good thing but it has not happened and it is not likely to happen in the foreseeable future.

Conclusion

Let me conclude: Being a civil society is perfectly compatible with being a national society; in fact it is impossible for it to be otherwise. On the other hand, a society in which nationality is driven into the extreme form of nationalism will set many obstacles on the path to being or remaining a civil society.

Hegel thought that every national spirit could dissolve after it reached the stage of universality. He did not go into detail on how the dissolution could occur. Habermas' arguments about constitutional patriotism do provide one illustration of how this can come about but he and those who share his view would like to destroy the idea of the nation and obliterate the traditions on which the nation rests. Without territory and without tradition there can be no nation; without a nation there can be no civil society. This is so, even where there is no direct attack on civil society.

There are other ways to destroy the national spirit. "Multicultur-alism," as it is thriving in the educational system of the United States, is a more intentional and perhaps more effective way of destroying the national spirit and the nation as a unity. I do not mean to say that any argument in favor of any form of "multiculturalism" is meant to destroy the idea of the nation. But it is definitely intended to undermine the idea of the dominant nation in the United States and of the national state by which it is supported. The destruction of the idea of the dominant nation in any society is, in fact, tantamount to the destruction of civil society. This in turn would do damage to all the lesser nations within a nation-state because it would damage the civil society which protects the lesser nations from the damage which they would suffer in "a war of each against all." This would be a result of the dissolution of civil society, it would be a further sapping of the foundations of civil society.

The growth and decline of the national spirit are difficult to promote. It seems to be easier to promote its decline. Paradoxically the decline of the nation or the national spirit is a product of the intensified nationalism of the lesser nations and of groups which have never before been nations.

Max Weber
and the World Since 1920

§

SOCIOLOGY is said by some of its present practitioners to be a
science aiming to discover comprehensively general laws about
human actions and institutions; these general laws are expected
to be applicable to all human actions and institutions in whatever
epoch and place. Other sociologists are less insistent on this view of
their subject, claiming that their first task is to obtain precise knowledge
of their contemporary society. In fact, most sociologists conduct their
investigations into their own contemporaneous societies; this is partly
a necessity of their preferred techniques of direct observation and
interview and is partly a result of their paramount interests in their
own societies. (It is also, in more recent decades, a result of the fact that
an increasingly large proportion of sociological research is supported by
governments that are interested in obtaining reliable information about
contemporary conditions in their own society.) There are exceptions
to this generalization; there are sociologists who study societies of the
past and who go outside their own national boundaries; they have
been increasing in number, but they are still a very small minority.
Most sociologists study contemporary Western societies.

The most eminent figures in the history of sociology have had a
much broader perspective than the practicing sociologists of the present

Previously published in Wolfgang J. Mommsen and Jürgen Osterhammel, *Max Weber and His Contemporaries* (London: Unwin Hyman, 1987), pp. 547–73. Reprinted by permission.

day who conduct studies of particular contemporary factories or towns or of living families. Some of these eminent figures were concerned about the stages in the history of mankind and the "laws" that described or determined the movement from stage to stage; others, like some contemporary sociological theorists, attempted to transcend history by the formulation of categories and hypotheses that were alleged to be valid for all societies in all times. (Of course, none of them was successful.) Nonetheless, all of these founding and contemporary sociological theorists regardless of whether they thought of general laws ostensibly of universal applicability, like the laws of physics or chemistry, which had no regard for epochs or territories, or whether they thought of laws of historical evolution, were, in fact, primarily interested in modern Western societies in their relative distinctiveness compared with societies in other times and in other parts of the world; they wanted to explain how the unique phenomenon of the typical modern Western liberal, democratic, capitalistic, national society came about and how it worked.

I

Max Weber, the corpus of whose work is, in my opinion, the most fundamental and most learned achievement of sociology, went further than any other sociologist in the pursuit of these combined aims of understanding human societies in a universal setting and modern Western society in its uniqueness. He produced the most differentiated set of categories for the analysis of all societies regardless of epoch and territory, he analyzed a number of particular civilizations and cultures—China, India and ancient Judaism—in order to contrast them with modern Western societies, and to discover what there was in them which disposed them to move along paths other than that taken by Western civilization in arriving at its modern pattern. Max Weber's general categories, which he intended to be applicable to all societies, were also intended to permit the discernment of the distinctiveness of modern societies. Although he did not believe in "laws of historical development" or in a "philosophy of history" that purported to describe a meaningful pattern in the temporal sequence of societies or civilization, he did regard "rationalization," which was present in some degrees and forms in all large-scale societies and in all civilizations and which he thought reached its most pervasive and most penetrating ascendancy in modern Western society, as both a universally applicable category and as a means of delineating the unique features of particular societies.

Efforts to be systematic, to eliminate contradictions, to establish consistency among observations and between observations and theories, and to make theories internally consistent are acts of cognitive rationalization. Not only the growth of the natural sciences but the numerous efforts to advance the social sciences are such acts of rationalization. Efforts to bring scientific knowledge into the chains of practical action in political, economic and social life are as much acts of rationalization as are the efforts to bureaucratize administration in every sphere and to order our knowledge of the world. "Scientific management" is a rationalization. Bureaucratization is a rationalization of the actions of corporate bodies: governmental, ecclesiastical, military, academic, industrial and commercial. Secularization is a form of rationalization; it is a movement towards a unitary view of the world and away from seeing the world as made up of unconnected fragments and sectors. Secularization is the elimination of belief in the powers of transcendent spirits and the ostensible replacement of such belief by the mode of analysis and action that seeks to understand and influence the world in accordance with empirical observations made consistently with rationally defined criteria of validity and rational, logical principles constructed on the basis of such observations and criteria.

Societies could be compared with respect to the degree to which and the form in which their institutions were rationalized; patterns of thought—religious, scientific and juridical—could be compared with respect to the degree of their rationalization; institutions could also be compared with respect to their degree of rationalization.

Max Weber characterized modern Western society, ideal-typically, as follows: (1) rationalized, privately owned, economic enterprises oriented towards market conditions and seeking to maximize the profitability of their investments, calculated in monetary terms; (2) these enterprises availed themselves of a rational scientific technology; (3) a formally free market for labor, allowing mobility and hence rationality in the allocation of labor; (4) citizenship with rights and obligations within the national state; (5) bureaucracy, i.e., rationalized administration in government, economic enterprises and other institutions; (6) a legal order and a corresponding judicial system permitting stability of legal norms and hence a far-reaching predictability of consequences; (7) representative political institutions associated with competitive political parties seeking the support of an electorate constituted by approximately universal suffrage; (8) a pervasive secularization (*Entzauberung*) of the view of the world and society: this comprised the extinction of magic, the refusal to admit the operation of "spiritual" forces, and the ascendancy of a rationalized, naturalistic, scientific outlook; (9) the rule that rewards should be rationally commensurate with achievement. This last feature was not explicitly listed by Max Weber in his enumeration of the features of modern society. Yet it was pervasively implicit in his characterization of the modern society that he studied. In contrast with the traditional society that placed such great emphasis on lineage or descent as a qualification for the possession of property, income, status and office, the modern outlook—contained in the Protestant ethic and in the spirit of capitalism that grew out of it—required that exertion and skill be the legitimate basis for reward. It should be added that Max Weber attributed much importance to the nation as a social and cultural formation. This is, however, more taken for granted than elaborately, systematically treated in his sociological writings; in his political writings it is given considerable prominence, but it is not analyzed with the careful attention that he gave to most other features of modern societies.

These were the attributes of modern Western societies, not fully or equally realized in all Western societies but still, to a far-reaching extent, sufficiently developed to make these societies unique in world history. This was Max Weber's view of Western societies as they functioned in his lifetime.

II

Max Weber died in 1920. Approximately two-thirds of a century have now passed since then. Western societies have changed drastically in many respects during the last sixty-five years. Industry has become much more productive; scientific knowledge has been drawn upon for the development of industrial technology far more than was the case at the time of Max Weber's death. All these societies are consequently much wealthier now than they were sixty-five years ago; the mass of the population lives at a much higher standard of material well-being than it did. Extensive provisions for welfare have practically eliminated poverty, as it was then conceived, from these societies. The sphere of the free market, in which enterprises seek to maximize their profits in competition with each other, still exists, but its sphere has been much reduced by an extension of governmentally owned enterprises and by a more penetrating and restrictive regulation by government. The market for labor, which economic theory assumes to be free, has been much eroded by legislation and by the strength of trade unions, which restrict entry into certain occupations, which restrain dismissal and which affect the rates of remuneration that would otherwise be fixed by competition in the market for labor; they restrict output and resist technological innovation by formal and informal agreements, thus limiting the rationalization of business enterprises. Citizenship, with its obligations to the payment of taxes and the performance of military service and its rights to preference over non-citizens in the enjoyment of certain guarantees and political activities, has undergone an uneven development. The obligation to the payment of taxes has been extended throughout the population, the refusal of military service has become more frequent and more tolerated; the differences between the rights of citizens and those of non-citizens have been much diminished at a time when the rights of all residents within the national boundaries have been much increased. There has been a great increase in the demands of individuals throughout modern Western societies for higher incomes, more governmentally provided amenities, and protection and greater freedom in private and public spheres. Previously subordinated and submissive groups, ethnic, regional and social, have become more assertive and demanding. The press, printed and electronic, has become more free, more inquisitive and more critical towards existing institutions and the authorities who rule them. Patriotism, which was once an attribute of citizenship, has been attenuated.

The technology of communications and transportation has greatly increased both the ease and the amount of travel; more of the citizenry can now be reached more speedily and more often by the new methods of electronic communication. Societies have become more integrated through the greater concentration of resources and authority in the hands of central government; they have also become more integrated in the sense of possessing a common body of knowledge of current events through a common focus of attention on central government and through the substance transmitted by a relatively few nationally pervasive organs of communication. The attention of the mass of the population has become more focused on the central government; there has been an increase in demands for the protection of what people assert to be their rights and, in each society, the mass of the population directs these demands towards its central government. Bureaucratization has grown enormously throughout the length and breadth of society.

Despite several setbacks in Italy between 1923 and 1945, and in Germany between 1933 and 1945, and in Spain from the late 1930s until the late 1970s, and in Portugal for a longer period, political democracy now prevails in all these countries as well as in those in which it was never eclipsed. Politicians have become more ready to attempt to gratify the demands of the electorate and to regard themselves as its instruments, while the electorate, for its part, has become more fickle in its loyalty and more skeptical about the merits of its political representatives. The relationship between the electorate and their elected representatives has become more labile, partly in consequence of a diminution of deference towards persons in positions of authority and of the establishment of the sample surveys of public opinion, which bring before politicians (both incumbents and candidates for elective office) the desires and evaluation of "the public." "Party machines" have been weakened by this greater assertiveness and demandingness of the electorate, and particularly by the agitation of intellectuals and social and political reformers who have gained in influence over the functionaries of party machines. Various forms of populism, most of them actually the agitation of organized intellectual and sometimes radical political groups claiming to speak on behalf of "the people," have placed professional politicians at a disadvantage in their relations with the mass of the population.

The higher educational level of the population—larger proportions of the relevant age-cohorts attend secondary schools and universities—has contributed to greater assertiveness and demandingness and to a more critical attitude towards politicians. Public demonstrations and agitation by particular interest groups have proliferated. Strikes were at one time a monopoly of the industrial working class. This is no longer the case. Employees in civil services and nationalized industries have become as ready to strike as employees in private industry. White-collar workers and professionals also strike on behalf of their demands for higher salaries, shorter working weeks and other benefits. Farmers and peasants have become more insistent in their demands on central governments.

The much greater "consumption" of mass communication, especially of television broadcasts, by the mass of the population has increased the sensitivity of politicians to the views of the public. Politicians are now more alert to how their "image" is represented in newspapers and periodicals and on television. Because the electorate is more concerned with issues of domestic policy, politicians have also become much more occupied with domestic issues than with the issues of foreign policy, although they cannot disregard these as much as many of them would like.

The demandingness of the populace is a demandingness addressed to government for services, payments and protection from whatever misfortunes can befall human beings. One major consequence of this has been the growth of the "welfare-state" and a very great enlargement of the civil service. In most European countries, the size of the public services has been further increased by the nationalization of various branches of industry and of particular firms. Socialists, communists and collectivist liberals press for more nationalization and for a more and more comprehensive regulation and direction of private business enterprises.

The power of bureaucracy has accordingly expanded immensely. The legislature enacts more laws than ever before, but the individual legislators are less powerful. In some systems, legislators are under the control of the cabinet and the party leadership; in the United States, they are increasingly under the influence of their own staffs, originally appointed to help them cope with the executive branch, including the civil service, on the one side, and their demanding constituents, on the other. In the United States, also, the federal judiciary has increasingly claimed jurisdiction over subjects that were unknown to it before.

The intellectuals in their many different intellectual and intellectual-practical activities have become more visible and more influential. University teachers have become much more active as advisers to governments and as incumbents of high political offices. Economic ideas generated in academic situations and in the course of academic debates have been assimilated into governmental policies, although not always with satisfactory practical results. Governments employ more social scientists, not only as staff members in the executive civil service but also for the promulgation and evaluation of policies. The ideas of academic social scientists have been incorporated into public opinion to an unprecedented extent. Politicians are more responsive to the opinions of such academics. The ideas of academics enter into public opinion through the media of mass communication. The academic community on its own side has become more politicized, and universities in many countries have become the platform for radical political ideas to an extent practically unknown in Max Weber's lifetime.

The amount of scientific research in physics, chemistry, astronomy, biology, medicine, agriculture and technology has increased greatly in volume, the number of scientists has grown vastly and the cost of research has increased disproportionately. The promotion and execution (as well as the control) of scientific research in the natural sciences have been taken into the agenda of governments; the chief support of such research comes from central governments, and governments thereupon take it on themselves to attempt to guide the direction of research into paths that they regard as being of practical economic, political and military value. In the course of this, natural scientists have come to occupy important roles in the institutions designated by governments to guide the direction of scientific research; natural scientists have acquired more influential roles as advisers to governments on problems and decisions that require scientific knowledge. Governments have created divisions of research within many of their departments or ministries and maintain many research institutions. The substance of the natural sciences is immune from politicization because of the nature of scientific knowledge, the strength of the traditions of the scientific community and the obstacles that are inherent in the efforts of laymen to control activities which are so complicated as to be intelligible only to those who have studied them for a long time; however, there has never been a time in the history of science when governments have attempted to intrude so much into the sphere of scientific work.

Literary authors also have become more politicized, frequently on behalf of radical causes. The same has been true of the recently much expanded sociological profession, whose members have tended to judge their respective societies from the standpoint of a Utopian egalitarian ideal. The ideal of most intellectuals who have become more or less active in politics has been an ideal of rationalization. Such people have generally been in favor of more control and planning by central governments in most spheres; most of those who are not so active or so favorable acquiesce in such programs of rationalization.

The progress of rationalization and, even more, of the ideal of the rationalization of society and of the scientific view of the world reaches deeply into the sphere of religion. A striking development of the past sixty-five years is the reduced position of the Christian churches in most Western societies, the decline in the prestige of their leaders and the faded state of Christian belief within the population at large. Regular attendance at services of worship has decreased; Christian belief and imagery come less frequently and less prominently into the idiom of the public speech of politicians. Whereas, at the beginning of the period under consideration, these societies were considered by their members to be "Christian"—without going further into what that meant—this is no longer the case. This has happened to some extent even in Latin countries of Southern Europe, where the Roman Catholic Church and Roman Catholic belief have, in the past, made fewer concessions to modern secularism. The pressure to conciliate secular desires and to accept secular beliefs has become strong in Roman Catholicism; it is, and has been, even stronger in the major Protestant churches and sects.

Priests and pastors and ministers of religion have become more assertive politically than at any time since the Restoration following the Napoleonic Wars, but now they do not act in defense or for the promotion of their churches and their theological beliefs. They do not act so much "in the religious interest" as they do on behalf of secular ideals of equality and popular sovereignty outside the churches. The clergy of the Roman Catholic Church, in which more has been required in the way of beliefs and observance, has also lost some of its confidence in the truth of the traditional theological teachings in which its predecessors had believed. The decline in the numbers of vocations and the increase in the number of priests who have requested release from their vows indicate this. In some respects, the crisis of authority in the Roman Catholic Church is more severe than it is in the Protestant churches, in which authority has always been somewhat more limited in its demands on the faith of the clergy and their flocks; the special position of the Papacy adds to the obligations of faith of Roman Catholics, as do the traditional demands of the Church for specific acts and abstentions by the faithful, and both are now more in question than they were in Weber's lifetime.

Ritual and ceremonial have been forced into more and more confined occasions; their elaborateness has been simplified where it has not been obliterated. Ritual and ceremonial have always been associated with the affirmation of authority, with the invocation of higher powers to legitimate earthly powers through the attribution of a sacred significance to earthly things. It may be said that the reduction and confinement of ritual and ceremonial is a manifestation of a secular, rationalizing outlook that denies the existence of the higher powers to which ritual and ceremonial appeal. It should also be said that there is a coincidence of secularist attitudes with attitudes that are hostile towards superordination and towards the exercise of authority and towards any superiority of status. Ritual and ceremony entail superior authority, earthly as well as transcendent, and when authority itself is so critically assessed, ritual and ceremony are bound to be distrusted.

The situation of Christian authority in the past sixty-five, and particularly in the past thirty-five years, is only one instance of the situation of authority more generally. There is more questioning of the authority of teachers and officials in universities and in schools, of the authority of officers in armies, of the authority of employers in factories and offices, of the powers of the police in dealing with suspected criminals, of governments vis-à-vis the press in the disclosure of confidential information and the protection of the press's sources of confidential information; these are all parts of the far-flung mosaic of the diminution of deference towards authority.

There is a passion for equality—the argument for it remains very vague—but the burden of proof has passed to those who are reluctant to accept the demand for equality; the argument for equality has become an argument resting on self-evidence. The passion for equality and the efforts to restrict the powers traditionally allowed to offices of authority are probably closely akin to each other; the common element is the postulate of the dignity of the individual human being. This passion and these efforts have gone hand in hand with the readiness to accord greater powers and a greater share of the national income to central government.

The emphasis on the irreducible dignity of every human being is linked to a belief that human beings also have unequal abilities, although those who support the first thesis sometimes deny that they believe the second. They obviously do believe that the equal dignity of human beings is not paralleled by their equal abilities, because it is characteristic of the arguments for equality that they also demand that governments occupy themselves with enforcing equality by a great number and a wide variety of costly and unprecedentedly intrusive measures. The equality of human beings, although alleged to be "natural," must be assured by measures that have behind them the coercive power of government. Although there is still a belief, more common in Max Weber's lifetime, that rewards should be commensurate with achievement—this was a common belief of the liberalism in which Max Weber shared—it is now qualified by the contradictory belief that inequality of rewards must be reduced in accordance with the postulate of the fundamental equal dignity of all human beings.

The belief in equality permeates the collectivistic liberal and social-democratic outlooks that have been dominant throughout most of the period since the death of Max Weber. It combines distrust towards authority, egalitarianism and secularism, and the belief that only governmental activity is capable of realizing the great ideals of the abolition of authority and the entrenchment of equality.

These have been the salient features of modern Western societies for the last sixty-five years, but they have not been the only features. In some of these societies—specifically in Italy and in Germany—regimes of quite different features have appeared, suppressing individual and civil freedoms, abolishing the institutions of representative government, the rule of law, the freedom of the press, the rights of expression, association and assembly, the competition of two or more political parties; in varying degrees, they have abolished the mechanism of the market, and persecuted ethnic and religious groups to the point of extinction. They have preached vehemently the pre-eminence of the national community to the exclusion of all other social formations save the state, and to the state they have assigned the responsibility of driving to an extreme the paramountcy of nationality within its own society and abroad.

In the other Continental European countries, and to only a very small extent in the United States and Great Britain, there have been organizations that mimicked the German and Italian groups inimical to the liberal-democratic social order, but they have remained very small and inconsequential minorities.

There have also been other political movements that wished to displace the liberal-democratic social order and to replace it by a totalitarian order of a sort somewhat different from that contended for by the Nazis and Fascists. These communist movements were intended to install regimes like that prevailing or thought optimistically to prevail in the Soviet Union, centralized and planned by a dictatorial center of a single party, without any freedoms, private or corporate. The economy was to be wholly controlled by the central political authority; private economic enterprise was to be wholly abolished except for very marginal activities. The communist ideal was territorially expansive: the communist parties of the Western countries sought to extend the power and pattern of the Soviet Union to their own countries. The communist movement has failed to attain its basic objective in any Western country either before the Second World War or after it. It attained great size in Germany before 1933 and in France and Italy after the Second World War. In other countries, including the Federal Republic of Germany, it has not been able to gain large numbers of adherents nor has it been able to exercise much influence except by infiltration into trade unions and by its often camouflaged appeals to intellectuals.

Nevertheless, all the Western countries where liberal democracy was established have been obdurate in opposing the efforts of the Communists, just as all but Germany and Italy and Spain were resistant to the Nazi and Fascist efforts to gain control.

The failures of the major movements of subversion—the Communists and the Fascists—have left behind them residues of small, unstable groups of individuals who refuse to reconcile themselves to the liberal-democratic societies in which they live. They refuse to live at peace with their societies; they engage in assassinations and the explosion of bombs in crowded places of symbolic importance. Germany, Italy and Ireland, the three countries of the West in which political violence was most pronounced after the First World War, have in recent times been scenes of such terrorist activities.

The institutions for the protection and enforcement of public order have had only partial success in the prevention of these violent disruptions of public order. Limited by legal restraints on the use of force and frustrated by the ingenuity and the numbers of the perpetrators of acts of terror and the help which they receive from ideological sympathizers, the police and security services have not been very effective. (Nor for that matter have they been able to cope with the greatly increased number of ordinary crimes such as armed robbery, burglary, rape and murder or with the great increase in the frequency of "economic crimes" such as embezzlement.)

Despite severe criticisms from within and attempts at subversion, most of the liberal-democratic countries have persisted and developed.

Even Germany and Italy, the two countries that could not resist the totalitarian movements within them, were able, once their tyrants were destroyed in the Second World War, to turn to the liberal-democratic path; they have, moreover, stayed there—the West Germans very successfully, the Italians less successfully but sufficiently so to remain clearly liberal-democratic. In all Western countries, collectivistic liberalism and social democracy have gained the ascendancy during the two-thirds of a century under consideration here.

In the last decade and a half, several developments in the direction of a reversal of these tendencies have occurred. In Western Germany, Great Britain and the United States, a more conservative body of political philosophers and publicists has emerged and more conservative parties have acceded to power. They wish to restore greater opportunities to private business and to make it possible for the initiatives of private enterprise to be successful; they wish their societies to rely to a larger extent on the market. They would reduce the share of the gross national product taken by government through taxation and leave more of it to private individuals and enterprises. They are less egalitarian in their fundamental ideals, less emancipationist in their attitude towards the expression of emotional impulses. They have more sympathy with traditional religious beliefs, and are more inclined to affirm the virtues of traditional family life, and of the responsibility of parents for the care of their children. In general, they are more willing to give the benefit of the doubt to established legitimate authorities in state, school and church, when these are in conflict with the desires of individuals. At the same time, they wish individuals to take more responsibility for providing for themselves and their families. They believe that rewards should be commensurate with effort.

Although they espouse the values of individualistic liberalism, i.e., the values of individual effort in work and the opportunities to gain the rewards of that effort, they would also restore to the family and church their previously esteemed positions. They would give more responsibilities to local and regional governments and would reduce the powers of central government. Yet they would maintain and strengthen the nation, that amorphous and inclusive society-wide collectivity, the most comprehensive consensus-bearing frame of all other individual and collective activities. They would therefore nurture patriotism, or at least not deride it.

This restoration of individualistic liberalism, in combination with the more traditional communal values of patriotism and authority of family and church, has been successful in electing governments that are in principle committed to such values. Nevertheless, it has not succeeded in restoring the patterns of society that were dominant in Western societies in Max Weber's lifetime.

III

Several other very great changes have occurred since Max Weber's lifetime. One is the establishment of so many new sovereign states in Asia and Africa, in what were former colonies of the Western societies that were the central focus of Max Weber's interests. The formation of the new states of Asia and Africa in the formerly colonial territories is one of the most prominent features of the world since Max Weber's lifetime. They are the creation of the influence of nationalism in the colonial territories and represent a changed attitude towards the paraphernalia of the powerful national state in the Western liberal-democratic societies.

The growth of colonial nationalism is very much a product of the experience and the culture of Western societies. Both the idea of a national society and the demand for its congruence with a sovereign state, although foreshadowed in Antiquity and the Middle Ages, came to prominence in Asia in the 1930s and in Africa in the 1940s and 1950s. By 1985, the "process of decolonization" was practically complete. The aspirants to sovereignty and the rulers who executed it were not willing to reinstate their pre-colonial condition. They wished to become "modern" almost in the style of the societies analyzed by Max Weber as specifically Western. They wanted a rational bureaucratic state, rational scientific industrial technology, modern institutions such as armies, universities, hospitals. Since they arrived late on the historical scene, they absorbed social democratic and quasi-communist aspirations. Hence, they desired economic planning rather than the market. Although they usually began with the desire for political democracy, parliamentary government, the rule of law, competitive elections with a plurality of political parties, freedom of expression and the rest of the panoply of political democracy, these concepts were the first victims of the hard life of self-government. In very many of these countries, civilian governments moved towards the one-party state: first civilian, then military. In some of the new states, the changes in regimes are rapid. Coups d'état in Black Africa have become as characteristic of the regimes there as they became in Latin America after those societies gained sovereignty about a century earlier. These changes in regimes were frequently justified by the newly ensconced rulers as necessitated by the urgent, all-overriding aim of economic development through the mobilization of all resources. The aim has not been realized except in those few states that have abstained from the temptations and pretences of a centrally planned economy. Although most of these states have increased their industrial and agricultural production, and have received considerable financial assistance from their former rulers and other Western societies and international organizations, their populations have grown more rapidly than their economies; their governments have expanded their bureaucracies and spent more than their resources. In consequence, inflation, corruption and resentment are rife on the part of those sections of the population who think that others are being disproportionately favored by governmental policies. All disorder and misgovernment notwithstanding, in most of the new sovereign territories the standard of living has risen for the new middle class and a larger percentage of the population has become literate. Urbanization has not destroyed the traditional culture: it has, in some respects, intensified attachment to it; ethnic conflicts have become aggravated and sectionalism has grown more rapidly than civic orientation.

The other great change in the world since Max Weber died is the industrialization of East Asia and particularly of Japan. Japan was already acquiring some of the features of Western societies when Weber was still alive: rationalized legal codes, newspapers, universities, rationalized military and economic organizations. But after 1920, and particularly after the Second World War, Japan adopted and developed much more of the pattern of modern Western societies, except in the traditionalism of its religious beliefs and practices—although here, too, secularization has made much progress—and in the greater reverence for authority.

The third major change since Max Weber's time is the establishment of dictatorial and totalitarian communist regimes in territories of the Russian and Chinese empires. Although both the Soviet Union and the People's Republic of China are very inimical towards Western liberal-democratic societies, and are particularly hostile towards the capitalist economies of the West, they both seek to promote the rational scientific technology of the West by reproducing it or purchasing it. They emulate the Western objects of their aggressive attitudes, claiming to have overcome illiteracy by universal education; they are emphatically secularized; they would extirpate the traditional culture; they are, at least in declaration, wholly scientific in their view of the world. Like the impoverished, disorganized and disorderly new states of Asia and Africa, the ideals which their elites allege to pursue are drawn from what they regard as the major features of modern Western societies. Although, in their political arrangements, they depart most widely from the pattern of those societies, they claim nonetheless to be democratic! Non-Western societies have, by and large, changed very much since Max Weber's lifetime; their changes have been engendered mainly through their ambition to become like Western societies.

Much of the modern Western society, of which Max Weber was the great analyst, has continued to exist: the belief in the necessity of economy and efficiency, the belief in the value of scientific knowledge and scientific technology, the belief that rewards should be commensurate with achievements, the belief that citizenship confers prerogatives which are not to be granted to non-residents living within the same national territory. These beliefs, somewhat eroded, and with some ebbing and rising, have many adherents, and even those who reject them do not do so wholeheartedly. Patriotism still persists, as do nationality and nationalism. Private enterprise oriented towards profit in a competitive market also still exists, quite vigorously. Religious belief still exists, as do believing priests and ministers, and believing laymen. The Western world is far from wholly secularized. Deference towards authority still exists, as does obedience to the commands of authority. The attitudes and institutions that have taken shape in the sixty-five years since the death of Max Weber, and particularly in the forty years since the end of the Second World War, have not by any means completely replaced the institutions and attitudes that prevailed earlier. Nevertheless, despite similarities and continuities, real changes in those societies have occurred. They are for the most part extensions and unfoldings of traditions already present in Max Weber's lifetime. Nothing has sprung into life by a disjunctive mutation. Nonetheless, the unfolding from a state of potentiality in a tradition is different from that same tradition when what was potential had still not become unfolded. (The formation in Asia and Africa and Eastern Europe of societies possessing some of the features of modern Western societies, or at least striving to do so, has not occurred in consequence of the unfolding of indigenous traditions.) The question that I wish to put is: are Max Weber's ideas, as we can construct them from his writings, adequate or helpful to understand the world of Western—and non-Western—societies, as it has taken shape since his time?

IV

In one respect, Max Weber's account of the society of his time remains more pertinent to the societies of our time than it was in that earlier phase of modern societies. This is his idea of the preponderance, the central importance, of bureaucracy. Max Weber was not the first to see this in its most general outlines. Alexis de Tocqueville, in the second volume of *De la Démocratie en Amérique,* published in 1840, had pointed out the unceasing progress of the regulatory power of central government. Max Weber gave a more refined analysis of the character of bureaucratic administration than Tocqueville or any other writer before or since. Our depiction and understanding of the present could not begin without Max Weber's account of bureaucracy as the characteristic mode of administration of a government legitimated, in his terminology, on rational-legal grounds.

Max Weber thought that bureaucracy would triumph over all other alternative types of administration because it was the most efficient. He thought that a bureaucracy could consolidate itself in power because it possessed expert knowledge and, because it could withhold that knowledge, it could gain the upper hand over the legislature. He thought that once a bureaucracy became dominant in a government it could not be dislodged from its position except by charismatic leadership on the part of the elected politicians. He did not, however, say just how this process of overpowering the stronghold of a bureaucracy by charismatic politicians would be effected. His account of why bureaucratic authority would be difficult to dislodge is still valid; his argument that a charismatic political leader can reverse the directions in which bureaucracy presses remains plausible. But the evidence for it is scanty, indeed for the very reason that bureaucrats have such tenacious resistive power, and not many politicians can overcome it. The experience of the Reagan administration in the United States and the Thatcher administration in Great Britain are instances of the difficulties experienced by powerful elected politicians in resisting and setting aside the power of the bureaucracy.

In his admiration for the efficacy of bureaucracies, Max Weber did not consider the possibility that a bureaucracy, expanded to such an extent in size and in the complexity and numbers of its tasks as bureaucracies have been in these past six and a half decades, might not be able to act successfully. The complexity of the tasks delegated to it and arrogated by it and the multiplicity of the interconnections of those tasks, as well as an illusionary faith in its capacity to carry out every task and any sets of tasks, have in fact resulted in many failures of bureaucracies to cope effectively with the tasks that they have undertaken. It is true that they do more than has ever been done before, but they often fall far short of their own objectives, which sometimes are not only not fulfilled but are in fact turned into results very different and frequently contrary to what has been sought.

What Max Weber had to say about bureaucracy obviously does not present an adequate account of the growth, vicissitudes, triumphs and failures of bureaucracy since his death. Nevertheless, he, more than any other writer of his own age and probably since, compelled observers to perceive the bureaucratic component of modern societies. His picture of the structure and the consequences—failures and repercussions— and the problems of controlling its growth and action are in need of revision, but only revision and not rejection.

According to Max Weber, the continuous expansion of rationalization was a major feature of modern society; bureaucratization is only one manifestation of this process. Rationalization is a process that takes many forms. It is operative in the organization of civil government and of armies; it is operative in economic life. It is no less present in the effort to understand the world by empirical scientific research and by systematic speculation; it is present in the organization of education and scientific research. It is certainly present in the organization of the media of mass communication as well as in the publication of literary and scientific works.

It is no less present in the substance of intellectual activities, above all in the study of nature, man and society. Here also Max Weber's analysis presents a fruitful approach to the understanding of modern societies, both Western and non-Western. One of Max Weber's most persisting observations about modern Western societies was his view that they had become *entzaubert*. Taken literally, *Entzauberung* is the denial of the validity of propositions asserting the existence of the powers that are dealt with by magical techniques; in that sense, it does not include spiritual forces that are not manipulated by magical techniques. In fact, however, Max Weber regarded the *Entzauberung der Welt* as the elimination of both magical and spiritual forces from the picture of the world; he regarded the refusal to acknowledge these powers as a culmination of one current of the process of rationalization. Other writers, less melodramatically and with less insight into its constitution and its affinity with other movements of belief and practice, have called this process "secularization." The process of *Entzauberung* was not complete in Max Weber's time but, discerning its steady expansion in the development of Western theological thought and, in modern times, in the various spheres of social life, Weber seems to have thought that, in the course of time, the eradication of belief in magical and spiritual forces would be complete.

Max Weber was not the first to anticipate such a development. It had been both a factual prediction and a desideratum for Condorcet; Comte took for granted that it would occur in the course of the nineteenth century or shortly thereafter, once the "positive" method found universal acceptance. Since most of the important sociologists of the nineteenth and twentieth centuries were not believers in the existence of magical and spiritual forces, and since they believed that the prospectively dominant and already visible trend of opinion in the most "progressive" societies was the increasingly unencumbered expansion of the dominion of reason and sense-experience, they anticipated a totally secular society, a society without religious beliefs. The expectation of a wholly secular future was, thus, not a discovery of Max Weber. His originality consisted in placing the secularization of belief in the wider setting of the rationalization of practically all spheres of life. He was not really consistent when he left open the possibility of a recursion to less secularized beliefs. His profundity consisted, however, in his assertion that the secularization of the world must inevitably leave unanswered the question concerning the meaning of cosmic and earthly existence. The ultimate meaninglessness of the world for those who believe that scientific knowledge is the only valid kind of knowledge was stressed in "Science As a Vocation"; he had already intimated that at the end of the *Protestant Ethic,* but he said nothing about the lasting and universal predominance of a view of the world that left that question unanswered.

Weber gave much attention to theodicy in the world religions: that is, to their efforts to provide a rational justification for the anomaly of the prosperity of the wicked on earth and the sufferings of the good. He is strikingly silent on the position of theodicy in the secularized rationalization of beliefs in his own time; he suggested that its place had been taken, in the outlook of the modern working man, by a naturalistic view of the world, which interpreted the anomalous injustices of the world as the products of a historically changing, economically determined social system. A belief in the rightfulness of a regime of equality in this world could be interpreted as a secular rectification of the anomalous injustice, which a transcendental theodicy placed in the next world.

Whether Max Weber thought of modern egalitarianism in this way cannot be asserted with confidence because he dealt very little with sacred beliefs, and such surrogates as they might have, in the modern society pervaded by *Entzauberung.*

Weber either thought that rather contradictory tendencies would be at work or else he had contradictory views. On the one side, there were religious dispositions, needs for redemption, purification, needs for explaining the meaning of the world, needs for rectifying the injustice that was generated by the evil of this world. On the other side, there was a naturalistic outlook, partly a product of the scientific rationalization of the world, partly a product of religious insensitivity and of the experience of coping effectively with the biological and ecological necessities of individual and collective survival in this world. Max Weber did not deal explicitly with the balance of these two tendencies in the modern world and, hence, it cannot be said that the period which followed his lifetime has confirmed or invalidated his view, since his own beliefs in this matter are obscure.

The fact remains, however, that the rationalization of the world has not by any means taken complete possession of the whole of any Western society. There are still many Christians in Protestant countries; there is an even larger proportion of observant Christians in the Southern European Latin countries and in North America. Among those who call themselves non-believers, many adhere to fragments of traditional Christian belief; many ostensible non-believers have recourse to traditional Christian ceremonials for christening, marriage and burial. Furthermore, charismatic religious enthusiasm thrives in most Western societies, not only among the less educated but among the more highly educated as well. It is perhaps even more common now than it was sixty years ago, although it was not rare then, especially in Protestant countries. The churches as institutions now have fewer prerogatives in the non-ecclesiastical sphere, but the activities of churchmen in that sphere are numerous and not wholly without influence among the many competitors for the attention of the public. There are probably no countries in the West today where secularized politicians think that they may disregard the views of the leading churchmen. The *Entzauberung der Welt* is far from complete in the sphere of religious beliefs. Despite Weber's apparent conviction about the drive towards *Entzauberung,* much of his discussion of the grounds of religious belief throws light on the recalcitrance of religious belief in the face of this movement of *Entzauberung.*

In non-Western countries, where the process of secularization never advanced as far as it has in the West, there has been a traditionalistic resurgence of religious beliefs. This has been especially true of the Islamic societies. This is a subject with which Max Weber did not deal. It goes without saying that he did not write about the syncretistic religious movements in Black Africa. Yet in both cases an approximation to understanding is afforded by his discussions of the Israelitic prophecy and his observations about salvational religions.

Science is a body of knowledge that corresponds most closely to the ideal type of rationalization. That is the way in which Max Weber saw it. Nevertheless, the entire body of scientific knowledge has never been wholly rationalized into a single unitary system. Such a unitary system of knowledge is, however, a postulate of scientific explanation; the growth of scientific knowledge is in part a subsumption of particular observations under more general, more abstract propositions. The now very numerous profession of science has for a long time been inclined to think that, in the course of time, a wholly rationalized account of the universe and of human existence will be produced; many non-scientists believe the same. They also believe that this rationalized body of scientific knowledge will also provide valid criteria of ethical judgement as well. These views are shared by many laymen.

Max Weber did no more than touch on the social and cultural consequences of the belief in the rationalizability of the world. He criticized the scientific position when he assessed the power of social-scientific knowledge to arrive at evaluative judgements, both political and moral; he criticized scientism more profoundly when he pointed out the incapacity of scientific knowledge to disclose the ultimate meaning of life and the ultimate criteria of choice in practical action. A realistic account of the world as we know it would require that the consequences of scientism for modern society and culture be reckoned with. It would have been consistent with Max Weber's views about modern Western society and culture to have observed this spread of scientism and to have discussed the relationship between bureaucratization and scientism. He did not do so, but what he did do, in fact, opened the possibility of our identification and understanding of the belief in scientific solutions to moral and political problems.

It should also be pointed out that belief in the ultimate scientific rationalization of the world has not been universally shared in modern Western societies, even by scientists whose thought was taken by Max Weber to be the prototypical rationalization of symbolic configurations. There have always been scientists who have not shared the scientistic view and, in recent years, many scientists have lost their confidence in the rationalizability of the universe by scientific discovery. Some assert the complementarity of religious faith—most often, Christian religious faith—and scientific knowledge. Others speak more vaguely of the "two spheres," the conflict-less and separate existences of faith and science. "Values" are repeatedly emphasized in the non-scientific discourse of scientists addressing laymen. The scientific rationalization of the world has many supporters, but there are also many who do not regard it as having been achieved in the present or likely to be achieved in the future.

Thus, the belief in the ultimate scientific rationalization of the world view might have lost some of its adherents in recent decades. At the same time, the belief in the desirability of the rationalization of the management and strategy of enterprises in industry and agriculture, and particularly of governments, has continued to gain adherents in the period under consideration. (Max Weber himself, with some qualifications, could be counted among these adherents.)

The promotion of the study of the social sciences and the support of social research (although it is partly prompted out of the social scientists' desire for rational understanding, i.e., the cognitive rationalization, of the real world) is supported by its patrons mainly because they think that it will help to "solve social problems." Earlier in the present century, it was thought that the "solution" would lie in making the problematic sectors of society subject to "rational self-control"; now it is thought to lie in the rational rearrangement of institutions and governmental practices. A large part of the history of modern social science is to be understood as one element in the hope of rationalizing society, both cognitively and practically. This is largely a matter of aspiration; the realization inevitably lags considerably behind.

Max Weber's effort to understand the world sociologically was part and parcel of that process of intellectual rationalization. He also went to some pains, in his essay on *Wertfreiheit*, to show what social science could contribute to the rationalization of decisions about practical social matters; he thought that, at least in principle, it could throw light on the costs of carrying out practical decisions; it could clarify, i.e., make more rational, the analysis of objectives, the means of achieving them and the consequence of using those means. His own attempts to understand the intellectual and practical potentialities of social science, despite vast changes in the scale and technical sophistication of social research, continues to provide the best point of departure for the analysis of the relationship between social science and social policy.

Weber's belief in the possibility and necessity of the scientific rationalization of society and the effort to apply it in practice is a ramification of his conception of bureaucratization. Rationalized bureaucratic practices and the application of scientific knowledge now affect larger proportions of the population than they did in Max Weber's time, and they affect them in more departments of their existence. This, too, is in accord with Max Weber's analysis; indeed he did in fact predict this expansion. They were not predicted in a particular form by Max Weber, but they are intelligible only in the setting of his analysis. Likewise, the developments in econometrics, systems-analysis, social psychology and "management-science" were unforeseen in their particulars by Max Weber, but their application can best be understood in accordance with his view about the continuing rationalization, i.e., bureaucratization, of modern societies. Nonetheless, the scope and penetration of bureaucratization are far greater now than they were in Max Weber's lifetime. Moreover, the aspiration to increase the rationalization of society is, if not more intense, then at least unabated. Our understanding of these changes, at least descriptively, has been rendered possible by the prior absorption of Max Weber's ideas. The fact that we raise these questions about the degree of rationalization means that we are putting questions and proffering answers to them that have been made possible by Max Weber's own questions, although he did not describe the situations that we now see.

The cognitive and moral disenchantment of the world has, it is true, not gone as far as the rationalization of the organization and management of corporate bodies and the state itself. That too is incomplete. Even though Max Weber's anticipation of the "disenchantment of the world" has not been realized, our assessment of the limitations of his view could not be rendered without our acceptance of the categories within which he interpreted the world, and within his setting of the problem. In fact, our grasp of the limitations of the process of disenchantment draws on Weber's own elaboration of the conception of charisma and his subsequent analysis of the range of variation of charismatic qualities, between attenuated and intense and between the dispersed and the concentrated distributions of charismatic qualities.

The concept of charisma is a necessary logical presupposition of the analysis of situations in which it is extremely attenuated; Max Weber's idea of routinized charisma was a step towards this further analysis.

Many years ago, I undertook, in the course of an examination of the economic policies of the poor, in recently colonial countries, to try to understand why the political leaders and the higher civil servants in these countries believed that they alone could provide the initiative for the economic improvement of their countries.[1] My knowledge of this matter was not a direct result of applying Max Weber's ideas about charisma; that idea came to me only while I was delivering an address to an academic society about economic policy and public opinion in underdeveloped countries. The idea came to me as I was reading my paper, which contained no reference to charismatic authority. Suddenly, in the course of delivery, the pattern of my thought about the making of economic policy changed; I formulated a distinction between "concentrated" and "dispersed" charismatic qualities. (Later, I added the distinction between "intense" and "attenuated" charismatic qualities.) It turned out to be illuminating to extend the idea of charismatic authority to the beliefs that educated higher civil servants and leading politicians held and to the contrast that they saw between their own

1. For example, see "The Concentration and Dispersion of Charisma: Their Bearing on Economic Policy in Underdeveloped Countries," reprinted in Edward Shils, *Center and Periphery* (ed.).

capacities and those of the rest of the members of their own societies. It could be said that the distinctions which I then formulated were already implicitly contained in Max Weber's work; that might be true, but only in the sense that Weber himself employed the distinctions in reference to particular situations, without making them explicit. Once made, the potentiality of extension—the extensibility of the idea—was realized.

The idea of attenuated charisma was implicit in the concept of charismatic authority as it was formulated by Max Weber, although he himself did not formulate such an idea. The idea of attenuated charisma permits a richer analysis of Weber's ideas about charisma and the *Entzauberung der Welt,* while at the same time enabling us to recognize the limitations of his original formulation of the idea of *Entzauberung.*

The concept of rationalization is similarly extensible. It is valuable for the assessment of the extent to which rationalization has in fact occurred, but it is also valuable for the analysis of situations in which the prospect of ceaselessly advancing rationalization has fallen short and seems bound to fall short of the extreme possibility implied by Max Weber. It puts problems to us regarding an inherent tendency towards self-annulment in the process of rationalization. The further it advances, the more likely its frustration. Max Weber did not discuss such questions directly, except in some passages regarding the limits of the formal rationalization of the legal system, arising from demands for substantive rationality. But he turned our attention to the extension of rationalization, and this itself raised questions about possible causes of its breakdown.

Max Weber was a liberal in the sense that he viewed with abhorrence the growing power of the state at the cost of the freedom of the individual. He was also an unsentimental supporter of the rudimentary welfare state as it existed in Germany in his time, although his grounds for giving support had more to do with its contribution to national solidarity and national strength than they had to do with humanitarian principles or sentiments. Weber was also a democrat, but again with a difference: he was not a democrat because he believed in the rights of man or in popular sovereignty—in fact he derided such ideas—but because he thought that representative institutions are the best of possible arrangements for training and selecting the political leadership which any national society needs to keep its position in the larger competitive world of national societies and to protect the freedom of creative individuals from the constriction of conformity imposed by a powerful bureaucracy. He was far from a "grass-roots democrat." Not only did he have no sympathy with the idea of popular sovereignty, he regarded its realization as plainly impossible. Max Weber believed in the possibility, under modern conditions, of mass democracy—a system of political parties competing for the support of an electorate defined by universal suffrage and then forming a government on the basis of the support given to one of the parties by a majority of the electorate.

Weber did not say why democracy was necessary "under modern conditions." Tocqueville explicitly acknowledged and described the irresistible, onward flow of greater "equality of condition." Weber did not speak in those terms. He did not sympathize with theories of the "rights of man"; he was far from a sentimental exponent of the virtues of the laborious poor; he expressed his contempt for policies concerned to eradicate the misery of the poor, which he disparaged as *Miseribilismus*. His acceptance of democracy probably was inspired by his belief in the value of the national state and of national culture; his democracy probably derived from his nationalism. He thought that the national state could be effective in the world if it were based on a coherent national society and that such a society depended on the attachment of all classes to it. The national society had to incorporate the lower classes, who otherwise would be alienated from it and hostile to it. Because of the large populations of modern societies, democracy had to be "mass democracy." The power of the mass of the electorate was confined, in this view, to a retroactive assessment of what the politicians in office had done and to voting for their retention in or dismissal from office. The only power of the electorate is the power exercised through voting; it has no substantive demands that a politician in office or contending for office must heed, satisfy or distract. "Mass democracy," Weber thought, could work only under the control of "party-machines" and of charismatic leaders. The electorate could initiate nothing, it could only respond to leaders selected by "party-bosses" or by the competition of outstanding individual politicians formed through and brought forward in the electoral and parliamentary struggle. The notion of an electorate that was an effective power with substantive demands of its own and which did more than merely ratify or approve the actions of the political elite was not conceived by him to be possible; certainly it was most unlikely. The idea of politicians quailing before reports of public opinion polls or trimming their sails to gain a few additional percentage points in such a poll, and of calculating their actions to satisfy the specific demands of particular blocs within the electorate had little place in his analysis of political democracy in modern Western societies. To think that political democracy could work in that way would have appeared to him to be the fantasy of sentimental populists and of unrealistically idealistic democrats. His studies of Russian and American politics made him very aware of populism, but he thought that populistic politicians were either sentimental, self-deceiving idealists or demagogues who flattered their audiences.

This was an important gap in Max Weber's views about political systems. A demanding electorate and politicians attentive to its demands were omitted from Max Weber's ideas about modern society. They are features of modern Western society that Max Weber's ideas did not really comprehend. The mass of the electorate is probably not as rational in the perception and pursuit of its own advantage as some theorists of democracy have believed it is, although the possibility should not be wholly dismissed. Nor is the electorate as concerned for the common good as some theorists have thought, although this possibility too should not be completely dismissed. However these things may be, the mass of the electorate, in modern Western societies, especially since the Second World War, is certainly demanding of benefits from its governments and its political leaders. Once the mass of the population became aware of the substantial benefits which it could receive from governments, its demands on government increased. The possibility that this could happen was never articulated by Max Weber.

Is there anything in the body of Max Weber's thought that could help us to fill this gap? I think that Max Weber's own ideas, if extended, contain in a fruitful potentiality the ideas needed to correct his own too limited view of the working of present-day political democracy. It seems to me that the extension of Weber's ideas about charismatic authority does offer such help in the task of attempting to explain the increase in self-assertiveness and demands of the mass of the population in Western societies in the present century. The ordinary man in these societies has increasingly come to believe himself to possess those attributes or qualities that entitle him to the deference of others and to the goods and services related to the enhancement of status that he demands. This does not, of course, explain why the dispersion of beliefs about one's possession of charismatic qualities has occurred so pronouncedly in the last three decades, and why it was so slow to emerge in Germany in Weber's time that he failed to observe it in its embryonic manifestations. (In concrete observation, Max Weber did see this phenomenon as early as 1895 in his inaugural lecture at Freiburg on "The National State and Economic Policy."[2])

2. In attempting to explain why German agricultural laborers were not willing to work as day-workers or seasonal workers on the large East Prussian estates, Weber referred to the conditions of work in the large estates in which there were only masters and drudges, who saw no prospect even for their remote descendants to do anything other than menial labor on someone else's land. "This dim, largely unconscious glimpse into the future contains an element of primitive idealism. One who does not grasp this, does not know the magic of freedom." Later, he says that it is "one of the

Although Weber did not examine the belief in "human rights" and in the dignity of all human beings as a force in conduct, he was well aware that the German working man had a sense of his own dignity that he wished to be acknowledged in German society. The trade unions and the Social Democratic Party were the beneficiaries of that aspiration to dignity. In his discussion of social classes and status groups (no more than a few notes) Weber does not assert any connection between the granting of deference and the acknowledgement of charismatic qualities. Nor does he treat it in his often very sharp observation of citizenship in modern societies. Yet, to make explicit and to emphasize that implied link not only makes Weber's analysis more coherent but it also deepens the discussion of modern political democracy in a way that Weber failed to do himself.

There is another important deficiency in Max Weber's writings, namely, his rather narrow treatment of the grounds for the increase in the power of governmental bureaucracy. Weber thought that bureaucracy became established mainly because rulers saw that it was more efficient and more economical in the use of scarce resources than other types of administration, and that it freed them as rulers from dependence on personal clients and vassals or great landowners, who were their rivals in the struggle for power in their realm. These explanations are sound historically, but they do not contribute much to the explanation of the bureaucratization of governmental administration in the nineteenth and twentieth centuries. It certainly does not explain the great expansion in the size and powers of governmental bureaucracies in the period since Weber's death.

Max Weber also spoke of bureaucratization as one manifestation of a deeper drive towards rationalization, which was integral to Western civilization. More important was his statement that bureaucratization became imperative as the tasks assumed by governments became more

most primordial dispositions of the human heart." *Gesammelte Politische Schriften*, 2d ed. (Tübingen: J. C. B. Mohr, 1958), p. 7 *(ed.)*.

elaborate, required more expert knowledge and skill, more probity and more efficiency. This is true, but why did the bureaucracy and the politicians accept such elaborate and far-reaching tasks and so many of them that the size and the powers of the civil services had to be so greatly increased?

It is at this point that Max Weber's failure to foresee the demands of electorates also carried with it a failure to explain the growth of the bureaucratic authority of government over society as a whole.

It is also at this point that we can see the ways in which certain fundamental ideas, which are implicitly contained in Weber's writings, can serve to correct the deficiencies of what is explicitly stated in them. Weber did not see that some of the impulsion for this drive towards the expansion of the power of central government comes from the electorate working through the legislative branch. Bureaucrats usually do not simply seize power against the will of other parts of the government and against the will of the electorate. It is true that they hold firmly to and try to expand any authority that is conferred on them, but it should not be overlooked that the authority that they have exercised increasingly over society has been conferred on them by actions of the legislature. These actions are impelled partly by the legislature's acceptance of current beliefs about the moral responsibilities and capacities of governments and partly by their desire to conform to the wishes of the more pressing sectors of the electorate, which share these current beliefs. The motive force is the electorate's demands for goods and services to which it thinks itself entitled and the politicians' competition for the suffrage of the electorate. Here, as elsewhere, the correction that I would add is not intended as a refutation of Weber's views but rather as an extension of his fundamental, enduringly valid insight into the characteristics of modern societies. As in so many other sides of an assessment of the relevance of Max Weber's ideas to the understanding of modern societies, his shortcomings can often be corrected by the extension of some of his more basic ideas.

In this review of the fittingness of some of Max Weber's ideas for the understanding of important developments in the Western world that have arisen in the sixty-five years since his death, I should also say something about the hedonism and "emancipationism," i.e., emancipation of impulse from the restraints of reason, convention, institutional rules and tradition, which seem to have displaced in some measure the Protestant ethic. The drive towards the rationalization of economic activity was derived by Max Weber from "the Protestant ethic," that body of normative beliefs arising from the urgent yearning for certainty of eternal salvation, which was the tradition received by various Puritan sects from Calvinism. It was from this source that, according to Max Weber, much of the motivating force for capitalistic enterprise had sprung; it was to be found in the Puritanical attitude towards work as well as in entrepreneurial initiatives.

The sense of obligation in the individual to work steadily and efficiently at a calling and the rationalized discipline of all his activity in the service of an end higher and more remote than immediate sensual gratification represented for Max Weber the most characteristic and unique feature of modern Western societies. Max Weber thought that this Protestant ethic was already in an advanced state of attenuation in his own lifetime; it was with reference to this attenuation that he spoke of the uninspired continuation of the process of rationalization that threatened to lead the world into a rationalized subjugation to bureaucracy—another facet of the comprehension of *Entzauberung* that would penetrate into every sphere of life.

Weber did not anticipate the stagnation or the disruption of the movement towards rationalization, even though it had lost its most powerful motive-force. The process of rationalization, with all the discipline which it entailed, would, he thought, continue; but it would have no meaning without the theological foundation which the progress of *Entzauberung* was undermining. It is certainly true that rationalization continues in institutions and in the quest for scientific knowledge. There are still many individuals to whom rationalization is a good in itself, or who expect substantial improvement from it in economic organization and in the pursuit of truth through scientific research.

In the conduct of individuals outside organizational and scientific activities, however, the self-discipline and the acceptance of external discipline that were manifested respectively in the "Protestant ethic" and in the "spirit of capitalism" have lost much although not all of their force. Emancipation from external and even from internal discipline is the condition that many persons nowadays regard as the right one. The elevation of the immediate gratification of impulse to the highest value certainly existed in Max Weber's time and he was well aware of it. He understood very well the new forms of romantic belief and sensibility at the turn of the century; he was well aware of the antinomic tendencies in modern literature and he was well acquainted with the culture of bohemianism to which he did not refer except in passing in his writings. (He referred contemptuously to *Literaten* but when he did so he did so with reference to the Utopian, doctrinaire or hypernationalistic political ideals of political publicists and literary men; he did not have in mind the "liberation" of impulse, particularly erotic impulse, which was being so highly praised by certain Bohemian intellectuals whom he knew.) He apparently did not think that the Bohemian culture of the free expression of impulse would ever find a large following; he did not quite perceive the significance of what he disparaged as the desire to be a "personality."

Nevertheless, this has happened, and what was once the culture of a very small circle within a generally self-disciplined society—or one which at least justified the principle of self-discipline in pursuit of careers and in familial and sexual relations—has now become much more widespread in most Western societies than it was in his time. In part, this could be deduced—after the fact—from Max Weber's views about the decay of the Protestant ethic, but it is also in certain respects antithetical to his ideas about the unceasingness of the process of rationalization.

Max Weber's writings on religion are full of penetrating remarks about orgiastic and mystical religiosity which breaks through or circumvents institutional religious practice and traditionally set religious beliefs. He also defined a basic category of individual action which he called "affectual." Yet, in the rest of his writings, he did not anticipate these phenomena consequent on the evaporation of the Puritanical motive underlying the movement of rationalization. Throughout his writings, sensual gratification and impulse-dominated conduct are regarded as overwhelmed by conduct directed by individual or group "interest" (meaning the desire for pecuniary benefits and advantages of power and deference) and by beliefs, mainly traditional, in the validity of certain norms or rules.

Weber was well aware that actions to gratify affective impulse and to enjoy sensual pleasures existed and could never be expunged from human life, but he seems to have thought that they were not likely to be very widely practiced in any society. He was probably more right than wrong in this view. Human beings can never become exclusively biological organisms, orienting their actions primarily towards biological gratifications. Nevertheless, such an idea has nowadays considerably more adherence in principle and in practice than it had in Max Weber's time; more individuals think that the gratification of impulse and the experience of emotions are of the highest importance. This is in one respect a by-product of the *Entzauberung der Welt,* but it is also a consequence of the relocation of the site of charisma. Max Weber's failure to attribute more importance in his writings to this element indeed presents a shortcoming in any literal application of his ideas to the world since 1920. Its correction entails, however, only an extension of some of his ideas and an elaboration of their potentialities. In a perverse way, contemporary emancipationism is a manifestation of the dispersion of charisma; it is a manifestation of the phenomenon to which Weber himself alluded in his understanding of those sects of extreme Protestantism that insisted that all individuals have within themselves a spark of divinity.

Max Weber, sympathetic though he was towards the industrial working classes, often although not always thought of the lower classes—the working and clerical classes—as rather amorphous, uninspired aggregations, except in times of crises when their charismatic receptiveness and their attractability by charismatic initiative were heightened. He thought that Puritanism had stirred, maintained and disciplined this sensitivity. Nonetheless, apart from this moment of creativity, the lower classes seemed to him to be singularly unproductive. Intellectuals, priests, prophets, charismatic persons were required, if they were to be animated; otherwise, they were only capable of responding, they could not initiate. There is undoubtedly some truth in this view, but it is like some of Weber's other ideas, which require correction if we are to understand this most recent age.

It certainly would be too much to say that the lower classes have become creative in the sixty-five years since Max Weber's death, but they have certainly become less inert and less confined to reacting to external situations. They make more "demands on life" now than they did formerly and this involves more demands on persons in positions of authority. The demands might be said to be largely for the enhancement of their material advantages—"interests" as the current idiom has it—but they are also demands with moral or ideal content. Even what they regard as the objects of their "interests" are things that they think they are morally entitled to have. They feel more justification for making these demands; suffrage is for them not merely a way of selecting leaders but of communicating, in however blurred and inchoate a manner, an indication to those leaders of what they want from them and of what they are "entitled" to, by virtue of their dignity as citizens and human beings. Modern democracy, for better or worse, is a phenomenon of the dispersion of charisma. Weber intimated as much in his occasional remarks, but he did not do so in his main sociological writings. The failure to state this explicitly, and to incorporate it into his analysis of social stratification, is one of the shortcomings of Max Weber's work. The correction of this failure is made possible, here as elsewhere, by the opening up of the potentialities of some of his own ideas.

V

Finally, I wish to refer to the applicability of Max Weber's ideas to the new states of Asia and Africa. Max Weber's beliefs did not foresee the end of the European empires in Asia and Africa. Weber did not interest himself in colonial societies; there are practically no references to modern Indian society in *Hinduismus und Buddhismus*. He was certainly acutely aware of "imperialism" and his brief discussion of the subject is full of shrewd and illuminating observations. But on the societies subjugated by imperialism he is practically silent.

Max Weber regarded it as in the nature of things for "great powers" to be expansive as a condition for "holding their own" in the universal struggle for existence. Expansion entailed—at least in most cases— colonies. He accepted the existence of colonies, although he thought imperial Germany had come too late upon the scene to acquire colonies. Colonies were not as central to Max Weber's sociological ideas as rationality, and it is not surprising, therefore, that he did not give much attention to social developments in colonial societies.

Nevertheless, it is not unreasonable to raise the question of whether we can find in his writing ideas that are fruitfully applicable to the understanding of the course of events in the new states of Asia and Africa. There are a few instances where the conception of charismatic authority is directly applicable: for example, in the cases of some of the great figures of the movements for independence such as Gandhi, Soekarno, Nkrumah, Ho Chi Minh. The tension between the charismatic leader and the bureaucratic party-machine needed for the organization of the movement and then for the ruling of the new state may also be interpreted directly in his terms. Apart from these instances, his writings are silent. Nevertheless, as in the analysis of the developments in Western societies after 1920, many clues to understanding can be derived from his fundamental ideas.

The most important of these clues come only from a considerable extension of Weber's explicitly stated ideas. Let us take as one example the ideals of the founders and the first leaders of the new states, particularly the idea of a unitary "modern" society, bureaucratically administered, with popular elections to a representative legislative body, a planned or rationalized industrial economy with bureaucratic governmental control over agriculture, a bureaucratically organized army, the employment of scientific technology in industry and agriculture. Such ideas were not indigenous; they were acquired from models perceived, correctly or incorrectly, as practiced in advanced societies such as the United States, Great Britain, France, Holland and the Soviet Union, which were the centers for the peripheral societies of Asia and Africa.

Now, the ideas of center and periphery are not to be found in Max Weber's writings, neither in his analyses of the working of modern societies nor in his much scantier analyses of the relations between societies. Yet, the ideas of center and periphery, as I have developed them in my own studies and as others have done since then, owe a great deal to the elaboration and extension of the idea of charisma.[3] The instabilities of the new states, the weakness of their internal "modern" center, the strength of the primordial attachments of the lineages, tribes, ethnic and linguistic groups in these newly constituted states, which in many respects scarcely form national societies, become more intelligible to contemporary students of the subject through an amplification, which Max Weber did not envisage, of ideas contained in his writings.

VI

In these observations, which are intended to show that Max Weber's ideas still have value for the understanding of relative developments in Western liberal-democratic societies and in other societies outside

3. See "Center and Periphery," in Edward Shils, *Center and Periphery,* and Edward Shils, "Center and Periphery: An Idea and Its Career," in L. Greenfeld and M. Martin, eds., *Center: Ideas and Institutions* (Chicago: University of Chicago Press, 1988) *(ed.).*

the circle of modern Western societies, I have had no intention of vindicating Max Weber's standing as a sociological interpreter of the modern age. It is far from my desire to assert that all that Max Weber said is true or that all that needs to be done is to go on studying his texts and interpreting them. I do not intend to imply that there is a "fundamental Weber" whose fundamental ideas have been misunderstood and distorted by those who have hitherto studied his writings. There are many features of Western and especially non-Western societies as they have developed since 1920 for which Max Weber's ideas do not provide any illumination. I think here, for example, of the Holocaust of European Jewry by the National Socialist regime, but there are others. There are also other features of these societies about which Weber's ideas were simply not correct; I think here of the limits on the capacities of bureaucracies to carry out any policies which are assigned to them or which they arrogate to themselves.

Nevertheless, it has seemed clear to me that there is more in Max Weber's ideas than what he formulated explicitly, and that what is below the surface of his texts contains possibilities for understanding the world as it is which are richer than what is on the surface in the text. This does not mean that any effort to study modern societies must begin with an exegesis on Weber's writings. On the contrary, all that I am recommending is that classics of the sort in which Weber's works are comprised should be read freely and not just exegetically. There is a place for exegesis in intellectual history, but not in sociological analysis. What I have tried to show in this paper, on the basis of my own experience with Max Weber's writings and my own studies, is that classics have a continuing intellectual value for understanding the world. They have a life beyond themselves.

Max Weber touched on the deepest elements of the existence of human societies. The elements he touched are of permanent importance. But these elements appear in human history in different forms and combinations. The elements themselves are difficult to define precisely; there are almost inevitable ambiguities. These ambiguities are sometimes obstacles to understanding and sometimes fruitful. Max Weber's ambiguities were more often fruitful than obstructive. They contained within themselves potentialities for extension to situations with respect to which they were not originally propounded. They are susceptible to reinterpretation, extension and above all correction; they have the great merit, because of their pregnancy, of permitting and even compelling these reinterpretations, extensions and corrections. That is why so many of Max Weber's ideas are still of living value for understanding a world that is, in so many ways, very different from the one in which he lived.

The very rough, very general portrayal of some of the chief features of the Western societies of the past sixty-five years, and the even sketchier references to non-Western societies which have been essayed here, and the no less unrefined assessment of the utility of Max Weber's ideas for the understanding of that society which he did not live to know, throw some light on the after-life—the *Nachleben*—of great works of social and political analysis. Their greatness, their standing as classics, consist not just in their simple and straightforward applicability to the historical situations that their authors themselves did not know, but in an application through interpretation which draws out ideas that were not originally and knowingly formulated in them.

It is in the nature of the subject-matter of political and social theory that it changes through time. It does not change in every respect. Societies remain societies bound by the compelling necessities that are inherent in the nature of human beings and the societies that are formed from them. No two situations are identical and no society remains the same through time. The quality that constitutes a classic of social and political analysis is its pertinence to the understanding of the unforeseen societies that have grown out of antecedent societies.

The analytical process or the logical structure of the drawing out of the potentialities of an idea is very obscure. This drawing out is done, even though it is very difficult to say how it is done. The value of an idea—not its only value—lies in its possession of such potentialities.

Such potentialities cannot be foreseen by their authors. They can only be seen by those who, at a time later than the time of their authorship, modified and adapted those ideas. Works that are constituted by such ideas are the classics in their fields. The classics are not merely historical monuments, fixed and settled forever. They must also be capable of a vital after-life through reinterpretation. Treated in this way, they are capable of directing thought on to unforeseen objects and to new tasks.

There are undoubtedly sociological questions of importance that Max Weber's ideas, whether in their literal form or in their potentiality—their unintended variant—cannot answer. That should be recognized. It should also be recognized that the labor of maintaining Max Weber's reputation is not a worthy activity. Max Weber's reputation does not need that vindication. There is no need for those who study Max Weber's works to adopt that protective attitude, which devotees of Marx and Engels have often taken when they sought to vindicate the theory of surplus-value or the theory of increasing poverty or of relations between "substructure" and "superstructure."

An intellectual tradition should not be regarded as sacrosanct. For those who live within it, as sociologists cannot avoid living within the tradition in which Max Weber is the greatest figure, the task must be to use it as well as it can be used. Its shortcomings must not be disregarded, but the fertility that it contains and the intellectual benefits that it offers to deeper understanding of the world—and not just of the text—should not be eschewed. Respect for a tradition should rest not just on the praise that it acquired in the past, but on its present merit as a point of departure for better understanding and deeper, more realistic knowledge.

The Modern University
and Liberal Democracy

§

A<small>T A TIME</small> when the governments of liberal-democratic societies attribute so much importance to universities, and when many publicists and university administrators and teachers respond symmetrically, it is desirable to give some thought to the relations between liberal-democratic societies and universities.

The first thing to be said is that the university as a particular type of institution is not a creation of liberal-democratic society. If we take the long stretch of seven centuries when universities became integral parts of European countries, and when despite numerous ups and downs in their achievements, they had many achievements in science and learning to their credit, it is obvious that the period of their establishment was not a period of liberal democracy. Some of the distinctive features of universities—of the universities of the past century and a half as well as those of earlier centuries—were settled in these early centuries. Instruction at an advanced level, the pursuit and transmission of fundamental truths, institutional autonomy and financial support by external powers, are now in practice and at least in declaration, characteristic of universities everywhere. These features were certainly fixed long before the emergence of the liberal-democratic order which took root over the past two centuries. They were the creations of the medieval and early modern churches, absolutist mon-

Previously published in *Minerva* 27 (Winter 1989): 425–60. Reprinted by permission.

archies and empires, princely states and oligarchical municipalities, and commercial republics.

The Impact of Liberal Ideas on Universities

The American universities and the American colleges which later became universities—for example, Harvard, Yale and Princeton—unlike the great European universities, were all founded in a time when what we now call liberal ideas were being much discussed by philosophers and publicists. Nevertheless, the ideas which presided over the founding of American universities and colleges in the earliest years of the eighteenth century, were not the ideas of liberal democracy. The private colleges established before the Revolutionary War and the formation of the United States were not intended to serve a liberal democracy. They were intended to instruct young men who would enter the clergy or who might play a part of significance in oligarchical colonial societies. Neither in their course of study, nor in their policy of recruitment, nor in the careers towards which they sought to guide the youths who were under their care, did they think of a democratic society. There was no expectation that colleges and universities would educate a large part of the generation between the ages of 15 and 22, nor was there any intention that the institutions of higher education in the colonial period would take their places as exemplars or propagators of liberal ideals. There certainly was no notion that they would enable their graduates to contribute to the wealth of their society. Fragmentary approximations began to appear in the eighteenth century. The universities and colleges of the newly independent United States offered curricula which were much influenced by the undergraduate courses of study at the ancient British universities, teaching mainly mathematics and classics. They did not regard the classics as subjects contributing to the training of citizens of a liberal society, although the study of Cicero, Aristotle and Locke did help to form the minds of the founders of the republic.

The American colleges and universities began to introduce subjects drawn from the Scottish universities—moral philosophy, political economy and the history of civilization. In this way they were affected by the Scottish Enlightenment. The first opening of American higher education to liberal ideas came with the establishment of the University of Virginia by Thomas Jefferson. (Jefferson had recruited and appointed teachers from Scotland. Some of these later returned to University College London, thus bringing to that college, which was already under Benthamite influence, Scottish ideas about higher education admixed with Jeffersonian liberal rationalism.) The writings of Adam Smith began to appear in the syllabuses of the American colleges and universities. With them came a breath of European liberalism in its beginnings.

LIBERAL SKEPTICISM ABOUT UNIVERSITIES

Liberal thinkers did not have an especially high opinion of universities, not did they think that they had any great part to play in liberal society. In France, neither Tocqueville nor Constant thought seriously about universities, and they had no great expectations that they would contribute much to the effective operation of free institutions. In Scotland, Adam Smith had a rather low opinion of universities and university teachers, although he was a university teacher for a great part of his life. He certainly did not regard universities as the intellectual engines of liberal society. John Stuart Mill did not expect any great help for liberalism or democracy from universities. (Von Humboldt's ideas about the *Grenzen der Wirksamkeit des Staates* were taken up in part by John Stuart Mill in his *Essay on Liberty*, but not his ideas about universities.)

The vocation of the university was differently seen in Germany. Belief in the formation of the character of cultivated autonomous individuals was much more the product of idealistic German philosophical thought. Fichte's idea of "the calling of the scholar" could be said to be a liberal idea, but it did not envisage the individual as a citizen in a liberal society as much as it did the individual as an end in himself. Freedom was necessary for the development of character, of a harmonious whole within the individual, rather than as a condition which would enable the individual to pursue his own freely chosen ends by the use of his own reasoning powers and his own cognitive assessment of the situation of his action.

The first influence of liberalism in European universities occurred with Wilhelm von Humboldt's memorandum on "the state of our learned institutions," from which emerged the University of Berlin. The liberalism expressed in the memorandum was the idealistic liberalism which looked to the universities for the formation of the character of the autonomous cultivated individual. The ideals of the unity of research and teaching (*Einheit der Forschung und Lehre*), the freedom of teaching and learning (*Freiheit der Lehre und des Lernens*) and of academic self-government (*akademische Selbstverwaltung*), were liberal ideals but they were not products of the individualistic liberalism of British provenience. Von Humboldt did not think of the practical utility of what is discovered and taught in universities, although he took for granted that they would produce higher civil servants educated in law. Nor did he think of universities as providing training for civility in the leadership of society. The highest good to which universities would contribute was the formation of individuality or character and the means to this was the disciplined, methodical search for truth, i.e., free and unhampered research. The ideal of academic freedom became an integral feature of universities of many countries in the nineteenth century, not least of those with quite a different tradition of liberalism.

Academic Freedom:
Humboldtian and Benthamite Liberalism

The academic freedom which became a major part of the program and constitution of the German university was a different sort of thing from what academic freedom became much later in the United States. As propounded in Germany, it was intended to culminate in the realization of the autonomous character. For that, freedoms of the kind mentioned were necessary. It also required the civil or political freedom of academics, but that was not an end—only a means. The justification for the political freedom of the academic later became a most important element in the argument for academic freedom, when that ideal began to be discussed in American universities in the last two decades of the nineteenth century and throughout the twentieth century. This was a significant change in part of the substance of a tradition consequent on the shift from idealistic to rational-individualistic liberalism.

Another point of contact between liberalism—individualistic and utilitarian—and the foundation of universities is to be seen in the history of University College London. This institution was founded by the liberal utilitarians led by Lord Brougham and George Grote, the historian of Greek liberty—under the inspiration of Jeremy Bentham. One of the main intentions of the founding Benthamites was to offer higher education for the offspring of the professional and business classes at a lower cost than at Oxford and Cambridge. Insofar as it was the intention of liberals to promote the middle classes, then the foundation of University College London could be said to have been a step in the direction of a liberal and to some extent democratic society. But the intention was not clear and unambiguous. University College London became the first institution of higher education in England to cultivate the full range of modern academic subjects, and its development was parallel to and in frequent contact with the German universities as they were developing in the nineteenth century under the influence of von Humboldt's liberal ideas and of the University of Berlin, which embodied those ideas. University College London was a liberal institution also in the sense that it deliberately refused to have any requirements of subscription to any church or religious belief as a condition of admission as a student or appointment as a teacher.

STATE AND PRIVATE UNIVERSITIES

In the United States, when the new republic launched itself on its career, state universities were formed mainly in the states (recently colonies) in which there were no dominant private established colleges. For example, Massachusetts, Connecticut, New Jersey and New York had no state universities until very recently, since they already had Harvard College, Yale College, Princeton University and Columbia College (called King's College during the colonial period). The first state universities, formed in the southern seaboard states, were little different from privately founded and supported colleges. Private colleges and universities continued to be created in the United States throughout the nineteenth century, even in states which had state universities. In Great Britain, the major modern universities—London, Manchester, Birmingham, Leeds and Liverpool—were founded by private initiative and they were also supported almost entirely by private patronage. Private patronage is still very important to American colleges and universities, even to some of the leading state universities.

Liberal-democratic societies are pluralistic societies; voluntary associations and free corporate bodies, privately founded and conducted, are parts of their constitutions. Yet the independent private creation of a university has, with the exceptions of the United States and Great Britain and territories which were once parts of the British Empire, been very rare. The Université libre de Bruxelles founded in 1834, the Vrije Universiteit of Amsterdam founded in 1880, the Libera università di Economia e Commercio "Luigi Bocconi" of Milan founded in 1902, probably had none to follow in their footsteps until the University College (University since 1983) of Buckingham in Great Britain founded in 1973, and several institutions in Western Germany.

It is sometimes thought that private universities and colleges in liberal-democratic societies enjoy a greater measure of autonomy and academic freedom than do universities which are supported by government and which are legally under the jurisdiction of the state. This would seem to be the case in principle. In fact, however, there are numerous exceptions. Although the modern British universities were private universities, in the sense that the term is understood in the United States, and their teachers have accordingly had exceptionally wide academic and civil freedoms, this was almost as true of the German universities—all of them state universities—from the foundation of the German Empire in 1871 until the accession of Hitler. In contrast with these, in the United States, there were some infringements of academic freedom and relatively numerous infringements of the civil freedom of college and university teachers, both in state and in private universities. The United States Constitution provided for the separation of church and state; many colleges and some universities were founded and governed by churches. In the institutions which were under ecclesiastical authority, there were many infringements on the freedom of their teachers in their teaching, their civil activities and in their private affairs.

The investigative commissions established by legislative bodies have not hesitated to take private universities into their purview; of course, the private universities have been less susceptible to the sanctions of legislation—only a few of them have had the courage to resist the demand for restrictions on academic freedom.

Liberalism and the Development of Universities on the European Continent

GERMANY

The German academic profession in the first half of the nineteenth century was not only permeated by the liberal ideals of the freedom of research and teaching; it was also liberal in its public political activities. The liberalism of the "Göttingen seven," who were dismissed for their criticism of the unconstitutional activities of the King of Hanover in 1837, lived on in the German revolution of 1848 when, in the liberal parliament meeting in Frankfurt, about one third of the deputies were university professors.

After the unification of Germany in 1871, political liberalism faded from the German academic profession but the liberal ideals of the unity of research and teaching, of the freedom of teaching and study, and of academic self-government did not fade. They persisted undiminished. Even in the period of the Weimar Republic, when many German professors were hostile to the liberal-democratic republic, these particular ideals remained largely unimpaired.

So strong was the conviction of the dignity of scientific and scholarly knowledge that any derogation from its traditions was resisted. There were limits on the consistency with which this conviction was observed in practice. Before the First World War, socialists were not looked upon as fit to teach in a German university. Jews too were frowned upon when it came to university appointments. There were genuinely liberal professors who tried to undo this limitation on the primacy of strictly intellectual standards, but they were not successful. The situation in these respects changed under the Weimar Republic, but at the end of that period the German universities lost nearly all the virtues which they had acquired from universities of the age of absolutism and humanism and princely states, and from the idealistic liberalism of the neo-classical period. During this time, which ran for more than a century, the German universities maintained certain features which although not liberal in origin, became part of the tradition of universities in liberal-democratic societies.

It should be pointed out that the German universities at the height of their devotion to academic freedom never questioned that they were "institutions of the state," and that the government retained the final and definitive decision regarding appointments and the establishment of new subjects and new chairs. It was accepted by academics that the statutes and by-laws of the university lay within the province of government, and were not merely to be approved and enacted, but also to be promulgated by the government. In comparison with the situation of American and British universities, the autonomy of the German university was relatively restricted, and these restrictions were accepted. But the restrictions very seldom intruded into the freedom of teaching and research of a teacher once appointed. The cases of infringement of academic freedom in Germany were invariably in-

fringements on the civil freedom of academics. One case is that of
Theodor Lessing. Two cases of infringement on the civil freedom of
academics involved *Privatdozenten* whose appointments were legally
not under governmental jurisdiction at all; these were the cases of Leo
Arons in the 1890s and of Ernst J. Gumbel in the 1920s.

FRANCE

The French universities did not enjoy the prerogatives conferred by
liberalism, either before or after the Great Revolution. They progressed
towards the freedom of research and teaching only very slowly. For
much of the nineteenth century, the central ministerial authorities—
French educational administration was very centralized—sought to
deny the freedom of teaching to teachers in the provinces. They also
denied the civil freedom of academics; university teachers who expressed political opinions distasteful to the government were dismissed.

Perhaps in response to these indignities, French academics in the
second half of the nineteenth century became more and more demanding of academic freedom. Thus, whatever might have been the
case among French academics previously, liberal attitudes became more
common among them by the latter part of the century. When, in
1893, almost 104 intellectuals signed the letter drafted by Emile Zola—
"*J'accuse*"—in support of the assertion of Captain Dreyfus's innocence,
for publication in *l'Aurore,* about one third were academics, mainly in
humanistic disciplines (including the social sciences). There were very
few academics among the public supporters of the government in its
condemnation of Dreyfus and its refusal to reopen the case.

The position of the academic, as well as the literary signatories of
"*J'accuse,*" was clearly a liberal one. It was a matter of equality before
the law, religious toleration, equality of opportunity ("careers open to
talent"), free scrutiny of governmental actions, the appreciation of the
power of public opinion, etc. All of these are among the primary and

derivative articles of liberal belief. There were undoubtedly conservatives and reactionaries in the Sorbonne and in the École normale supérieure and in the École pratique des hautes études, but the running was made by the liberals and democrats who were also often socialists. They were secularists, if not anti-clerical. They were in short the embodiment of the academic ethos of the Third Republic. Albert Thibaudet was right to call the Third Republic the *république des professeurs*. This was a period of academic freedom inside and outside the universities, i.e., in the content of teaching and research and in the expression of political attitudes. French scientific activity was marked by outstanding individual achievements, but neither the government nor the public did much to promote and increase the scale of that activity by greatly increased support. Although *de facto* autonomy increased in the universities—they became corporate bodies instead of an informal cluster of separate faculties only in 1893—the ministry of education kept a firm and highly centralized control over syllabuses, requirements for degrees, the creation of new chairs and other aspects of university autonomy. Indeed, the universities, especially the provincial ones, were financially neglected by the government and by the wealthy classes.

The *grandes écoles* were favored institutions which operated at a high intellectual level. They were intended to prepare intellectually outstanding men for the civil service, for the technological departments of government and for teaching in secondary schools. In brief, these great intellectual institutions within which intellectual freedom flourished *de facto,* with correspondingly high achievements, were to some extent continuations of the traditions of the absolutist regime.

France was, like Germany, notable for the fact that its universities were state universities. One exception was the École libre des sciences politiques founded in 1872 in response to the defeat by Prussia in the war of 1870–1871, by private initiative (Emile Boutmy) and by private financial support (the Duchess de Galliera); the other was the Institut catholique founded in 1875.

Liberalism and Academic Freedom in the United States

In the United States, liberalism, verging towards collectivistic liberalism, gained ground among university teachers, although the majority, especially in natural scientific and technological subjects, had relatively little interest in politics, did not share in and, above all, were not sympathetic with the collectivistic liberal view. As university teachers became more liberal in their political views, so the university became a more liberal institution in a more liberal society. The establishment of the elective system and the greater diversity of courses of study in the education of undergraduates increasingly displaced the fixed and narrow curriculum of the earlier period. Specific religious qualifications for academic appointments—within the universities and colleges of Protestant foundation—were less frequently invoked. Jews and Roman Catholics continued, however, until the end of the period between the two world wars, to be considered very charily. Until the 1930s, Negroes were never appointed outside predominantly or exclusively Negro universities and colleges; when the situation changed in that decade, it changed only very slightly. It is not that there were many aspirants among the Roman Catholics and Negroes. Jews on the other hand were available in large numbers but, until the 1930s, they too were seldom appointed in the universities.

Academic freedom, in the sense of the civil freedom of academics, was occasionally sharply reproved in the United States until after the Second World War. There were many cases of the infringement of the civil freedom of academics in the early part of the century, and this in turn heightened the demand by academics for their protection from such infringements. This led to the formation of the American Association of University Professors in 1915; its main concern was with the protection of university and college teachers from infringements on their academic freedom, and particularly from infringements on their civil freedom.

Between the two world wars and after the Second World War, there were a number of investigations by legislative bodies, federal and state, into allegedly subversive organizations and activities, and university and college teachers not infrequently came within their purview, resulting in embarrassment in many cases and in dismissal in a small number. We may say that to the extent that in American society there were such departures from strictly intellectual criteria of academic appointment on grounds of religious belief or ancestry or racial features, and that such infringements on the civil freedom of academics as occurred in the United States, to that extent the United States departed from the model of a liberal-democratic society.

The Intended Function of Universities in the Liberal-Democratic Age: The Infusion of Ordered Knowledge Into Society

One motive for the establishment and expansion of universities in the United States was an aspiration to realize one of the ideals of liberalism, namely, to introduce rationality and soundly based knowledge into the management of the affairs of society. Another motive for the establishment of universities and colleges in the United States, both private and public, was respect for the spiritual sphere and an acknowledgement that a society must make provision for the cultivation of the spiritual sphere; these attitudes long antedate the origins of liberal society. (In the Middle Ages, the church was the predominant object of such respect and acknowledgement; universities in time began to share that position. This motive also included the desire for an educated clergy. The desire of rulers for officials who would free them from dependence on aristocratic families, and who would be loyal and relatively rational administrators of the royal will, was another motive.)

The belief in the value of reason and sound empirical knowledge for society had been given a vivid presentation by Francis Bacon in *The New Atlantis*, at the threshold of modern times. English liberalism, in the form of the Benthamite maxim of "Investigate, agitate, legislate," did not reach the universities of its home country for a long time, but in Scotland, Adam Smith's and Adam Ferguson's teaching and writing represented a step in that direction. It was, oddly enough, in Germany, where the Baconian and Benthamite beliefs in rational statecraft—in the case of Benthamism, working through intellectual influence on public opinion, and of public opinion, in turn, on government—were philosophically repugnant, that the idea of the guidance of government through social inquiry found a firm footing in the work of the Verein für Sozialpolitik in 1872. This institution, with its steady flow of meticulously documented monographs on the economic and social problems of German society, acquired a firm footing in the universities. Germany was at that time a less liberal and less democratic society than Great Britain, yet it was in Germany that the specifically liberal idea of empirical social inquiry as a means of illuminating public opinion and thereby guiding government settled in the universities. The British Social Science Association, which had rather similar aspirations, had no impact on the British universities. The next society to take the social sciences into its universities was the United States.

Universities in the United States took to the entire range of the social sciences with much enthusiasm. The movement which began in the last quarter of the nineteenth century, first at Johns Hopkins University and then at the University of Chicago on a much larger scale and in a much wider variety, gradually spread to other universities, at first mostly the state universities in the Middle West, and somewhat later to the older Eastern universities.

The inspiration for this kind of social investigation—now established as an indispensable part of a liberal-democratic society—was first experienced by American academics during their period of study in German universities from the 1870s onwards. American academics saw in the Verein für Sozialpolitik a model for the enlightening influence of social investigation of public and political opinion. This was at the bottom of the teaching of economics at Johns Hopkins University; it was there that American academic collectivistic liberalism first became rooted and from there that its seed spread to other American universities. The more traditional individualistic liberalism of British, especially Scottish, political economy also took root in the American universities. The latter kind of liberalism in the universities—mainly in departments of economics—was as interested in influencing governmental policies as was the academic collectivistic liberalism, but it wished to influence them in the opposite direction, namely, in the direction of fortifying the workings of the competitive market and individual enterprise.

The foundation of the National Academy of Sciences in 1863 was another step towards realization of the ideal of liberal enlightenment, by proffering scientific advice to government on the basis of knowledge gained through scientific research. This took place before American universities were producing much knowledge of that kind. Nevertheless, two of the moving spirits in the foundation of the academy were Asa Gray and Louis Agassiz, both of them professors at Harvard University.

The American universities never attained the predominance in training for the highest levels of the civil service that was achieved by the German universities and the University of Oxford. One reason why the universities did not come to the forefront as sources of recruits to the higher civil service was because the "spoils system" remained for a long time the chief method of recruitment for the civil service; the higher positions in the service just below the cabinet were filled by the incoming party with persons who had become eminent as politicians and as lawyers. Nevertheless, the reform of the civil service at all levels—which aimed at the recruitment of officials by competitive examinations, to which only persons with a specified amount of education were admitted—was the work of university graduates who had studied in Germany and who had in mind both the German and the British civil services (the latter after the reform of 1853).

The highest positions in the German civil service had been reserved for graduates of the law faculties of German universities. The policy of looking upon the universities at the institutions which train young persons in rational judgement and technical knowledge for public service is far older than any liberal-democratic society; to aid this policy was one of the tasks of European universities in the age of the formation of the absolute monarchies of prerevolutionary Europe. The British reforms both at home and in India were the product of Whig and radical liberalism, which intended to replace primordial criteria of recruitment, by recruitment on the basis of performance in competitive examination to which admission was restricted to young men with high academic qualifications. The recruitment of highly educated experts for the service of the rulers was originally a policy of absolute monarchies; joined with the liberal principle of "careers open to talent," it later became an article of faith of more or less liberal-democratic regimes. The universities played a vital role under both kinds of regimes.

The Universities and Specific Features of Liberal-Democratic Societies

DISPERSION OF AUTHORITY

One of the chief features of the liberal order is the autonomy of corporate bodies. The autonomy of universities is consistent with the principles of liberalism and with the pattern of a liberal-democratic society. (It is less well situated under conditions of collectivistic liberalism or populistic democracy.)

The tradition of the autonomy of universities is one of the oldest of all the traditions of universities. It is nearly as old as universities themselves. It is much older than liberal-democratic societies. While the substance and most of the methods of teaching, and the subjects and techniques of research, have changed almost beyond recognition, the tradition of autonomy has persisted. It is perhaps all that is left from the medieval tradition of corporate liberty.

Nevertheless, it has never been complete. Universities have been dependent for practically all of their history on external financial support, and this has affected the degree of their autonomy. They have had to concern themselves with the external demand for the services of their graduates, and for the requirements of the professions for which their students have had to be trained. They have also intermittently been forced to submit to the powers of the rulers of their societies, and they have had to adapt themselves to the demands of external opinion. Despite these constraints, the universities have managed through most of their history to enjoy a very considerable measure of autonomy.

This autonomy became well entrenched in the course of the nineteenth century—earlier in the Netherlands and the Germanic countries—but it was never complete. In the liberal-democratic countries, it reached a high point in the first half of the twentieth century, within the limits permitted by the constitutional and political traditions of their respective societies. In the first two thirds of this century, central governments of liberal-democratic societies by and large abstained from intruding upon the sphere of autonomy of universities. Intrusions have begun to become more substantial since the middle of the 1960s.

This has happened in nearly every liberal-democratic society. In Germany, the central government, which had hitherto always abstained from dealing with universities, except in the inter-war period to provide funds for research through the Notgemeinschaft der deutschen Wissenschaft, enacted the *Rahmengesetz*, which has imposed a certain degree of uniformity on the university laws of all state governments; there is also now a central admissions office for all German universities. Similar actions have occurred in other countries as universities and their research have become more costly. In the United States, an executive order of the federal government has intruded very influentially into decisions regarding academic appointments. Most universities have been compliant with the ambiguous demands of the central government, and some have recently gone beyond what has been governmentally required in the suspension of the application of intellectual criteria in academic appointment.

It is not that central governments have taken action against the resistance of universities to these trends of central control at the cost of autonomy. On the whole, academics and academic administrators have been rather supine in the face of these intrusions into what had previously been regarded as the legitimate autonomy of universities.

Indeed it is not unreasonable to go further and to say that a great deal of the impetus to the movement towards greater centralization of authority in the government, has come from academics of liberal-democratic societies, and particularly from economists, political scientists and sociologists. Many of them have been the prophets of collectivistic liberalism and have denigrated traditional constitutional liberalism. This does not mean that academics have not been jealous about their academic freedom, and especially about their civil academic freedom. On the contrary! Nevertheless, much of that civil academic freedom has been exercised on behalf of policies of centralization.

SEPARATION OF CHURCH AND STATE. CONSEQUENCES FOR UNIVERSITY AUTONOMY AND ACADEMIC FREEDOM

The liberal ideal contained at its very center the idea of religious toleration. Toleration entailed, if not necessarily the legal or constitutional separation of church and state, at least the right of diverse religious communities to believe and worship in accordance with their own reasons and visions—as long as they respected the widened limits of public order. The realization of the liberal ideal of the separation *de facto* of church and state has made a very great difference to universities. In general, it has strengthened the corporate autonomy of universities and the freedom of individual college and university teachers. It has done so by decreasing—not eliminating—the capacity of any major religious community to intrude into the affairs of any university not established, governed or supported financially by itself.

The autonomy of universities originally was, to a great extent, indebted to ecclesiastical powers which wished to protect the universities from their rival earthly princes and from municipal authorities. That autonomy was not, however, an autonomy *vis-à-vis* the church. Nevertheless, the idea of a more far-reaching autonomy came into existence.

In the oligarchical states of Germany, a *modus vivendi* between the states and the universities was found; this except for a small qualification regarding chairs of theology, excluded the churches from any direct or constitutional influence on universities. In France, the progress of autonomy was unsteady, but the more the regimes moved towards the separation of church and state, the greater the autonomy *vis-à-vis* the church became. In England, after 1870, the church ceased to play any direct part in the affairs of universities although, in ancient universities, the Church of England was always a visible presence without any formally assured powers.

In the United States, which, alone of the major liberal-democratic countries, has had from the very beginning a constitutional separation of church and state, ecclesiastical bodies continued to exercise influence in colleges of their own foundation until well into the twentieth century.

Yet with all the differences in constitutional provisions and in the role of churches on the highest governing bodies of universities, the modern university has come to enjoy an almost complete autonomy with respect to religious bodies. This is true even in universities which are still legally governed by churches; even in these, the churches, without the reinforcement of constitutional establishment, have in many instances renounced much of their former power to dominate their universities.

The invaluable gift of the autonomous university with which the societies of modern times, and then the liberal-democratic societies of the nineteenth and twentieth centuries, were endowed by the Middle Ages has needed revision. It has needed this revision in order to improve it and to bring it to a higher degree of realization of the idea of freedom of investigation and teaching. It is not that teachers in mediaeval universities were uniformly servile agents of an ecclesiastically or officially prescribed syllabus and pattern of thought; teachers frequently strayed from the path of orthodoxy. That is why many universities were forbidden to teach theology and why that subject was confined to particular universities which, it was thought, were easier to control.

Nevertheless, the preoccupation of powerful intelligences with ordered knowledge could not but lead to new interpretations of traditional ideas and therewith to discoveries. What was needed by these powerful intelligences was the assurance that their lives and careers would not be damaged by infringements. The idea of academic freedom gradually became installed as the mark of a proper university. It has continued to be so up to the present. Some of this may be attributed to retraction of the churches of their older claims to authority in intellectual matters.

MARKET ECONOMY AND PRIVATE PROPERTY

Traditional or constitutional liberalism, which restricted the powers of government, supported the freedom of contract and hence the market economy. This too has had many consequences, most of them beneficial for universities. Universities have prospered from the market economy. The market economy has made the wealth of which universities, whether governmentally or privately supported, have been the beneficiaries. The universities could never have done the many things they have accomplished in research and teaching, and in the participation of academics in public life, if the economies of their respective societies had not been so productive. Nor could universities have accomplished so much if private business men had not given large monetary gifts to universities and created philanthropic foundations which have also made large gifts. They have benefited too from the capacity of persons made wealthy by the market economy to pay taxes assessed at high rates from which universities have been supported by governments.

There are, however, other sides to the relationship. One side to the relationship between universities and the market economy is rather different. Academic economists have not been as generous to the market economy as the market economy has been towards the universities. Economics—theory and research—was more sympathetic to the market economy before it became an academic subject. It did not cease to be so once it was given a place in the teaching programs of universities. Nevertheless, academic economists—teachers and students of economics—also became more critical of the imperfections of the market and more insistent on the desirability of some governmental intervention to hold in check the injurious effects of the market on those who had failed in it. The humanitarian opinions and activities of academics have helped to darken the reputation of the market economy and have encouraged efforts to supplant it entirely or to restrict its freedom.

Some academics in the United States and Germany have denounced the market as an immoral institution. At the same time, other academics have not yielded to such arguments. The economists of a few major academic institutions contended strongly for the market, even when its reputation in academic circles and in government was at its lowest ebb. Over the past 40 years they have been vindicated.

This touches on another side of the relationship. Business men have at times been sensitive to the criticisms made by "socialists of the chair" and other academics of the market economy and the regime of private business. In the United States in particular, where they have usually made up a large part of the membership of boards of regents, they have allowed their displeasure to become known. This has sometimes resulted in infringements on the civil freedom of academics.

THE RULE OF LAW

The training of lawyers was from the very beginning of universities one of their major tasks, and the teaching of law to future lawyers has remained an unceasing activity of universities. (Great Britain, and to a smaller extent the United States, were for long exceptions to this generalization, but have become much less so in the course of the present century.) In Germany the practical rule of law, and especially the doctrine of the rule of law, was to a large extent the brain-child of university professors of law. Yet it must be recognized that the "free school of law"—*die freie Rechtsschule*—in Germany, and "sociological jurisprudence" in the United States, were also to a large extent professorial creations.

The universities have benefited from living under a regime of the rule of law which has restrained the power and ambitions of civil servants and, in the United States, of state legislators as well. They have benefited also from the self-restraint of the judiciary in dealing with universities. By and large, until quite recently, judges have abstained from exercising jurisdiction over universities out of respect for university autonomy. Academics and students have become more litigious in recent decades, the courts have accepted jurisdiction more frequently. Their recent record with respect to academic autonomy is mixed.

GOVERNMENTAL AND
INTERNAL REPRESENTATIVE INSTITUTIONS

Representative institutions are essential to liberal democracy. Universities, even those with academic self-government ("*akademische Selbstverswaltung*"), lived for most of their history without internal representative institutions. When they were ruled by rectors or by presidents, there was seldom provision for representation of the teaching staff in the governing body of the university. The rector or the president ruled—insofar as church or king or emperor permitted him to do so—without the aid of a council, although he might seek the advice and support of deans of faculties, as later in American universities, where the heads of departments were his agents and not the representatives of the teaching staff. Academic self-government had a place for internal representative institutions but that place did not become open for a long time.

Oxford and Cambridge colleges had no need for representative institutions since the fellowships were small; all fellows were members of the governing body. Of course, the head of the college was sometimes

288

a tyrant and was often indifferent to the governing body; sometimes he disregarded it. (Bentley as master at Trinity College, Cambridge, was one of the most notable examples.)

The German faculty senate was not a representative institution inasmuch as all the teachers, except for *Privatdozenten* and assistants, were professors. The senates became more representative when extraordinary professors were allowed to elect representatives from among their number to sit in the senate alongside the ordinary professors, who were automatically members of the senate in their own right.

The modern British universities began to develop internal representative bodies when readers, senior lecturers, lecturers and assistant lecturers elected colleagues of equal rank to represent them alongside the professors in the senate. American universities came late upon the scene of internal representative government. The powers of these bodies, when they did come into existence, were at best consultative. They had little or no legislative power, either positive or negative. Representative bodies of the teaching staff are now widespread in universities throughout liberal-democratic societies.

Governmental representative institutions provide for the civil freedom of academics, as well as of all other citizens. The participation of academics in governmental representative institutions goes very far back in Great Britain. There the ancient universities were represented by seats reserved for them in the House of Commons and filled through elections by an electorate consisting of masters of arts of the universities. The appearance of the modern universities was met by the provision of one seat in the House of Commons for London University and another seat for all the other universities combined. No such arrangements have existed in other countries; they no longer exist in Great Britain. As representative institutions grew with the spread of liberalism, university teachers began to stand for election to national and state legislatures. I think that this began earlier in Germany and in Italy than in other countries. Nevertheless, in the present century there have been many academics who, either on leave or having resigned their academic posts, have stood for election to national legislatures and have sometimes been elected. If they persisted in parliamentary careers, they usually always discontinued the intellectual side of their academic careers, although they sometimes nominally retained their appointments.

By and large, academics have approved of parliamentary government, although many of them, especially in Germany, looked on the growth of democracy with misgivings. At a time when many of them were liberals, representative institutions had a place in their articles of faith. Conservatives too accepted them. In the 1920s, with the triumph of the Bolsheviks in Russia and the rise of fascism in Italy, the criticism of popularly elected parliamentary bodies became more widespread; academics, however, were not usually among their more vehement critics. Even in the United States, where academic intellectuals stood apart from "party"—and "machine"—politics, they were not severe critics of the national legislatures and they were not especially active in seeking to reform them. Woodrow Wilson was an outstanding exception. The interest of academics in the United States was much more drawn to the reform of the civil service.

Even when many academics were most hostile to liberal-democratic societies, from the 1930s to the 1950s, they did not especially single out parliamentary bodies as objects of hostility. Those who took a more or less Marxist view regarded such bodies as part of the "executive committee of the bourgeoisie." Nevertheless, during the administration of President Franklin Roosevelt, when many important reforms were enacted by the Congress, they followed them avidly and accepted their legitimacy. However, in the United States not many academics have sought elected office, although their numbers have increased since the Second World War. The reason for this reluctance to seek electoral office in the United States has been that selection as a candidate has generally required an apprenticeship in local or state politics. This was not welcome to any but a few. The opportunity to exercise power seemed more attractive when it was offered in the form of an appointment to a high position in the executive branch. This was very true in the time of Franklin Roosevelt when American academics, for the first time in the history of the country, entered government in relatively large numbers. (There had been such an entry during the First World War but it was on a proportionately much smaller scale, and it diminished markedly in the post-war decade.)

Here and there, distinguished academics have risen to high office in liberal democracies, for example, Woodrow Wilson, Thomas Masaryk, Amintore Fanfani, Luigi Einaudi and Raymond Barre. But, on the whole, the electoral process does not attract them, in part because it is too arduous and too distracting from the academic mode of life. Academics are much more inclined towards serving as advisers, as members of specially appointed commissions, and in periods of national crisis, as temporary civil servants at a high level.

Intellectually, they have tended to disparage legislatives and legislators. The popularity among academic social scientists of the idea of the "bureaucratization" of "mass society," is an expression of a denial of the value of representative institutions. The fact that so many leading and less leading academics in France and Great Britain before the Second World War, and in most liberal-democratic societies after the Second World War, admired the Soviet Union so passionately, is evidence that many of them did not really consider representative institutions to be all that valuable.

FREEDOM OF EXPRESSION OF BELIEFS
AND ACADEMIC FREEDOM

Although academic freedom is not the same as civil or political liberty, it has greatly benefited from the expansion and consolidation of the latter in liberal-democratic societies. Much of the progress of genuine academic freedom and of the civil freedom of academics is owed to increased acknowledgement by the educated public of the dignity of learning, of learned institutions and of the profession of learning.

Freedom of expression in teaching, research and publication was needed if the universities were to achieve what they wished and what was expected of them. This is what the unevenly emergent liberalism provided. It did not have an easy birth. It was probably the universities of the Netherlands, the Universities of Leiden and Utrecht, which led the way. Most other countries lagged behind, some very far. The French universities of the *ancien régime* were among the most retrograde in Europe in this respect. The Revolution, which appeared to break the *ancien régime,* did not improve the situation. The age of Napoleon was scarcely an improvement and the successive regimes which followed were little better. The German universities exhibited a closer approximation to academic freedom in practice in the eighteenth century. Perhaps even more important for the establishment of academic freedom was the promulgation of the ideal by von Humboldt and some other German thinkers. By the end of the nineteenth century, the freedom of research and teaching and publication had become a standard for the assessment of universities through the Western world. This does not mean that it is always observed.

METHODICALLY GAINED AND ORDERED KNOWLEDGE

The liberal ideal accepted, indeed it stressed, the indispensability of rational reflection drawing upon the most reliable information or scientific knowledge for the making of private and public decisions. The market was regarded as the best mechanism to make available the knowledge needed for reaching private decisions about exchanges of goods and services. The market required a wide dispersion of that knowledge.

The liberal ideal also proposed or required a wide dispersion of the knowledge needed for public decisions. The original intention of academic social sciences was to make available the results of social science studies to the widest possible public. It was the expectation that on the basis of such knowledge produced by academics and transmitted to the public, individuals could adapt themselves, i.e., they could control their own actions in ways which would enable each to realize his or her individual objective, and to enable participants in collective actions, especially those in which authority is exercised, to perform in ways which would be optimally beneficial to all concerned.

The growth of scientific knowledge has not, however, turned out to be compatible with the liberal ideal of the equal distribution of knowledge to the adult public. The liberal ideal of a rationally and mutually adjusting collective life is not so readily adaptable in the affairs of large societies with a high degree of concentration of authority, and a fairly high degree of specialization of institutions and of occupational specialization within institutions.

The idea of representative institutions is a concession to inequality in the distribution of knowledge. It was in that respect also a departure from the ideal of complete *Mündigkeit* of all individuals. The development of modern scientific and technological knowledge has placed a strain on the liberal ideal because it renders inevitable a varying, but always rather high, concentration and specialization of knowledge. The problems created for liberal democracy by the growth of knowledge and its distribution have not been resolved.

This anomaly is a ramified consequence of liberal democracy. It is liberal-democratic society which has given such a free scope of action to the universities, and it is the universities which have generated so much scientific and scientific technological knowledge. The universities, which have been to such a great extent the beneficiaries of liberal democracy, grew up and flourished at various times under other social and political regimes, but they have flourished especially under the regime of liberal democracy. By their very efflorescence and their fidelity to the task laid upon them by the multiplication of knowledge, they have created a situation which might become a troublesome embarrassment to liberal democracy, as well as to themselves.

The esteem in which universities have been held in liberal-democratic societies has been strengthened by the belief that the universities, as centers of scientific research, have contributed and will continue to contribute to the economic well-being of their societies. In the early nineteenth century, before universities had become sources of practically beneficial and economically profitable knowledge, they were esteemed as parts of the spiritual sphere in which the churches were beginning to renounce their claim to monopoly or at least preponderance. The universities owe much of their standing to this latter belief in the intrinsic value of methodically gained and ordered knowledge.

REWARDS COMMENSURATE WITH ACHIEVEMENT

The superiority of individual achievement as a claim to preferment and reward over the criteria of birth, religion, race, etc., is one of the major features of modern liberal-democratic societies. This has many sources. One of them is the metaphysical-moral belief in the value of the individual human being as an intrinsically valuable entity; it has gradually gained the upper hand over belief in the legitimacy of status derived from lineage and role within the family. The value of individual intellectual achievement is almost inherent in universities, although there have been times—for example in Oxford in the eighteenth century—when individual intellectual achievement was only one value among others, and not usually the main one.

In the nineteenth century, however, this changed. It was not merely the assimilation of the ethic of individual achievement from the surrounding individualistic liberal society. The change came about from within the universities when increasing emphasis was laid upon intellectual achievement through research. In the course of that century, when degrees and prizes were awarded, when honors were conferred and when appointments were made, they were made for the intellectual achievement of individuals.

Thus in consequence of the spread of the ethic of intellectual achievement, universities became purified. Idlers and spellbinding placeholders became relatively more rare as the capacity for an actualization of individual academic achievement became more widely regarded as the proper criterion for admission, graduation, appointment and promotion. The application in matters of appointment of the criterion of past and prospective academic intellectual achievement has always been appreciated in universities, but it has not always been applied in practice. For a long time, religious affiliation and affirmation were either explicitly or implicitly treated as being among the criteria of academic appointment, admission to university, sitting for examinations and proceeding to degrees. These have gradually been abandoned in universities in liberal-democratic countries. Intermittently, political criteria have been applied at the cost of academic intellectual criteria.

In the United States, where for a very long time Negroes were never considered for academic appointment, the governmental program of affirmative action and a perverse egalitarianism have reversed but not nullified the earlier situation. At the same time, the program of affirmative action imposed by the federal government, the politicization of universities by their own teaching staffs and the agitation by small circles of students, have weakened adherence to the criterion of academic intellectual achievement in the award of marks and the making of academic appointments.

HUMANITARIANISM, LIBERAL DEMOCRACY AND THE UNIVERSITIES

Humanitarianism is not usually associated with traditional or constitutional liberalism. They are frequently thought to be antithetical to each other, and in some aspects they are. But they have much in common. Both extended the boundaries of society and incorporated previously peripheral sectors of society; both accorded much value to the individual; both espoused a puritanical ethic, regarding the working, self-supporting individual as the norm. Nevertheless, it is wrong to say that liberalism of the traditional or constitutional sort and humanitarianism are identical.

Nor would it be correct to say that humanitarianism and democracy are identical or always harmonious with each other. But like liberalism and humanitarianism they overlap with each other. Liberalism and democracy together have incorporated a good part of the humanitarian program of the nineteenth century. In this, the universities of liberal-democratic societies have played a great part. At the same time, the espousal of humanitarian attitudes has helped to change the universities within themselves and in their position in society.

Humanitarianism had nothing to do with universities in their early centuries. The improvement of the conditions of life of the society, and especially of the lower classes, was not thought to be anything of interest to universities. It might have been to some extent the coming of political economy under a variety of names into universities—first in the German and Italian universities in the seventeenth and eighteenth centuries, and then in the Scottish universities in the eighteenth century—which marked a turn of attention of some academics towards the wealth of societies and their populations, and to the physical conditions of the people. (Political arithmetic had a transient connection with Brasenose College, Oxford, through William Petty, who was a fellow there while serving as professor of anatomy in the university, but there is no evidence that he taught political arithmetic while at Oxford.)

It was really in the nineteenth century that persons holding academic appointments began seriously to consider the wealth of nations, and incidentally the condition of the poor.

The Verein für Sozialpolitik in Germany with its numerous academic members had a deep impact on universities in the United States. The establishment of the Johns Hopkins University in 1875, the University of Chicago in 1892 and the London School of Economics in 1895, greatly widened the institutional provision for inquiries into the conditions of the poor. (Previously in those countries, such inquiries had been conducted by private individuals and private charitable societies.) This new field of academic work was often associated with the emergence of a divergent current of liberalism, namely, collectivistic liberalism, which in the course of time pushed aside the great liberal tradition which required the free control and disposition of property as an essential feature of the competitive market and the regime of liberty. This new collectivistic current of liberalism brought academics, especially in the social sciences, into public agitational activities.

In universities, both in the United States and in Germany—in France and in Great Britain the universities were much slower—the provision of teaching in the social sciences gave much attention to "social conditions." Social science departments of universities—some universities were very reluctant to create them—were from the beginning intimately related to activities outside the universities to improve the conditions of the poor, orphans, widowed and deserted women, prostitutes, alcoholics, immigrant labor, and the whole panoply of activities and conditions called "vice" and "poverty." The turn towards humanitarian concerns among academics fostered the study of economics and "social economics" in the universities and, early in the present century, the establishment of "schools" within the universities for the teaching of "social work" or "social administration." (This happened especially in some universities in Great Britain and the United States.) The surge of humanitarian beliefs in academic circles was accompanied by actions of academics on behalf of "social reforms." These actions were intended to arouse public opinion and to impel governments into measures to alleviate poverty and to control "vice."

From at least the last decade of the nineteenth century, university teachers appeared in reformatory and civil activities performed outside the universities. Academics served on commissions of inquiry appointed by governments and they carried out investigations of their own, sometimes with the aid of students. They also agitated for reforms. These agitational activities, directed towards the larger public, raised questions about the propriety of such activities and sometimes, particularly in the United States, precipitated small crises of civil academic freedom. It also brought with it an increased participation of academics in academic activities which inquired into or which purported to "solve" social problems.

From the early twentieth century, critics of the universities, especially critics of radical progressivistic inclinations, had censured the universities for their failure to find places in their student bodies for the offspring of the working classes and from the poorer sectors of their societies, more generally. Numerous statistical studies had demonstrated in the decades before the Second World War that the students of universities came mostly from the middle and upper middle classes and more specifically from the families of members of the learned professions—the clergy, medicine and law, business enterprisers and higher civil servants, and in the United States from the families of more prosperous farmers. Neither university administrators nor university teachers worried much about these facts.

After the Second World War, governments and publicists, and particularly the expanded breed of higher educational publicists, began to take these matters to heart. Everywhere the numbers of university students increased, first through support for demobilized members of the armed forces, then through determined efforts by governments to further the admission into universities of candidates who, without financial support from outside their families, could not attend them. As a result, after the first surge of students who had been kept from university studies by their service in the armed forces, there was a further and almost uninterrupted surge. This was made up to a large extent of students who benefited from grants by governments and by the universities from their own resources.

In the United States, with its large Negro population, and demand for an increase in the percentage of students from "minorities," the insistence has been greater. It is not so pronounced in other liberal democracies, but it is likely to increase in those societies, given the increase in the major countries of the numbers of "foreign workers" who are mostly Asians and Africans.

The admission of such students represents more than a mere increase in the absolute size of student bodies which brings with it severe problems in the supply of qualified teachers, the provision of physical facilities, refectories, hostels, etc. The introduction of many students from cultures alien in their traditions of language, religious belief and outlook in life, and often with a secondary education inferior to that of earlier generations of students, makes the situation more difficult.

A similar demand for the appointment of university teachers from the "minorities" has occurred. This has been associated with a readiness to suspend or qualify the application of strictly academic or intellectual criteria in academic appointments.

Those changes in the composition of the student bodies and the academic teaching staffs have brought with them demands for changes in courses of study and syllabuses. "Black studies" and "women studies" are among the new subjects introduced. There has also been a demand to change the content of teaching away from emphasis on Western civilization and to give more attention to the "contributions" or work of Asian and African authors and female writers, who it is argued— quite wrongly—have not been sufficiently appreciated in teaching.

RATIONALITY, RATIONALIZATION AND THE UNIVERSITIES

Liberalism, both constitutional and collectivistic, has laid emphasis on the superiority of reason over custom, knowledge over ignorance, in the conduct of institutions. Each current of liberalism has stressed its greater efficiency and rationality. Scientific knowledge and rational analysis as the basis of practical action have been fundamental in liberalism.

Between the two world wars, there was much worry about the adequacy of representative institutions and the other institutions of liberal democracies to deal effectively with the problems of contemporary liberal-democratic societies. The firm grip of the Bolsheviks on the empire which they extended, the abolition of liberal democracy in Italy by the fascists in Italy, and the tribulations of liberal democracy in Germany and its overthrow by the Nazis against the background of the apparently insuperable economic depression, shook confidence in the capacity of liberal-democratic institutions to act effectively. The powers of analysis and discussion, indeed of rationality itself, were thrown into doubt. Irrationality found spokesmen inside the universities as well as outside.

On the whole, however, within the universities persistence in the pursuit of scientific knowledge and the use of such knowledge in the polity and in economic life held the upper hand in the liberal countries. The prophets of irrationalism were scarcely represented in the universities of the liberal-democratic societies. The critics of capitalism and of representative institutions, the proponents of socialism and communism, stressed the superior rationality and the more scientific character of their preferred types of society.

The Second World War silenced the doubters about the capacities of scientific knowledge in the service of practical ends. After that war, the scientific side of universities—now greatly extended—brought a new eminence to universities. Governments began to spend much larger sums of money on scientific research and scientific education. The chief beneficiaries were the universities which appreciated greatly the benefits and thought little about the costs of these greatly increased expenditures.

When governmental expenditures on science and universities were relatively small, little public attention was directed towards them. The prestige of scientific knowledge and of the universities were generally very high in the first two decades after the Second World War, and the great expenditures were neither begrudged nor closely scrutinized. This seemed to be a very happy moment in the relations between universities and liberal-democratic societies. However, it was only a prelude to a continued but more captious largesse, and a greater demandingness. No largesse could ever be generous enough to meet the much expanded demands of scientists and universities for financial support on a scale which was sufficient to meet their ever expanding demands. The intensified scrutiny which accompanied the largesse was not wholly in accordance with the traditional freedom of academic scientists to choose their problems and to do their work without having to worry about very detailed accountability.

The reversal of the tradition of scientific freedom was never as far-reaching as it could have been. Academic scientists retained a great deal of their traditional freedom, but they lost some of it. In fact, the relationship between universities and the governments of liberal-democratic societies had become more differentiated, intimate and intricate than ever before.

Concurrently, new scientific discoveries and their applications in scientific technology in private industry and commerce also became much more intimately connected with each other. Scientific discoveries in certain fields have turned out to be much more immediately and specifically applicable than had been the case up to the beginning of the Second World War. This has made industrial and commercial entrepreneurs more eager to profit by the application of scientific knowledge and to encourage such research by the provision of financial incentives. Thus, academic scientists have been drawn into connections with private business enterprises more closely than they had ever been. The academic scientists have been attracted by the prospect of additional support for their research which was becoming ever more costly; in some cases they have been attracted by the prospect of private enrichment.

These new relationships have been embarrassing experiences for other reasons as well. The demand for funds for research is insatiable; at the same time, universities have become more costly to administer as they have grown in size and in the scale of their teaching and research activities. University teachers and administrators are in search of funds in ways which they have never been before. Universities have never before been expected to pay their own way, except for institutions of marginal intellectual importance which have supported themselves mainly from the tuition and other fees paid by students. Nowadays, at least in Great Britain and the United States, they are being pressed by their own administrators to engage in money-earning activities to meet their increased costs—as well as to contribute to the economic growth of their societies. These situations have added to the difficulties of conducting autonomous universities with internal freedom along traditional lines.

AMBIVALENT AND HOSTILE ATTITUDES
TOWARDS TRADITION

Neither the liberal, nor the collectivistic liberal, nor the democratic streams of thought which have entered into contemporary liberal-democratic societies, have looked with affection on traditional beliefs and institutions. It is true that each of them has appealed to its own traditions, but they have been very critical towards the traditions of others and they have all tended to deny the value or supportability of tradition. Their ideal of society would be one in which traditions were set aside by scientific and rational analysis, popular will and calculations of collective-individual advantage ("interest").

The scientific and technological parts of the academic world have had little patience with tradition; many of their practitioners deny that they have had traditions of their own. Social scientists likewise have lacked understanding of the traditional elements of their own societies. The specialization of humanistic scholarship, while studying traditions and practicing their transmission in their own research and teaching, placed the more fundamental understanding of the nature of tradition into a marginal position. All this notwithstanding, many academics in liberal-democratic societies have had a genuine appreciation of the traditions of their own universities, and a sense that there were traditions which ought to be continued. These attachments to the traditions of their universities, and hence their attachment to the universities, did not make them indifferent to the importance of traditions in society.

The developments of contemporary liberal-democratic societies have had a deleterious effect on these attachments to university traditions. The appearance of the mass university, the increase in size of administrative staffs, the large classes and seminars, as well as the high degree of specialization and the increased frequency of close collaboration with colleagues in other universities, have had a debilitating effect on the morale of university teachers and students. The creation of so many new universities has offered a poor soil for the growth of university traditions.

The student disturbances in so many liberal-democratic countries in the 1960s and 1970s, the idea that a university is a "constellation of interests"—the basic idea of the *Gruppenuniversität*—the numerous conflicts among teachers arising from the disturbances, and the increased intrusion of central governmental bureaucracy in the internal affairs of universities, have had disaggregative consequences.

On top of all this, the birth of the ideal of individual emancipation from the ties of institutions—itself a noxious outgrowth of liberal democracy—has accentuated these disaggregative tendencies within universities.

What Universities Have Given to Liberal-Democratic Societies

The universities have contributed to their liberal-democratic societies through training for the various professions which have helped those societies to function, and they have affirmed—although far from unqualifiedly—certain beliefs which are constitutive of liberal democracy. On the most practical side, they have trained physicians, scientific research workers in medicine, biology, agriculture and the physical sciences. They have trained all types of engineers, who, taking over the task from engineers trained by apprenticeship and periods of study in very specialized institutions, have continued, together with chemists, the elaboration of the technological apparatus of the modern economy and contributed to its productivity. They have trained medical research workers, have made it possible to control many diseases and, with the agricultural research workers who have increased agricultural productivity, they have lengthened the life-span of human beings in many countries and not just in the liberal democracies. They have provided both systematic theoretical and relatively precise particular knowledge about the workings of economies and societies. They have trained a very large fraction of the persons who have administered modern governments and business enterprises, more or less efficiently and honestly. They have trained the lawyers needed to apply the law and to represent individuals and institutions in the conflicts which are inherent in a free pluralistic society, and to bring them to peaceful solution. They have increasingly educated the journalists who supply the factual information needed by citizens and rulers.

They have not only performed research and applied the results of research, they have also offered expert advice to governments and large organizations and perhaps helped them, by their advice, to function more efficiently, and thereby maintained the morale and confidence necessary for the effective functioning of liberal democracy.

Universities, by their research and teaching, have greatly increased the stock, breadth and depth of knowledge of nature and of man; they have increased our knowledge of the history of human societies and civilizations and of the achievements of mankind in religion, art, literature, etc. They have, directly and indirectly, through the lower levels of the educational system, given to the citizens of liberal-democratic societies some knowledge of the history of their own societies and the ability to see themselves as participants in them. They have made human beings in modern liberal-democratic societies cognizant of the place of their civilization among the civilizations which appeared in world history. They have above all enriched their knowledge of their own civilization. They have disciplined many minds by making them aware of how truths are discovered and of the moral discipline which is required for attainment of those truths. They have given to many the exhilaration of discovery and contemplation of the intricacy and coherence of the world, or at least of sectors of it. They have enabled some human beings to grasp the dignity of rational, methodical thought and reflection. On a level intellectually less important but not less important for a liberal-democratic society, they have enabled many individuals to improve their lot in life by offering them the training and certification to enable them to enter the occupations to which they aspire.

What Universities Have Not Given to Liberal-Democratic Societies

What have the universities failed to do? They have failed to replace a lost religious faith in many human beings whose lives have become more troubled—intermittently—by their inability to hold confidently a view of the world which gives meaning and value to cosmic and human existence. That, however, is a task the universities never undertook. As long as the churches were able to do what it was in their province to do, the universities worked alongside them in a division of labor which left the final truths of cosmic and human existence to the churches, while the universities attempted to understand and explain according to the methods of valid and reliable empirical knowledge. When the churches declined in credibility, the universities, except for those "grown-up children"—as Max Weber called them—who thought that scientific methods could supply answers to all the questions which serious inquiring minds could ever ask, continued to perform with increasing success the tasks which were appropriate to them. The universities have in fact taught theology for most of their history, but have done so under ecclesiastical supervision. They still teach theology but the other departments of the university do not regard the maintenance of theological belief as their responsibility. Hence to charge the universities with the failure to replace religion would be to charge them with a failure which they share with the churches. The protection of the traditional religion was never the responsibility of the whole university; it was the responsibility of the churches and of the divinity faculties.

WISDOM

A society without wisdom is bound to go astray, and a liberal-democratic society is no less liable to do this than any other type of society—perhaps more so, as university graduates who have not received some of the intellectual preconditions for wisdom come to constitute an increasingly large fraction of the adult population. This is where the humanities are failing to serve the good of a liberal-democratic society.

The study of the great works which are the subject-matter of the humanities may foster the growth of wisdom in those who study them. Wisdom cannot be taught and the students are too young and too inexperienced to give birth to it. It can be elicited only by those who have a mind for it, and that can be achieved only in the years of maturity. Still the study of the great works—the "canon" now disparaged by teachers of the humanities—can lay the foundations for it in youth, if teachers are attentive to the opportunities offered by teaching. But that is not the way in which teaching is done nowadays by many teachers of the humanities.

Humanistic studies moved from the task of finding and living in accordance with the right pattern of life through the study of the great intellectual works of antiquity, to the pedantic emendation of texts of important authors, and later to the pedantic study, in great detail, of unimportant authors and events. The transformation came about gradually and unwittingly. At first, the secondary task of humanistic scholarship was the discovery and collation of surviving manuscripts, with the aim of making the text as pure as possible, that is, as close as possible to the state of the text when it left its author's hand. This was a work of tremendous importance. It was also a task which challenged great intelligences and called for impressive qualities of memory and imagination.

When, with the increasing sensitivity to contemporaneous truths, the study of modern language and literatures came into the programs of academic humanistic studies, the emendation and purification of texts aiming to establish what an author had really said declined in prominence. The invention of the printed book had rendered much of that important activity superfluous, as far as modern languages and literatures were concerned. There were not many modern authors as great as Plato and Aristotle or Horace and Virgil, and the study of the contemporary recently living great authors offered little in the way of an exemplary pattern of life in accordance with which a scholar could hope to form and live his own life. Nor did modern authors offer the same legitimate opportunities for philological textual study and emendation.

In consequence, and with the attendant increase in the number of research students writing dissertations for the doctorate, from quite different causes, innumerable doctoral dissertations were produced and many of them were published. They had to be as detailed as the much richer documentation of recent events permitted. The small number of worthy subjects and the great number of persons to work on them, with the obligation of making an original contribution to knowledge, resulted in a widespread trivialization of subjects. Such "original" research led to the production of a flood of boring books and an inevitable weariness and uninterestedness of much postgraduate research, which had to continue long after the dissertation was completed. The requirement of long lists of publications as a criterion of academic appointment and promotion accentuated this drudgery. The academic calling became a profession in which the bare fact of publication was the sole mark of merit. Research became increasingly specialized and self-contained. It looked upon its objects without the benefit of any large perspective.

It is no wonder that as humanistic scholars who had become experts without vision and with no end in life except promotion and more publication, teaching sank in importance alongside this all-consuming treadmill of exhaustive and exhausting research. The vision of a way of life faded away nearly completely. That is one of the causes of the crisis of the humanities which has been aggravated by the wantonness of a desperate profession. What is now called "theory" in the humanities is the misguided effort to find new tasks for the humanities.

The movement towards "theory" in the humanistic disciplines has received an influential embodiment in the technique of "deconstruction," which has recently gained the ascendency. Its derogation of the "canon" is an effort to deny the validity of the tradition which ranks literary works in accordance with intellectual and literary criteria other than individually variable likes and dislikes. It is against the traditional canon. What it is really trying to break is the tradition of Western liberal-democratic society. It is a form of antinomian political radicalism with scraps of Marxism and psychoanalysis, supported in the most far-reaching and subtle form in some of the work of the philosopher and historian Michel Foucault. It is hostile to intellectual traditions, even to knowledge itself which, because it has been received from the past, is regarded as "oppressive." Even language, according to this new movement, is "oppressive" because it provides established forms for expression.

This antinomian body of beliefs is prominent mainly in the humanistic disciplines and particularly in the study of modern literatures. It has, however, made inroads into the social sciences, and even into the classical and oriental parts of the humanistic disciplines. In the social sciences—not in economics—the work of "deconstruction," i.e., of devaluation, takes the form of "unmasking" and "demythologizing."

The current efforts made in the humanistic disciplines to overcome their desiccation by launching themselves into "theory" cannot be accused of narrowness. They are very broad. Their leaders hold forth on all sorts of subjects which they have not studied, e.g., economic history, sociology, philosophy, comparative religion, etc., etc. There is no subject which they do not venture into to rediscover their own image of the world. Nor can it be said against them that they are not interested in a way of life. They are interested in a way of life—it is nothing other than complete emancipation from all traditional ways of life. Humanistic "theory" is very political but its politics are those of antinomianism—although probably in any particular situation their views are those of the radical or emancipationist variant of collectivistic liberalism. This is not very fertile ground for the growth of wisdom or for the growth of civility, either within the university or within society. In any case, they find liberal-democratic society utterly abhorrent. It embodies all that they would destroy.

Their political sympathies are generally populistic and anarchistic. In the United States, this hostility to the tradition of liberal-democratic societies has another facet: the accusation against the great literary and philosophical works of Western civilization as "sexist, racist and imperialist." (The discussion about the required course for undergraduates at the Leland Stanford University, which has been amply documented in *Minerva*,[1] exhibits the aggression of the critics and the compliance of those who otherwise know better.)

This is of course not the entire picture. Traditional modes of scholarship are still strong in many of these fields, but the practitioners of those modes are timorous and on the defensive. Although these practitioners of the traditional modes of study do not wholeheartedly support the antinomian views, they are reluctant or afraid to oppose them. Only a small minority speak out against them and they are pilloried as dogmatic reactionaries.

Thus within the universities in which they hold remunerative appointments and in which they exercise their authority over students, they oppose the traditions without which universities could not exist. Needless to say, they are irreconcilably hostile to liberal-democratic society.

---

1. "The Discussion About the Proposals to Change the Western Culture Program at Stanford University," Reports and Documents, *Minerva* 26 (Summer–Autumn 1989): 223–410.

CIVILITY IN THE UNIVERSITY AND IN SOCIETY

Specialization is an inevitable and fruitful condition of scientific discovery. But it has dangers for the university and for liberal-democratic society. Hyper-specialization is often attended by an attrition of perspective, i.e., of breadth or comprehensiveness of curiosity and understanding. Specialization is like the leather-tanner's view that "there is nothing like leather"; for the leather-tanner there is nothing in the world as worthwhile as leather. Specialization is incivility in intellectual treatment of the realm of material substances, it is indifference to the larger scene. Pedantic specialization in the academic disciplines is part of the attrition of civility within a university; nothing in the university is of interest to the specialist—neither the work of other parts of the university, nor the university as a whole. Only his own department or his own research project interests the specialist. This is one of the sources of the damage from which universities are suffering at present. Indifference to what is happening in one's own university is a companion to indifference to what is happening in one's own society, an indifference qualified only by an unthinking partisanship, pervaded by clichés.

Scientists, pure and applied, and technologists have, through their specialized research, already made great contributions to liberal-democratic society. They have also presented it with problems which are beyond their capacities to solve. The problems generated by the advances in biomedical sciences and biomedical technology are unprecedented. They have raised questions about the prolongation of human life and the manipulation of species with which no societies have ever been faced before. Scientists, having contributed their mite to the abandonment of traditional religious beliefs and their associated ethical beliefs, now find themselves confronted by problems which they are ill-equipped to solve. It is not that the traditional religious beliefs and ethics offer any clear solutions. It is only that the new problems disclose the moral threadbareness of the scientific and technological professions.

They also disclose the moral threadbareness of the population as a whole in facing problems of a sort which have never been faced before.

It is not that there have not been some great scientists and physicians who have also been humane and generous persons and who have taken seriously the future of their respective societies and of all mankind. There was such a wave of naïve but genuine civility at the end of the Second World War among scientists who had been engaged in the work which was directed towards the invention and construction of nuclear weapons, but this did not last. It fell into the groove of collectivistic liberal partisanship and helped to make internal discussions about nuclear weapons more vehement and less civil. (I refer here to the Federation of American Scientists; the American Association of Scientific Workers had always been a "front" for the Communist Party, than which nothing was more uncivil.)

The once widespread notion that scientific training purged an individual of prejudice and partisanship and that scientists could therefore speak for the whole, since scientific knowledge itself offered such knowledge of the common good, has turned out to be a generous delusion. I do not intimate by this statement any slur on the character of scientists, many of whom are guided by a disciplined love of truth which is exemplary.

The vast majority of scientists are probably little interested in public affairs except insofar as they affect resources for scientific research and training; they are also little interested in what goes on in their universities. They are not antinomians in the way which many members of the departments of the humanistic disciplines have become. However, public spirit is not among their striking features, nor is academic citizenship.

Social scientists by their professional obligations know more about societies than their colleagues in the natural sciences and the humanities. They have also become very specialized as the social sciences have become more scientific. Their specialization within each discipline tends to be focused on "social problems," i.e., the poor, the outcasts, the broken reeds of society. That is the tradition of empirical sociological research; that is the tradition which they have inherited. This focus of attention is kept in place by the readiness of governments and philanthropic foundations to support such research.

This partiality of vision has laid them open to the ravages of the last few decades. Sociology, anthropology and political science all have somewhat more intellectual discipline than do the present-day practice of the humanities, but they have not been resistant to the infectious spreading from the humanities and from the radical epidemic of two decades ago. Whereas among natural sciences a high degree of specialization may be accompanied by indifference to or ignorance of society, among social scientists it produces a superficial view of society. Superficiality is conducive to incivility. Those social scientists whose procedures were more rigorous or more "scientific" have been less susceptible to the infection of uncivil radicalism than those with purportedly "theoretical" interests. There, antinomianism found more acceptance.

The Universities as Bearers of Civility

This is a very rough but approximate account of the relationships between the universities and the main features of liberal democracy. It is clear that the universities owe a great deal to liberal democracy and that liberal democracy owes a considerable part of its successful functioning to universities.

Liberal democracy needs civility, i.e., a concern for the common good. What have the universities contributed to this? Before attempting to answer this difficult question, it is desirable and reasonable as well to suggest that civility—which involves detachment from conflicting interests, and an imagination capable of envisaging a solution which is more than a compromise between the conflicting interests and which takes into account consequences for third parties—is a rare quality and it is probably never found unalloyed. It is mixed with partisanship within the mind of the individuals who possess it.

Despite their often crude and unashamed espousal of partisanship, civility is probably most often found among politicians with long experience because it is they who see the entire society somewhat more frequently than other persons, except experienced lawyers who often have a comprehensive perspective over the entire society. What about academics? Can they achieve and exercise the civility needed by a liberal-democratic society for its maintenance?

Karl Mannheim thought that the *"freischwebende"* intellectuals— the detached intellectuals, free of obligations of devotion to political parties—might be capable of speaking for the common good. He thought that they could do so by amalgamating the partial perspectives of the contending parties into a single wider perspective. For this he was almost everywhere ridiculed. (In the recent revival, by radical sociologists, of interest in his ideas about the sociology of knowledge, this is one aspect of his work which has been allowed to rest in oblivion.)

Yet, Mannheim's idea should not be rejected without further ado. It ought to be seriously examined. Scientists and academics achieved the high status which they long enjoyed because it was thought that being disciplined to observe and analyze, despite their own personal predilections and pride, they possessed the objectivity necessary for dispassionate judgements, as true as the evidence allowed.

Governments over the past half century have frequently turned to academic scientists to do research on particular problems. They have also been invited to give advice to politicians and administrators at the higher levels of authority because there was confidence that scientists could rise above vanity and partisanship. They have been asked to tell what "science" knows on particular problems and to recommend alternative policies. They have even been encouraged to recommend the adoption of particular policies, because there was confidence that they would assess fairly arguments for and against any particular policy and that they would bear in mind the interests of the entire society.

Their association with universities was thought to be a further guar- antee of disinterestedness. The university was believed to be an exigent institution; nothing less than truth was to be expected from it or from those who were members of it.

In serving governments on advisory capacities in this manner, academics conformed with the liberal-democratic ideal of infusing sound scientific knowledge into the conduct of practical affairs. They were able to do this because of the good reputation universities had acquired as institutions devoted, in an utterly disinterested manner, to the discovery and enunciation of truth.

The advice given by academic scientists has not always been good advice, in the sense that the results of policies based on their advice did not turn out as had been hoped. Often the advice given by academic scientists, including social scientists, has been disregarded because the persons advised received contradictory advice from other advisers, or because they themselves had opinions of their own which were inconsistent with the advice they received. Nevertheless, the advice of scientists was frequently sought because it was thought that scientists were politically disinterested, desired to serve the common good, and were capable of objectivity in judgement.

Politicians and administrators, i.e., laymen without the discipline and knowledge provided by scientific training and experience, cannot themselves assess the validity of the knowledge drawn upon by their scientific advisers. The validity of the results of research gained by scientific methods can really be judged only by other scientists who have mastered the field into which the investigation falls. Scientific studies are often so highly specialized that even an authority in one field of science often cannot pass judgement on the knowledge gained in another field. Certainly very few laymen can verify the scientific assertions made by a scientist. If a layman consults scientists who have divergent views about the same subject, he is scarcely in a position to adjudicate their differences and to decide correctly by himself which one is right.

It is important that the scientists be regarded by the laity as trustworthy. Being a scientist has been thought to be a guarantee of trustworthiness. Universities have been respected because they dealt with what were thought to be very important subjects and because it was also thought that those subjects were dealt with honestly and impersonally, that is, without concern for private pecuniary gain or for fame. That is why in the course of the nineteenth century, liberal-democratic societies and those which were less liberal and less democratic fostered the development of universities. They believed that universities, like the church and judiciary, were necessary for society; they attributed a high moral value to them. It was thought that they served the ideal of the disinterested search for truthful knowledge. The functions of universities were not just practical; even when they performed such functions, they were esteemed for producing the truthful knowledge which was necessary for practical functions such as the care of health or the practice of law. But the main function—seldom if ever adequately articulated—was the custodianship, transmission and enlargement of the various bodies of truthful knowledge.

Universities were maintained because the centers of their respective societies wanted them, not necessarily for their own practical or spiritual benefit, but because they thought that universities were needed for society in the way in which religious institutions, literature and art, justice and internal peace, majesty and ceremony, were needed. A society without these things would be an incomplete society.

Universities moved forward as the churches diminished in their centrality. The universities overlapped in their function with the function of the churches which was to link the society with a transcendental realm, i.e., a realm which transcended the material interests of individuals and of the various groups making up society and which held forth a higher ideal. The universities, like the churches before and alongside them, represented to their societies an objective value or values beyond the interests or desires of any given group within the society.

The universities and their academic staffs usually did not think in these terms which envisaged the university as an earthly church. But they did accept that the universities should stand above or beyond the practical interests of any class, and that they must make the scrupulous methodical pursuit of truth in research and in teaching their first obligation.

This was an important function to perform in a liberal-democratic society. The liberal component of the market, the aspiration towards individual achievement and the working of the mechanisms of the allocation of rewards commensurate with achievement, sometimes produced injurious consequences which had to be moderated by the idea of the moral order of the whole of society. Similarly the democratic element in liberal democracy had a tendency towards populism, which placed the desires of the populace and of its proponents and their conception of its interests above all else. This too is not the only thing in democracy, but there is a tendency in that direction which has to be kept in check for the concern of the whole.

What Can the Universities Do for Liberal-Democratic Society?

Liberal democracy is the ideal form for societies which are highly differentiated, in which the various individuals and sectors of society, each of which has interests and ideals which are in conflict with the interests and ideals of the others have an opportunity to strive to realize some part of their interests and ideals. This differentiation is an inevitable consequence of the size and tasks accepted by the society. It is also the ideal form of society for vigorous individuals with ambitions and ideals of their own. Liberal democracy is a regime which acknowledges this differentiation of ideals and interests. Other types of regimes, and particularly totalitarian societies, attempt to suppress them and attempt to bring under their own central authority those which cannot be suppressed, and to deny the existence of those types of differentiation which they cannot suppress and which they cannot dominate.

Because it is differentiated and calls for differentiation, liberal democracy requires some measure of consensus, i.e., a collective self-consciousness embracing most of society. Not everyone in the society needs to be completely civil to the rest of society or to a particular group at all times. Even if it were desirable, it is neither necessary nor possible. The centers of society must be more civil than the peripheries, although these peripheries too must possess some civility; there must be sub-centers of higher degrees of civility scattered throughout the society. A liberal-democratic society is incompatible with complete consensus; complete consensus would render liberal democracy largely superfluous. In any case, complete consensus is an impossibility. It does require a measure of consensus or collective self-consciousness. This collective self-consciousness is sustained by a common language, the strength of a common authority making and applying law over a common, bounded territory. It needs traditions which keep before it an image of a long, common past. It needs emblems of effective centers and sub-centers. It needs institutions and individuals who are emblems of the whole and who can speak and act in ways which bring forward the image of the whole so that it overshadows its parts.

The different sectors of liberal-democratic societies must be kept in a peaceful balance or equilibrium with each other. It is not possible for this balance or equilibrium to be achieved or maintained only by the rational bargaining of individuals and corporate bodies with each other and by explicit compromise. Some differences of interests can be bargained over and fixed by contract, but not all can be rendered compatible with each other by this technique.

The concern for the whole is a transcendental value. It is not only transcendent of the material interests, of the various sectors of society; it is also transcendent with respect to power and the desire for it, with respect to authority and the desire for it, and with respect to prestige and pride and the desire for them.

Can the universities perform this function nowadays when they are needed more than ever, now that the churches have renounced their aspiration to provide for mankind an objective transcendental ideal which stood for the whole in time and society?

I do not think that the universities, either the greater or the lesser, are representing this civility to their respective societies. They are not very civil inside themselves, having become disaggregated by earnest specialization and by a self-indulgent antinomianism. The tendencies which make them uncivil internally make them uncivil in their activities and beliefs regarding the public sphere.

Concluding Observations

My conclusion from all these observations is that the universities in the liberal democracies will continue to perform important functions in training for those professions which require, for admission and practice, knowledge of the matters which universities can and should properly provide. They will continue to do important research, although as the results of intellectually important, as well as practically useful, research can nowadays be more speedily converted into practically useful and profitable activities, more of such research will be done outside the universities.

They will continue to nurture and display a relatively small number of persons of exemplary devotion to truth in their respective fields. All of these are functions necessary to the well-being of liberal-democratic societies. They will continue to provide consultants and advisers.

As to the provision of an infusion of civility in liberal-democratic societies, I do not see the universities performing this function. They have become too uncivil—internally—and also too self-indulgent and lacking in firmness of character to withstand the pressure on universities of external incivility. Administrators of universities are usually too weak in character; they are harassed by costs which exceed revenues and by the ceaseless desire to increase their activities and to stay on the right side of uncivil proponents of external and internal demands. If universities were less before the eye of the public, it would be better for them and for their liberal societies. But I do not think that this is likely to happen in the near future.

I think that, for the time being, liberal-democratic societies which cannot do without many of the functions which universities perform for them, must make do with a very small contribution from them to the exhibition and diffusion of civility throughout their societies. They will have to do as well as they can with the civility produced by some politicians and lawyers and by the saving remnant of ordinary citizens scattered throughout liberal-democratic societies.

The Virtue of Civility

§

S INCE MONTESQUIEU, writers on politics have been aware that there might be an association of particular moral qualities and beliefs with particular political regimes. The association between virtue and republican governments, although duly recorded by students of Montesquieu's thought, has however been passed over. The disposition to participate in politics, the sense of political potency or impotence, certain traits of personality such as could be summarized in the term "authoritarian personality," etc., have all been studied by theorists of democracy. Virtue or public spirit or civility has been neglected.

I would like to take up Montesquieu's theme once more. I wish to enquire into the place of virtue or what I call civility in the liberal democratic order, which Montesquieu referred to as the republican type of government. Latterly the term "civil society" has come to be used very loosely as equivalent to "liberal democratic society." They are not entirely the same and the difference between them is significant. In civility lies the difference between a well-ordered and disordered liberal democracy.

I

The idea of civil society is the idea of society which has a life of its own, and which is separate from the state, and largely in autonomy

A much shorter and different version of this essay appeared previously as "The Virtue of Civil Society," *Government and Opposition* 26 (Winter 1991): 3–20. Reprinted by permission.

from it, which lies beyond the boundaries of the family and the clan, and beyond the locality.

The idea of civil society has three main components. The first is a society containing a complex of autonomous institutions—economic, religious, intellectual and political—distinguishable from the family, the clan, the locality and the state. The second is a society possessing a particular complex of relationships between the state and a distinctive set of institutions which safeguard the separation of state and civil society and maintain effective ties between them. The third is a society of refined or civil manners. The first has been called civil society; sometimes the entire inclusive society which has those specific properties is called civil society. In other words, sometimes the term is used to refer to the whole, sometimes it is used to refer to the distinguishing part of the whole.

First of all, regarding the separation of state from society in a civil society: that part of society with which we are concerned here consists in individual and collective activities which are not guided primarily by the rules of primordial collectivities and which are not directed by the state. They have rules of their own, both formal and informal. The state lays down laws which set limits to the actions of individuals and collectivities but within those ordinarily wide limits, actions are freely chosen or are performed in accordance with explicit agreement among the participants or are based on calculations of individual or collective interest or on the rules of the constituent collectivity. It is in this sense that civil society is separate from the state.

II

Civil society is not totally separate from the state. It would not be a part of the society as a whole if it were totally separated, just as the family, distinctive though it is, is not totally separated from civil society and the state. The state lays down laws which set the outermost bound-aries of the autonomy of the diverse spheres and sectors of civil society; so, civil society lays down limits on the actions of the state. It does this through political institutions and the organs of public opinion. These include elections of representatives, through consultation and representations of interests and ideals before the state, through petitions and through public opinion expressed in political speeches and writing. Civil society and the state are bound together by the constitution and by traditions which stress the obligations of each to the other as well as their rights *vis-à-vis* each other. The rights of individuals and collec-tivities with respect to each other are provided in the constitutions and the laws and traditions.

A civil society is a society of civility in the conduct of the members of the society towards each other. Civility regulates conduct between individuals and between individuals and the state; it regulates the conduct of individuals towards society. It likewise regulates the relations of collectivities towards each other and the relations between collectivi-ties and the state.

The term "civil society" has appeared relatively suddenly upon the intellectual scene. It has hovered in numerous variants on the edge of discussions of society ever since antiquity; sometimes it entered more centrally. It was a term of ancient jurisprudence. It was a fluctuating presence in medieval political philosophy where it was distinguished from ecclesiastical institutions. In the seventeenth century it was con-trasted with the state of nature; it was a condition in which men lived under government. In the eighteenth century it came into its own, as a type of society which was larger than and different from a tribe. Adam Ferguson, when he wrote *The History of Civil Society,* meant a society of less barbarous manners, a society which practiced the cultiva-tion of the mind by arts and letters. Civil society was seen as one in which urban life and commercial activities flourish. Adam Ferguson regarded associations for commercial ends, associations which were not primordial, as characteristic of civil society. In the views which prevailed in the eighteenth century, civil society was pluralistic; minimally it was a society with numerous private activities, outside the family and not assimilated into the state. Without referring to it by name, the pattern of the civil society was most fully delineated by Adam Smith. The outlines of the civil society were sharpened by the German romantic precipitation of the idea of the "folk," a complete antithesis of the market. The "folk society" was a small local society, dominated by tradition and history; it was society at the stage where "status" governed action; the individual had no standing on the basis of his individual qualities and achievement. It was a society of agriculturalists and craftsmen in small communities largely self-contained. These views were elaborated to contrast with the individualism, rational thinking and commercial activities of territorially extensive societies.

In the nineteenth century the notion of civil society was most elaborately considered by Hegel in his *Philosophy of Right;* Hegel drew much from Adam Ferguson and Adam Smith. For Hegel the civil society, or rather the civil part of society, was distinguished from the family and the state. It was the market, the commercial sector of society and the institutions which were necessary to the functioning of the market and the protection of its members. It was conducive to the realization of the interests of individuals but it also, through corporations, formed individuals into super-individual collectivities and integrated them into a single larger collective self-consciousness which was fully realized in the state. Like all other usages of civil society in modern times, Hegel placed the right to the private ownership of property as the indispensable feature of civil society. Montesquieu, although he did not speak of civil society, said that "civil law" guaranteed to individuals the right to security of their possessions. Hegel used the term "*bürgerliche Gesellschaft*," which has been translated as "bourgeois society" and as "civil society." The German term combines autonomy from the state and the right of private property. This has always been an integral component of "civil society."

From Hegel, the idea of civil society came into the thought of Marx. For Marx, it came to mean something different from what Adam Ferguson thought of when he wrote *The History of Civil Society*. Commerce was only one feature of civil society according to Adam Ferguson. Marx's conception of civil society, developed more than a half century after Adam Smith's analysis of the market, was an extension of Smith's views, and of the successors of Smith, to the "factory system." The division of labor, exchange, and private ownership of the instruments of production, already crucial in Hegel's thought, and the society divided by the property-owners and the propertyless—which Marx added from earlier writers of the eighteenth and nineteenth centuries—were the heart of the civil society envisaged by Marx. Marx disregarded Adam Ferguson's stress on the refinement of manners in modern civil society; this rejection has always remained characteristic of Marxism. Marx likewise disregarded Adam Smith's views about moral sentiments, just as he rejected Hegel's views about the unification of individual minds in the *Geist*. He gave his attention to the commercial or economic aspect of civil society. Marx followed Hegel in his use of the designation "*bürgerliche Gesellschaft*," but he used the term to refer to all of society and not solely to refer to a part of it. Marx made "civil society," in the narrower Hegelian sense, the determinant of the whole society. Marx equated "civil society" with "capitalistic society." For Marx, civil society was certainly not a society of more polished manners; it was not even a society held in coherence by the mutual dependence of partners in a relationship of exchange. It was rather a society in which the propertyless mass of the population was coercively held in subjugation by the owners of the instruments of production. The relationships of production and the division of society into the propertied classes and the propertyless classes were the defining features of civil society. All else was derivative from that.

In all these variations and shifts in meaning, from the eighteenth century onward, the term "civil society" retained certain central features. One: it was a part of a society distinct from and independent of the state. Where it had not yet reached the point of independence from the state, it was argued that it should become so. Two: it provided for the rights of individuals and particularly for the right of property.

Three: civil society was a constellation of many autonomous economic units or business firms, acting independently of the state and competing with each other.

An additional feature, not much emphasized in the nineteenth century—perhaps it was more of an overtone—was the idea of a political community. This carried with it the idea of citizenship. This is an aspect which was not stressed by the Scottish writers or their Germanic continuators. Nevertheless, it was there, carrying forward the image of a *polis,* of a municipality, of citizens with rights to public office and to participation in discussions of and decisions about public issues. This was an inheritance received from the jurisprudential and political philosophies of classical antiquity to early modern times. "Civil" was contrasted with "natural." It was the condition of men living in society, living in accordance with rules.

In the nineteenth century, the term "civil society" has been used to refer to a part of society and to refer to the entire society which possesses such a part. That part is not found in all societies and so not all societies are civil societies.

III

Despite the coerced ascendancy of Marxism in the Communist countries of Eastern and Central Europe, for nearly three quarters of a century in the Russian Empire and for nearly a half century in Poland, Hungary, Czechoslovakia and the Balkans, and its repression and distortion of the idea, the two central features of the idea of civil society— private property and independence from the state—with the overtone of citizenship, have never been extinguished from memory. "Civil society," meaning a market economy running separately from the state, and citizenship, meaning the exercise of civil capacities, i.e., participation in the affairs of the collectivity, i.e., rendering judgement on them and sharing in decisions about them, did not entirely fade from memory.

The idea of civil society which has been reanimated in Eastern Europe also bore within itself the elements of Ferguson's view of civil society as a society of polished manners. Polished or refined manners meant respect for the dignity of the members of society. A society of refined manners was one in which the members acted with consideration towards each other, with an acknowledgement, institutionally embodied and assured, of the dignity of the individual, derived from his humanity and from his membership in the political community. Refined or polished manners are the antithesis of rudeness of bureaucrats and the gross brutality of the police. The Communist, like the Nazi and Fascist, treatment of political opponents and the Communist and Nazi rhetoric in addressing or speaking about their opponents were the polar opposite of civil manners.

I do not know just at which moment the idea of civil society, as a contrast with Communist society, emerged in the Communist countries, nor do I know which particular persons were the first to put it into circulation. I am not acquainted with the extent to which the idea of civil society has been theoretically elaborated in those countries since the beginning of the erosion of the Communist regimes. All that I can say is that the invocation of the idea seems to have flared up and expanded in the Communist countries. From there, its echo has spread into the countries of the West which have been more or less civil societies for several centuries, although with only rare use of the term in common discourse or by academic political scientists. Its greatest popularity in the West over the past two decades seems to have occurred among dissident or disillusioned Marxists; it probably also owes some of its moderately favorable reception to the recrudescence of individualistic and constitutional liberalism and the appreciation of the superiority of the relatively free market to a centrally, governmentally planned economy.

This is not an accident. Marxist-Leninists declared themselves to be enemies of civil society. Although they sought to extinguish civil society and its idea, they did in fact preserve the idea of civil society while suppressing civil society itself. The polemical rhetoric of Marxism-Leninism preserved the idea, just as the idea of the devil was preserved in the theology which attempted to circumscribe and render him powerless.

When intelligent individuals in the European countries had had enough of the patent failures of their Communist regimes and were encouraged in their exasperation with them to demand something different from and better than those regimes, they turned towards the idea of civil society. The idea of civil society had remained alive in Marxism in its vilification of bourgeois society.

IV

According to Lenin—and not incorrectly—two of the sources of Marxism are British political economy and German idealism, meaning Hegelian philosophy. British political economy saw society as a market of individuals competing with each other, each aiming to maximize his own benefits. Marx extended this to the point where private ownership of the means of production turned into the struggle between the private owners of property in the means of production and the propertyless. Capitalistic or bourgeois society replaced "civil society"; the term *bürgerlich* survived the changed interpretation. It also retained some of its earlier connotations.

The Marxist distortion of the idea of civil society into bourgeois society was therefore not so complete that the remnants of the ideas which it had taken from British political economy and German idealism and transformed could no longer be recognized. Distorted and obscured, they could still be recovered by those who were sensitive enough and reconstituted into a plausible pattern of a desirable society. It was a pattern which could be sharply contrasted with the reality of Communist society and it could be sought as an alternative end.

This distinction between the state and society survived in Marxist-Leninism; it could be recognized in a perverse form in Lenin's conception of the state as the executive committee of the ruling class, i.e., of the ruling class of bourgeois society—and the complementary conception of the dictatorship of the proletariat. The idea of the dictatorship of the proletariat—the most numerous class of society and its historically destined heir—is the Communist version of the distinction between society and the state. But just as the Communists denied that they were separate from each other in bourgeois society, so they sought to overcome any separation between them in Communist society through the device of the dictatorship of the proletariat. The Communist Party did not claim to be the state; it only sought to control it completely. It always attempted to maintain that state and party were legally distinct from each other, with the former subordinate to the latter. To adapt Lenin's adage to the Communist regime, we could say that the Soviet state was the executive committee of the Communist Party. In the Marxist-Leninist view, the proletariat which was the essential part of society, was quintessentially embodied in the Communist Party; this society, through its agent, the Communist Party, prevailed over the state—as it did in bourgeois society. The distinction between the state and society, acquired from Hegel by Marx and revised by him, has been rehabilitated with destructive vigor by the internal critics of the Communist regimes. The ideal of a civil society has been invoked to vindicate the emancipation of society from the state and from the Communist Party which dominated it.

The compulsory teaching of Marxism-Leninism in the Communist intellectual institutions has been hoisted by its own petard. Crudely and unintentionally, Marxism-Leninism permitted the tradition of the idea of civil society to persist. The dissidents in Communist countries revived the idea of the civil society which had survived at the margin of the Marxist-Leninist view.

The difference between the Marxist or Marxist-Leninist conception of the relations between state and society on the one hand, and the idea of a civil society independent of the state which has been espoused by the Eastern European critics of communism, lies in their respective conceptions of society. The Marxist-Leninist idea refused to admit the existence of autonomous collectivities within society. Marxism-Leninism, true to its Hegelian ancestry, believed that society is the realm of particular interests but it believed that there were only two interests in bourgeois—civil—society and that these two interests continued into the early stage of communism. The multiplicity of interests has been outrightly denied by official Marxism. Its rejection of the multiplicity of interests and ideals, self-generating and self-maintaining, was derived from a metaphysical conception of a deeper stratum of social being, the "real interests" which could be apprehended only by the nominally proletarian "representatives" of society; the Communist Party alleged to be the embodiment of this essence of society. According to Marxism-Leninism, what was called civil society was in fact a highly stratified, coercively maintained arrangement, the ruling class of which, as a means of its self-protection and self-aggrandizement, had used the apparatus of the state to protect its property and therewith its exploitative dominion over the rest of society. According to the Communists, Communist society is the dominion of the most essential part of society over the state which has no will or force of its own. In the hands of the Communist Party, however, the state pervades and dominates every part of society. Practically no part of society is to be left free of the state which is the instrument of the Communist Party. The essence of society exercises complete coercive control over the factually existing society. The idea works through the state; the only difference from the Hegelian view is that the state acting on behalf of the idea, abolishes "civil society."

The Marxist-Leninist interpretation of Hegel's idea rejected his notion of the pluralism of civil society; it changed his notion of reciprocal autonomy and interdependence of the state and society by making the state entirely dependent on the ruling stratum of society and placing society completely under the control of the state. Marxist-Leninists retained enough of the fundamental categories of its intellectual inheritance to permit that inheritance to be discerned and retrieved.

V

The rebirth of the idea of civil society in Eastern Europe took the form of a determination to establish the autonomy of civil society from the state; it was also a declaration of the internal pluralism of civil society.

The place of corporations in Hegel's idea of civil society was ambiguous. What was not ambiguous was the place of private business firms; they were the main feature of civil society. There is however much more to civil society than the market. The hallmark of a civil society is the autonomy of private associations and institutions, as well as that of private business firms. Alongside of business firms, there are moral, religious and intellectual institutions and societies, as well as civic and political associations.

The pluralism of civil society is two-fold. Its pluralism comprises the partially autonomous spheres of economy, religion, culture, intellectual activity, political activity, etc., *vis-à-vis* each other. These spheres are never wholly autonomous in their relations with each other; their boundaries are not impermeable. Nevertheless, the spheres are different from each other and, in the objects they pursue in a pluralistic society, they are also largely autonomous. The pluralism of civil society also comprises within each sphere a multiplicity of many partially autonomous corporations and institutions; the economic sphere comprises many industries and many business firms; the religious sphere comprises many churches and sects; the intellectual sphere comprises many universities, independent newspapers, periodicals and broadcasting corporations; the political sphere many independent political parties. There are many independent voluntary philanthropic and civic associations, etc.

One of the institutions is the market. A market economy is the appropriate pattern of the economic life of a civil society. (Hegel saw this quite clearly; indeed, he made the market the decisive, if not the sole, feature of civil society.) The pluralism of institutions and institutional spheres requires the market economy quite apart from its necessity as the only way of working of a system of private ownership of the instruments of production and from its greater productivity than other modes of organizing economic life. The market is also an important pre-condition of a civil society because its own autonomy guarantees the autonomy of other institutions as well as business firms. (It should also be pointed out that the market economy being more productive than alternative modes of organization of economic activity engenders affluence, which is in many respects contributory to the security of civil society; this feature, however, is not the primary argument for the market economy as part of civil society.)

The Hegelian tendency to define civil society as coterminous with the market, and the Marxian inversion of the relations between *"Geist"* and "material conditions" have contributed to the deformation of the idea of civil society. They have led to the diminution of the significance of the other spheres, making the other spheres appear to be derivative from or dependent on the market.

Features of the market system do appear in other spheres. The market is neither a prototypic pattern, nor is it causally determinative. Individual scientists and scholars do compete with each other for the establishment of truths which they think they have discovered by their research; they do seek critical and informed confirmation by their peers of the truthfulness of the propositions which they assert. The chief difference is that there is no exchange in any reasonable sense of the word, since the scientist does not seek primarily what is in the power of his audience of fellow scientists to give him, namely, confirmation. His fellow scientists are not purchasing truth; critical assessment and approbation are not the same as purchasing power. The formation of scientific consensus is the objective of a scientist; prestige, prize, reputation are only incidental consequences of a persuasive presentation of his results of original research. It is truth that is the objective of the actions of a scientist and it is to its truth that the scientific audience will attest. The agreement of his peers is only an instrumental condition for the accrediting of the discovery. Even if the scientist thinks that credit for making the discovery is what he arrives at, he is compelled to aim at the truth. He will not otherwise receive any credit. If he seeks credit for truth, he will be discredited. The "truth" is not central to the market.

There is a somewhat closer approximation to the principle of the market in the political sphere in which politicians and their parties compete with other politicians and their parties for the suffrage of the electorate, offering them goods and services once they are elected.

Civil society does not include the state but it presupposes its existence. It presupposes a particular kind of state, namely, a state of limited powers. Among these powers are the powers to enact laws which protect the market. Civil society requires that the state (or government) be limited in the scope of its activities and that it be bound by law but that it be effective in executing the laws which protect the pluralism of civil society and its necessary liberties. Civil society consists, among other things, of institutions which hedge about the state, which sustain it and delimit the scope of its activities and powers. Civil society requires a distinctive set of political institutions.

The civil society must be more than a set of markets and market-like institutions. What else does it need to be a civil society? It must possess the institutions which protect it from the encroachment of the state and which keep it as a civil society. A civil society must have a system of competing political parties. It requires the competition of political parties, seeking the support of universal suffrage with periodic elections for the election of representative legislative bodies which once elected must have a modicum of autonomy *vis-à-vis* the electorate. It must possess an independent judiciary which upholds the rule of law and protects the liberty of individuals and institutions. It must possess a set of institutions for making known the activities of government; it includes a free press reporting freely on the activities of government. (The press includes here the printed press, radio and television broadcasting, published learned investigation, critical discussion and assessment of the activities of politicians and bureaucrats and of the forms of political and governmental institutions). These are the primary institutions of civil society because they are the safeguards of the separation of civil society from the state.

Essential to the functioning of the primary institutions are the supporting institutions: voluntary associations and their exercise of the freedoms of association, assembly and representation or petition. Individuals must enjoy the corresponding freedom to associate, assemble and petition. A civil society must provide for private contracts which assert binding obligations and the judicial enforcement of such arrangements; it should provide for collective bargaining and wage-contracts. Naturally, freedom of religious belief and worship, association and education are part of civil society. Freedom of academic teaching and study, of investigation and publication are also part of the complex pattern of civil society.

These are the institutions by which the state is kept within substantive and procedural confinement. The confinement, which might be thought to be negative, is sustained on behalf of a positive ideal, the ideal of individual and collective freedom.

Civil society postulates and accentuates the pluralism of autonomous spheres and autonomous institutions acting within and between such spheres. Civil society accepts the diversity of interests and ideals which will arise in any numerous society. It allows diversity of the objectives pursued by individuals and institutions—but not by all and any means whatsoever. Civil society guarantees the rights of individuals and collectivities to private property, lawfully acquired; it guarantees the rights of privacy of individuals and collectivities. It guarantees the rights of individuals and collectivities in the religious, intellectual and political spheres. But civil society imposes limits at the line where the practice of these rights becomes uncivil.

A civil society must impose limits on movements or organizations which would subvert it. It must impose limits on conspiratorial activity. It would be contrary to the ethos of a civil society, i.e., to the rule of civility, to permit the abrogation or abolition of civil society. Civil society provides for the individual pursuit of gain, just as it provides for the criticism of the existing social and political order but it would prohibit actions which would abrogate the civil order of society by breaking laws and acting to establish, gradually or suddenly, an uncivil society.

VI

Liberal democracy is the most general class of society, variants of which, among others, are mass democracy, "retrospective" democracy and civil society. Mass or populistic democracy is a variant of liberal democracy. It is at another pole from civil society insofar as it considers one section of society, albeit the majority of the population, as the properly sole beneficiary of policies regarding the distribution of goods, services and honors. Mass democracy would disregard representative institutions, replacing them by demonstrations and plebiscites. Mass democracy is conducive to demagogy and to the extension of governmental powers for the provision of substantive justice. Still, another alternative is the "retrospective" democracy formulated by Max Weber in his conversation with Ludendorff in 1919 and by Joseph Schumpeter, in which the electorate confirms or dismisses its rulers in accordance with whether it is satisfied with their accomplishments during the most recent electoral period.[1] Civil society differs from mass democracy in its concern for the interests and ideals of all sections of the population and not just for one. It differs from "retrospective" democracy in its constant scrutiny and assessment of government and its refusal to allow it to extend its range or depth of activities.

1. Max Weber, *Zur Neuordnung Deutschlands: Schriften und Reden 1918–1920. Gesamtausgabe* (Tübingen: J. C. B. Mohr, 1988), Abt. I, Band 16, p. 553; and Joseph Schumpeter, *Capitalism, Socialism and Democracy* (London: Allen and Unwin, 1943), pp. 269–83.

VII

Insofar as they work, more or less effectively, to maintain liberal democracy, it may be said that the institutions of liberal democracy "embody" civility; they could not work without a certain minimum of civility. The latter are likely to be in a minority but their presence and activities make a great difference. Civil society is maintained through the self-reproduction of its institutions; this self-reproduction is the work of persons who accept the obligations of their posts, those who conform with the rules of the institution since they are advantageous for them and by the stiffening influence of persons with a fairly high degree of civility.

Civility is an attitude and a pattern of conduct. It is approximately the same as what Montesquieu called virtue. Montesquieu said, "Virtue, in a republic, is a very simple thing: it is love of the republic." It is "love of one's country." "Love of the republic in a democracy is love of democracy. . . ."[2]

Civility is an appreciation of or attachment to the institutions which constitute civil society. It is an attitude of attachment to the whole society, to all its strata and sections. It is an attitude of concern for the good of the entire society. Civility is simultaneously individualistic, parochial and "holistic." It is solicitous of the well-being of the whole of the larger interest.

More fundamentally, civility is the conduct of a person whose individual self-consciousness had been partly superseded by his collective self-consciousness, the society as a whole and the institution of civil society being the referents of his collective self-consciousness.

"Civility," like "civil society," has had an upsurge of popularity in recent years. Unlike civil society, which has been much spoken about in the recently Communist countries and in the shadow of Marxism

---

2. Montesquieu, *De l'Esprit des lois* (*Oeuvres*) (Paris: Dalibon, 1822), II, pp. 213–14.

by persons who have become discontented with both, civility has been little spoken of by those seeking to escape from Marxism. It has been somewhat more spoken of in liberal democratic societies. In British and American societies, journalists have taken it up so that it is now in fairly common usage, after rather long disuse. Its history is obscure. In 1937, Walter Lippmann, in his book *An Enquiry into the Principles of the Good Society,* devoted a short chapter to "The Civil Society" (pp. 318–24) but he does not refer at all to "civility." After the war, Ernest Barker published a collection of essays under the title *Traditions of Civility* but did not go past the title in his treatment of the subject. In 1955, I published an essay under the title of "Ideology and Civility," in which I contrasted civil politics with ideological politics; by civil politics I meant political activities and attitudes which did not regard differences as irreconcilable.[3] A little earlier in the same year, Professor Raymond Aron entitled the final chapter of his book *L'opium des intellectuals,* "*la Fin des idéologies.*" He took up the same theme but he did not, except by implication, enter into an analysis of "civility" as a political attitude and a mode of political action. My own essay naturally came closer to the present meaning of the term which remains, even now, very ambiguous. In that essay I carried forward ideas I had put forth in a small book, entitled *The Torment of Secrecy,* which I had published a little while before and in an essay called "The End of Ideology?," published around the same time, on the incompatibility of the extremist sectarian politics of communism and populistic, apocalyptic anti-communism with the less divisive, more consensual politics of civility.[4] None of these writings found much in the way of ready acceptance. The last essay, "The End of Ideology?," did arouse enraged negations from more or less Marxist intellectuals whose faith in Marxism was faltering but who could not bear to hear it criticized.

3. Reprinted herein *(ed.)*.
4. Having first appeared in 1956, *The Torment of Secrecy* (Chicago: Ivan Dee, 1996) was recently republished *(ed.)*.

It is interesting to me that in the noise raised by the defenders of ideology—they knew that Marxism would be the main victim of any enlargement of the practice and influence of civility—the idea of civility was not discussed. Neither the opponents of the alleged thesis of the end of ideology, nor Professor Daniel Bell, who was an innocent by-stander and who was roundly assailed in the course of an extensive exchange, spoke about civility.

In 1973, Mr. Ferdinand Mount published an excellent essay, entitled "The Recovery of Civility."[5] It was mainly about civility in the sense of good manners and courtesy towards political opponents as well as towards political allies. He said that "civility . . . implied . . . inclusion in the same moral universe."

About a decade ago, the word came into a wider usage. It came to be used loosely to criticize conservative critics of collectivistic liberalism. It was aimed frequently at zealots such as religious fundamentalists, opponents of higher taxation, critics of governmentally supported abortions, etc. It was used to criticize for their lack of civility those who were opposed to collectivism. The objects of criticism, i.e., those charged with lacking civility, had imputed to them "demagogy," "uncaringness," "narrow selfishness," "dogmatism," etc. The word was, in short, employed to criticize vehement critics of collective liberalism. It was, as far as I know, the collectivistic liberals who brought the term civility into a wider usage, although it was certainly not initiated by them. Since collectivistic liberals did not interest themselves in civil society— the Soviet Union, the "peoples democracies" and the third world countries were more to their taste—they did not attempt to bring together civility and civil society, which has prized autonomy *vis-à-vis* the state, the market and private property.

The term "civility" has usually, both in the past and in its recent revival, been interpreted to mean courtesy, well-spokenness, moderation, respect for others, self-restraint, gentlemanliness, urbanity, re-

---

5. *Encounter* 41 (July 1973): 31–43.

finement, good manners, politeness. All those terms have generally been reserved for the description of the conduct of individuals in the immediate presence of each other. In all of these usages, there are intimations of consideration for the sensibilities of other persons and particularly for their desire to be esteemed. Thus, it would be antithetical to civility to refuse esteem or deference to another person. Civility would avoid insults to another person. Civility is basically respect for the dignity and the desire for dignity of other persons. Civility is conduct which accords, however superficially and however conventionally, esteem to others, either for particular properties or in general. Civility treats others as, at least, equal in dignity, never as inferior in dignity.

VIII

What does civility have to do with civil society? What place do good manners, courtesy, etc., have in a civil, i.e., pluralistic society of many, partially autonomous and competing individuals and associations? What does the civility of good manners have in common with the civility of civil society? Let me begin by saying that both postulate a minimal dignity of all citizens. The dignity which is accorded to a person who is the object of civil conduct or good manners is dignity of moral worth. Good manners postulate the moral dignity of the other person who is seen face-to-face, and in public discourse about individuals and groups who are not immediately present. It makes no reference to his merit or dignity in general, in all other situations. Civility as a feature of civil society considers others as fellow-citizens of equal dignity in their rights and obligations as members of civil society; it means regarding other persons, including one's adversaries, as members of the same inclusive collectivity, i.e., as members of the same society, even though they belong to different parties or to different religious communities or to different ethnic groups. Civility in the former sense is included in civility in the latter sense. But in the latter sense, it includes concern for the good of adversaries as well as for the good of allies. Therein lies the difference between civility understood as good manners or courtesy and civility as the virtue of civil society.

The two kinds of civility are different from each other; they are also similar to each other. I am also interested in their interdependence; one contributes to the other. Civility in the sense of courtesy mollifies or ameliorates the strain which accompanies the risks, the dangers of prospective loss and the injuries of the real losses of an economically, politically and intellectually competitive society in which some persons are bound to lose. Courtesy makes life a bit more pleasant; it is easier to bear than harshness. Softly spoken, respectful speech is more pleasing to listen to than harsh, contemptuous speech.

There is much said nowadays in disparagement of politeness; it is said to be artificial, hypocritical, lacking in genuineness or spontaneity. It is, however, generally recognized, even in this age which condemns artificiality, that impoliteness, such as is said to be common in New York City, is far from gratifying to those persons who are its objects. New Yorkers probably would like to have a little more politeness in their transient encounters with other New Yorkers, even if it is hypocritical. Civility in manners holds anger and resentment in check; it has a calming, pacifying effect on the sentiments. It might make for less excitability. Civil manners are aesthetically pleasing and morally right. Civil manners redound to the benefit of political activity.

Civil manners reach into politics in legislative assemblies, in public political meetings, in committees of legislative bodies—in all situations in which individuals can see each other and hear each other and in which individuals are addressed directly by other individuals, each of whom is present as the representative of a political group or as the exponent of a political view. They make relationships among the members of such institutions more agreeable. They make opposition less rancorous; they make opponents less irreconcilable.

Civil manners are beneficial to the working of civil society. Civil manners contribute in many situations to the peaceful working of the institutions of civil society and to the relations between them. The absence of civil manners introduces an unsettling effect on institutions; it makes people uneasy.

IX

Yet there is more to civility than good manners and conciliatory tones. Civility is a mode of political action. It is a mode of political action which postulates that antagonists are also members of the same society, that they participate in the same collective self-consciousness. The individual who acts with civility regards the individuals who are its objects as being one with oneself, as being parts of a single entity. Civility rests, at bottom, on the collective self-consciousness of civil society. Of course, individuals participate in many collectivities and they are also individuals. They participate in many collective self-consciousnesses and they also have their own individual self-consciousness, but in a civil society, they participate in, they are parts of, the collective self-consciousness of society.

The image of the common good is inherent in the nature of collective self-consciousness. Collective self-consciousness does not obliterate individual self-consciousness; collective self-consciousness has influence on conduct only through the activity of individual self-consciousness. In the other direction, no individual can live without a modicum of collective self-consciousness. No society could exist without it. Collective self-consciousness is generated wherever there are enduring relationships.

Collective self-consciousness, which is a cognitive state, as seeing one's self as part of a collectivity, has within it a norm which gives precedence to the interest of the collectivity over the individual or parochial interest. All societies engender some degree of collective self-consciousness. This does not mean that the collective self-consciousness always prevails over the individual's self-consciousness. On the contrary, the opposite is very frequently the case. Nor does it by any means imply that the more inclusive collective self-consciousness always takes precedence over the less inclusive collective self-consciousness. Nevertheless, the existence of the inclusive collective self-consciousness has a restraining effect. It is never obliterated, even in a society in a state of civil war. It is the inclusive collective self-consciousness which prevents society from degenerating completely into the state of nature.

The late Carl Schmitt said that political activity of a society is organized around the poles of friends and enemies. This is true of societies which are on the verge of or are already engaged in civil war. This is the antithesis of civil society. Civility is a mode of conduct which protects liberal democratic society from the danger of extremes of partisanship which it, itself, generates; civility limits or diminishes the real losses which are bound to be inflicted on a society in which conflicts are both inherent—they are inherent in all societies—and provided for by its liberal democratic constitution. Without such civility, a pluralistic society can degenerate into a war of each against all.

Civility works like a governor of civil society. It limits the intensity of conflict. It reduces the distance between conflicting demands; it is a curb on centrifugal tendencies. Civility is a phenomenon of collective self-consciousness, is a mode of attachment of the individual or the sub-collectivity to the society as a whole, i.e., the most inclusive collectivity. It is attachment to those particular institutions of civil society which provide opportunities for the open contentions of interests and the conflicts of ideals, and which at the same time hold them in check. Civility, by its attachment of its individual bearers to the society as a whole, places a limit on the irreconcilability with which parochial ends are pursued. Attachment to the whole reduces the rigidity of attachment to the parts, whether it be a social class or an occupational or ethnic group or a political party or a religious community.

All societies, the highly differentiated as well as the relatively homogeneous, are sites of conflicting interests in the sense that, at any given moment, when one part obtains more of anything, there is less for the other part. (Of course, when a third party external to the society is the object of military conquest and the taking of booty, all parts of the society might benefit. But there still remains the issue of the division of the spoils; if one part of society takes more of the booty, the other part receives less, even though its situation is better than it was previously.) These conflicts and contentions do not occur or are not severe as long as total demands do not greatly exceed total supply of the valued things which will satisfy them.

Ideals and beliefs too have limited opportunities for their realization; the realization of the ideals of one group would usually preclude the realization of the ideals and beliefs of other groups within the same society. Where contention among the advocates of the diverse ideals and beliefs is free, there will naturally be more public contention than in an unfree society.

Contention is unsettling to a society. It is unsettling not only because it raises desires for gains and fears of losses but also because it causes its participants and others in the same society to regard contention as inevitable and necessary. It supports the view that life is exclusively a matter of "dog eat dog." It makes for a hardening of contention and an irreconcilability of differences in interests and ideals. The tendency of contention to be expressed in a hyperbolic rhetoric aggravates fear of the other parties to the conflict. It makes for distrust.

Civil society is bound to be a scene of open conflicts. All societies are full of potential conflicts; most of these potentialities are not realized because of considerations of prudence or fear. Societies which are highly differentiated are especially disposed towards conflicts arising from ideals and interests which cannot be made compatible with divergent ideals and interests. A pluralistic society provides for the pursuit of these divergent ideals and interests; that is what its pluralism consists in. Where these ideals and interests have such objects as public observance or determinate gross-national products as other ideals and interests, there are bound to be conflicts between those who pursue these conflicting interests or ideals. The interests of the contending parties cannot be realized simultaneously; the same is true of ideals. The rules of pluralistic society not only permit these conflicts; they even arouse them to greater intensity. Civility diminishes the intensity of these conflicts.

There are some conflicts between different groups within a society which are unceasing. In their public manifestations, they are not however of constant intensity; they wax and they wane. This is equally true whether they are conflicts about incompatible interests and conflicts between mutually contradictory ideals. Civility on the part of those who participate in these conflicts reduces the probability of their flaring up.

X

Although autonomy *vis-à-vis* the state is one of the features of a civil society, the autonomy is far from complete. Civil society operates within the framework set by laws. The laws of such a society are, among other things, intended to hold conflict in check by compelling adherence to agreements, and by inflicting sanctions on actions which criminally damage other persons. Laws require that rights within the civil society be respected and that duties be performed.

A civil society is a society where law binds the state as well as the citizens. It protects the citizens from arbitrary and unjust decisions of high political authorities, bureaucrats, the police, the military, and the rich and the powerful. A civil society is one where the law prevails equally against the impulses of citizens to seek their own immediate advantage. The effectiveness of the laws both in the state and in civil society—and the family—depends in part on the civility of individuals. Of course, the effectiveness of the laws depends upon the executive organs of the state but it cannot be effective through the actions of those organs alone. The executive organs of society cannot cope with all the situations and actions to which they refer; even the best police force cannot detect, trace and capture all criminals, to say nothing of juvenile delinquents. It is true of course that if the investigative parts of officialdom and the police are very successful in tracking and finding most of those who have infringed on the law and if they succeed to have them found guilty on the basis of sound evidence and punished accordingly, the high degree of probability of detection and punishment might have a deterrent effect. This alone would be insufficient. The tendency towards law-abidingness must be reinforced by belief in the legitimacy of the laws or the regulations. Legitimacy in a pluralistic, civil society depends on the civil attachments of the bulk of the citizenry to the central institutions of society.

The foregoing considerations refer to recurrent situations and to existing laws and regulations. New situations are constantly emerging. Societies are never at rest. They are incessantly forced to move into new situations. Sometimes they are thrust into these new situations from internal dispositions and impulses and sometimes by changes in their external environment, frequently from both in combination. Sometimes they move because of newly emerging demands which are responses to changes generated within one part of the society to which other parts must adapt themselves. Techniques of doing things, material and social, change as part of an effort to be more rational or more powerful. New strata appear and some sections of the population become larger, more clamant, more audible, and more demanding for a larger share or a higher status than what they have had heretofore. There are other sections of the society which prefer to be left as they are, with their own position intact, their possessions and incomes undiminished, their status preserved; they too have to respond to actual changes or demanded changes which would deprive them of what they possess. Such changes usually heighten parochial or sectional self-consciousness. New situations generate new conflicts and accentuate old ones. They make it more difficult to be civil. They promote resistance to civility.

XI

Milton Friedman is right. There is no such thing as a free lunch. Someone must pay for it. A civil society, which is necessarily pluralistic, can no more escape from this ineluctable fact of earthly existence than any other type of society; it is inevitable that most will struggle to avoid loss and that the losers will often be resentful against the winners.

Here is where civility in the sense of political courtesy and substantive civility have their tasks laid out for them. The civility of good manners provides procedures or modes of speech in the expression of demands which mollify sentiments of antagonism. Substantive civility which is of concern for the common good of the society as a whole supports the partial renunciation of demands, and the moderation of ideals.

XII

Substantive civility is the virtue of civil society. It is the readiness to moderate particular, individual or parochial interests and to give precedence to the common good. The common good is not susceptible to an unambiguous definition; consensus about it is probably not attainable. It is however certainly meaningful to speak about it. Wherever two antagonistic advocates arrive at a compromise through the recognition of a common interest, they redefine themselves as members of a collectivity the good of which has precedence over their own particular objectives. The good which is accorded precedence by that decision might be no more than the continued existence of the collectivity in which they both participate. The common good is acknowledged wherever a more inclusive collectivity is acknowledged.

Every action in which thinking of and attempting to reduce the prospective loss inflicted on one section of a society when another section would benefit from a particular event or policy is an act of substantive civility. It is always possible to consider the consequences of any particular action in the light of its effect on the wider circle within which a decision is made. Every action which bears in mind the well-being of a more inclusive collectivity is an action on behalf of the common good.

The pattern of society as such—not any particular institution exactly as it is—is the minimal common good. The common good is a pattern which permits or enables the living of a good life, by individuals, collectivities and the entire society—or at least a better life than they otherwise might live. The civil society is the common good. Civility is the concern for the maintenance of the civil society as a civil society. Civility is therefore a concern to reconcile—not abolish—divergent interests.

The concern for the common good also takes into account the diversity of future interests and ideals as well as the diversity of present interests and ideals. The necessity to balance present and future interests is very similar to the need to balance contemporaneous interests and ideals. In thinking of the future, it would in principle be necessary to have to think of various points in the future. But the state of society at any moment in the future certainly eludes human intelligence, and the remoter the future, the more unencompassible. The future cannot be foreseen except in the case of some events of the very near future, and even then, very uncertainly. Who can foresee the multiplicity of desires and potentialities which might emerge at various moments in the future? Yet, the future cannot be totally disregarded and it too must be taken into account in the determination of the common good.

XIII

Max Weber spoke very eloquently about conflicts of values in his lecture on "Politics as a Vocation." Such conflicts cannot, according to Max Weber, be reconciled into a logically harmonious pattern; what can be done is to act in the light of what the attainment of each value costs in terms of each other's value. The adherent of the ethos and politics of responsibility—he called it *Verantwortungsethik* and implied the category of *Verantwortungspolitik*—has however to arrive at a decision. He has to make the best decision possible, arrived at by the weighing of each value and its costs. There is no formula for making benefits and costs homogeneous so that an arithmetic sum of a maximal of realization can be arrived at.

In another essay, written by Max Weber as an occasional political pamphlet during the First World War (*Parlament und Regierung im neugeordneten Deutschland*),[6] he argued for parliamentary government as a school for the selection of political leaders with sufficient force of character and sufficiently great persuasive powers to be able to maintain their parliamentary majorities or to keep their parties coherent and positive when in opposition. The task of such leaders is to fuse into a single coherent collectivity the diverse circles of adherents such as are drawn into association with a political party.

These two works of Max Weber, when brought together, define the task of a civil politician. Speaking on behalf of the whole is the task of the politician of a civil, i.e., liberal democratic society. They also define the task of the civil citizen; the citizen has the task of promulgating an objective which is broader than that of a leader of a political party. It is to seek consensus about an objective which will benefit the entire society and which will be sought by the entire society. Of course, the word "entire" is excessive; the support of the entire society is impossible and unnecessary. What is needed is sufficient consensus to permit government to work effectively towards the common good. (The effectiveness of government is also dependent on its practical

6. Max Weber, *Zur Politik im Weltkrieg, Schriften und Reden 1914–1918. Gesamtausgabe* (Tübingen: J. C. B. Mohr, 1984), Abt. I, Band 5, pp. 421–596. An English translation appears as Appendix II in Max Weber, *Economy and Society* (Berkeley & Los Angeles: University of California Press, 1978).

knowledge and its capacity for realistic judgement, not just on the consensus of its supporters.)

A society possessing the institutions of civil society needs a significant component of ordinary citizens and politicians who exercise the virtue of civility. How large must that component of civil citizens be? How much civility does a liberal democratic society need to be a civil society? Where in the society must civility be located?

Of no society can it be expected that all its citizens will have a very high degree of civility. The capacity for civility—the capacity for imagination and cognition of the properties of one's fellow men and the capacity to entertain and give precedence to the inclusive collective self-consciousness within oneself over one's individual self-consciousness—is probably rather unevenly distributed within any society. There are some persons in whom civility preponderates; there are others in whom it is usually at a low ebb. For a civil society to benefit from the former it is important that many of them should be in authoritative position. There are certain roles in society in which civility is particularly important for society. The higher judiciary, senior civil servants, leading legislators, eminent academics, prominent businessmen, influential journalists, and others like them, nationally and locally, must have relatively high degrees of civility. At least some of the leading members of each of these professions should have it; their civility should furthermore be visible. There must also be a scatter of persons of moderate degrees of civility throughout the society. There must be at least small degrees of civility in most citizens. There must be areas of concentration and larger areas of dispersion of civility.

Civility not only has immediate effectiveness in the actions of those who possess it; it also has radiative or reinforcing effect. Those who have a larger degree of civility animate the civility of those who have less, and so on downward in a pyramid of civility towards those with least civility and least responsiveness. A spark of civility exists in the breast of most individuals even though it is not strong. It is certainly strengthened by the scatter of civil persons throughout any modern society and particularly by the presence and visibility of civil persons in the institutions of civil society.

What we ought to hope for is enough civility in the participants in those institutions to maintain them effectively as civil institutions— and not as sites of intense conflicts between irreconcilable interests and ideas espoused by uncompromising parochial groups and inflexibly egoistic individuals. Civility can only be an ingredient of a civil society; it can serve to offset the perpetual drives towards the preponderance of individual self-consciousness and parochial collective self-consciousness.

Even those persons who are highly civil are not likely to manifest their civility with equal intensity on all occasions. Most human beings have some parochial attachment to their immediate and extended families, to their locality, to the social class, to their profession, their religious community, their generation, ethnic group, etc. These attachments, like civility, are unequally distributed among occasions and among individuals. They cannot be entirely abrogated or suppressed; nor is it desirable that they should be. Even persons with a very large measure of civility will possess attachments to their other parochial or less inclusive collectivities. Civility does not require their complete renunciation but it does require that they yield precedence on many occasions.

The primary institutions of civil society cannot always be filled exclusively with persons with a very high degree of civility. It is however very important that judges and high civil servants should be civil so that they may hold in check the parochiality, i.e., the sectionalism, group and individual selfishness, or partisanship of the leaders of political parties, regional, ethnic and national groups, etc., within the larger society. Legislators are not likely to be highly civil for much of their legislative activities, especially in societies in which elected representatives are regarded and regard themselves as the advocate of the interest of their respective parties, of their supporters and of their own constituents. It would be contrary to the nature of pluralistic political systems for it to be otherwise. It is reasonable to expect a fairly high degree of civility in religious bodies and in the academic professions, although this expectation is often disappointed. Likewise in the legal profession and in the teaching of law. This is certainly not always the case.

To summarize: the center and the main sub-centers of society need to be civil to a greater extent than the peripheries. But in the peripheries to these is a need for some civility to offset the partisanship of persons at the centers and sub-centers. It is in the nature of a civil society that the circles of peripheries, which are closer to the centers, will be relatively more civil than those more remote from the center.

XIV

No human being can be completely possessed by his civility. That would entail the suspension of his individual self-consciousness, his biological nature and his disposition to parochial attachments. Similarly, a completely civil society would cease to be a pluralistic society; it would probably not be a society of individual and collective freedom. It would simply be a society in which all individual and collective actions were aimed at the same collective goals, which would be goals of benefit to the collectivity and about which there would be no disagreement. All actions would be directed towards the common good. There would be no activities directed towards sectional or parochial ends. There would be no parishes or any other subdivision with their own interests and ends.

It would be contrary to the nature of man and the nature of society for all the members of society to possess to such a high degree the virtue of civility. Selfishness and parochiality are inexpungible from human life. However, there is no danger that they will be expunged. The larger danger is that they will be too powerful to keep the society reasonable and coherent.

XV

The idea of the common good and its other variants, like the idea of the good of society, are frequently invoked. They are frequently invoked with the intention to deceive. But even where they are honestly invoked, they are ambiguous. It is very difficult to define them precisely. For this and for more important reasons, there are bound to be in any civil society, diverse conceptions of the common good, conflicting with each other in varying degrees. The proponents of one conception of the common good might denounce the proponents of the other conceptions.

This does not invalidate the conception of the common good. In disagreement though they might be, they also recognize that there is a difference between parochial interests and the interests of more inclusive collectivities. What they disagree about is the weight to be assigned to different valued conditions, which they evaluate somewhat differently. Disagreements are aggravated by disagreements about facts. (This is inevitable in the present state of disruptive powers of the social sciences.)

Thus the ideal of the common good is a practicable ideal, even though there is likely at any given moment disagreement about its substance and even though it can never be completely realized.

XVI

What are the prospects for the realization of civil society to a greater degree than now exists? I will forego any discussion about how Western liberal democratic societies already modestly civil can be more civil. It is not because they have reached the ideal state. I wish rather to consider the prospects of civility and of civil society in two different situations.

The reemergence of the discussion of civil society has been concurrent with efforts to establish civil society in numerous countries in which it had been suppressed, resisted and denounced for many decades and where its proponents were persecuted. Does the recent demand for the installation of civil society correspond to a likelihood that the demand will be realized?

The accomplishments thus far in Eastern and Central Europe are real but they should not be overestimated. In Central Europe, in Poland, in Czechoslovakia, Hungary and the Baltic countries, communism was a foreign imposition. It was, it is true, aided by a substantial minority of domestic accomplices, some of whom acted from wrong, but firmly believed, ideals, others of whom were time-servers who became place-holders. The success of the effort to free themselves from totalitarianism in those countries has been largely a consequence of the loss of conviction of the Soviet elite about its own legitimacy, accentuated by the ever extending disclosure of its incompetence and failures of the planned economy and its now obvious disorder and unproductiveness.

It remains to be seen whether the effort to replace Communist totalitarianism by civil society will come upon such obstacles that the readiness to submit to the discipline of a civil society might be much weakened. There is no strong and widespread pre-Communist tradition of devotion to civil society in any of these countries, except for Czecho-slovakia; in Hungary and Poland, under different and difficult circum-stances, small circles of politicians and citizens attempted to act with civility but they availed very little against uncivil groups. All these countries have as one pillar of a civil society a strong sense of nationality. It was this which preserved them during periods when uncivil foreign rule was imposed on them. Nationality is the closest thing to a whole society; the national state is its proper form of realization. It therefore offers an object of civility. Nevertheless, the problem remains unsolved. For one thing, there are divergent conceptions of the common good of the nation. The other is that expectations have been aimed so high that failure to fulfill them is likely and in consequence the legitimacy of incumbent authorities will be diminished. Many persons might slide back into apathy or cynicism, the antitheses of civility. In addition to this, a number of different nationalities, equally demanding of being civil societies, are recalcitrant to being parts of the civil society of the numerically preponderant nationality.

Furthermore, as in the West, the intellectuals in large measure still regard, despite their hostility to communism and to Marxism and Marxism-Leninism, the "social ownership of the instruments of production" as the *sine qua non* of a good society. That is an idea which has until recently been increasingly pervasive in the educated classes over the course of the last century. Although in the public intellectual debate, there has been a great surge forward of adherence to the idea of the market economy, the leaders of that forward surge are probably still a minority. The major positions in intellectual institutions are still held by proponents of the social ownership of the instruments of production, including many persons who disliked the Communist regimes. They are, it is true, somewhat shaken by the renunciation of centrally planned, state-controlled economies in the Communist countries; but it is doubtful whether their fundamental antagonism to their own societies and to the principle on which their own economies are conducted, has lost its vital force in their minds.

Furthermore, the task of transforming the nominally "planned" but in fact bureaucratically congested economy into a market economy is very difficult. Unsatisfied, often unrealistically formulated, demands threaten to have divisive and demoralizing effects.

It is certainly not in order to celebrate the enduring triumph of civil society. It will as in the past have a long hard row to hoe. The bearers of civility will have to be very tenacious. The tasks they face are immense. Not all of these tasks are directly connected with being a civil society. Means of controlling inflation, of providing employment, of providing adequate supplies of foodstuff, are not primarily problems to be resolved by civility, although their chances for solutions might be increased by a wider diffusion of civility in the mass of the citizenry and among political leaders.

XVII

Still the advantages of nationality and patriotism—by no means unambiguously advantageous—are not inconsequential. Being a national society is a step—not an inevitable step—towards becoming a civil society. As national societies, they offer to their members a readily available object of reference for the inclusive collective self-consciousness which is the foundation of civility.

When we turn from the countries of Eastern Europe to the countries of Western Europe we face a different situation. About Eastern Europe, we face the question about whether they can engender enough civility to permit an undistracted effort to resolve some of the very difficult problems of creating a productive market economy and a pluralistic but consensual system of political parties. In Western Europe, we face a situation in which a number of moderately well functioning national economies and polities—largely civil societies—can be formed into a single European civil society.

Societies tend to be national societies. Well functioning multinational societies are relatively rare, certainly rarer than well functioning national societies. What are the prospects of European civility? They are, I would say, poorer than the prospects of civility in the Eastern European societies because Europe has no significant territorial referent such as the Eastern European societies possess, namely, its "own" territory. Europe has been a cultural phenomenon for a small elite of intellectual and religious intellectuals and administrators since antiquity. But on the whole, and particularly in modern times, it has been kept in a less effective position alongside of the more powerful national collective self-consciousnesses of the various European national societies.

The European Commission does not have the advantage of effective nationality to help it in its course. The European Commission has a bureaucracy which is probably regarded by the citizens of most Western European countries as alien; it is not thought of as existing at all by most of the population of the Western European societies. The bureaucracy in Brussels is well aware of the European Commission and so are European businessmen, and so are many civil servants of the Western European societies, but it is doubtful whether they accord to it the legitimacy which they attribute to the governments of their own national societies. The parliament of the European Community is faint and its powers are not prominent in the minds of Western Europeans. The European Commission itself and its rotating chairman gathers no moss of traditionality around it; it certainly shows no signs of becoming the object of a reference of European national collective self-consciousness. It has neither the charismatic qualities seen in great personalities nor does it have the charismatic qualities inhering in great and visible power. Invisible and intermittent or segmental power does not gain the attribution of charisma.

For Europe to become a single, albeit very differentiated, civil society, it will have to come forward much more prominently in the collective self-consciousness of European individuals. European civility might already exist, very incipiently, but it has a very long way to go before it can attain even the fluctuating strength of the civility which is in operation in the present Western liberal democratic societies.

All the more necessary is it to argue for the virtue of civility. It has more work to do than it ever had before. It must prevent gains within societies and within the European continent from being lost. It must go standing up for the common good of which civil society itself is one of the most fundamental constituents.

Principal Works of Edward Shils

Papers

Three volumes of the selected papers of Edward Shils have been published to date:

The Intellectuals and the Powers. Chicago: University of Chicago Press, 1972.

Center and Periphery: Essays in Macrosociology. Chicago: University of Chicago Press, 1975.

The Calling of Sociology and Other Essays on the Pursuit of Learning. Chicago: University of Chicago Press, 1980.

In addition, a collection of eleven of Shils's papers, having to do with the fundamental constitution of societies and the way in which the higher functions of the mind enter into that constitution, have appeared in:

The Constitution of Society. The Heritage of Sociology. Chicago: University of Chicago Press, 1972.

Finally, two collections of Edward Shils's papers on higher education have appeared in:

The Calling of Education. Chicago: University of Chicago Press, 1997. Edited by Steven Grosby.

The Order of Learning and the Contemporary University. New Brunswick, N.J.: Transaction Publishers, 1997. Edited by Philip Altbach.

Books

Toward a General Theory of Action. Cambridge: Harvard University Press, 1951. With Talcott Parsons et al.

The Torment of Secrecy. Glencoe, Ill.: Free Press, 1956; Chicago: Ivan Dee, 1996.

The Intellectual Between Tradition and Modernity: The Indian Situation. The Hague: Mouton, 1961.

Political Development in the New States. The Hague: Mouton, 1962.

Tradition. Chicago: University of Chicago Press, 1981.

Universities, Politicians and Bureaucrats: Europe and the United States. Cambridge: Cambridge University Press, 1982. With Hans Daalder.

The Academic Ethic. Chicago: University of Chicago Press, 1983.

Jews and Christians in a Pluralistic World. London: Weidenfeld & Nicolson, 1991. With Ernst-Wolfgang Böckenförde.

Remembering the University of Chicago: Teachers, Scientists, and Scholars. Chicago: University of Chicago Press, 1991.

Cambridge Women: Twelve Portraits. Cambridge: Cambridge University Press, 1996. With Carmen Blacker.

Portraits: A Gallery of Intellectuals. Chicago: University of Chicago Press, 1997.

Selected Books Translated

Karl Mannheim. *Ideology and Utopia.* New York: Harcourt, Brace, 1936. With Louis Wirth.

———. *Man and Society in an Age of Reconstruction.* London: Kegan Paul, Trench, Trubner, 1940.

Max Weber. *The Methodology of the Social Sciences.* Glencoe, Ill.: Free Press, 1949. With Henry A. Finch.

———. *On Law in Economy and Society.* Cambridge: Harvard University Press, 1954. With Max Rheinstein.

Essays and Articles

Edward Shils was the founding editor of the quarterly journal *Minerva: A Review of Science, Learning, and Policy.* The journal has appeared regularly since 1962 and was edited by Shils up to his death. The above represents only a partial list of Shils's scholarly output. In addition to his articles in *Minerva*, Shils was a regular contributor to such journals as *Encounter, Survey,* and *American Scholar.* Many of his important articles and papers remain to be collected. Of these, the following might be of particular interest to the readers of this volume.

"Authoritarianism 'Left' and 'Right.' " In *Studies in the Scope and Method of "The Authoritarian Personality,"* edited by Richard Christie and Marie Jahoda. Glencoe, Ill.: Free Press, 1954. A devastating review of T. W. Adorno et al., *The Authoritarian Personality.* New York: Harper, 1950.

"Government and Universities in the United States." *Minerva* 17, no. 2 (1979): 129–77. Shils was selected in 1979 by the National Endowment for the Humanities to be its Eighth Jefferson Lecturer. The three lectures that Shils gave were published in *Minerva* under this title.

"Raymond Aron: A Memoir." In *History, Truth, Liberty: Selected Writings of Raymond Aron,* edited by Franciszek Draus. Chicago: University of Chicago Press, 1985.

"Intellectuals and Responsibility." In *The Political Responsibility of Intellectuals,* edited by Ian Maclean, Alan Montefiore, and Peter Winch. Cambridge: Cambridge University Press, 1990.

"Henry Sumner Maine in the Tradition of the Analysis of Society." In *The Victorian Achievement of Sir Henry Maine,* edited by Alan Diamond. Cambridge: Cambridge University Press, 1991.

Index

Autonomistic liberalism: and achievement, 154; collectivistic liberalism contrasted with, 125–27, 139, 143, 159, 177–78, 181; and conservatism, 176, 180–83, 186, 187; deficiencies of, 174; definition of, 125n; development of, 138–39; and equality of opportunity, 151; and foreign policy, 143; and market economy, 187; and natural benevolence, 157; and plebiscitary democracy, 160–61; and political parties, 174; and private business enterprise, 132–33; and progressivism, 162; and radicalism, 148; renewal of, 187; and socialism, 175

Autonomy: of civil society, 320–22, 330, 337, 343; of market economy, 331; of nations, 209–11; of spheres, 330, 333

Babbitt, Irving, 106
Bacon, Francis, 279
Balkans, 325
Baltic countries, 352
Barker, Ernest, 336
Barre, Raymond, 291
Barrès, Maurice, 31, 106
Belgium, 202
Beliefs: of autonomistic liberalism, 127; of collectivistic liberalism, 127–30; in ideological politics, 25–26, 63–64; rationalization of, 247; and tradition, 104–9

Bell, Daniel, 337
Belloc, Hilaire, 26n
Bentham, Jeremy: and academic freedom, 271–73; and egoism, 157; and foreign policy, 143–44; and governmental secrecy, 164; and individual freedom, 133; and universities, 270, 280
Bentley, Richard, 289
Bernal, J. D., 44n
Bevan, Aneurin, 27n
Black Africa. *See* Africa
Blacks: in American universities, 278, 295, 298; awareness of plight of, 135–37; discrimination against, 174; as *Lumpenproletariat*, 16; as Negro problem, 32; as part of criminal and delinquent class, 91; riots of, 136–37; Tocqueville on, 16–17
Bohemianism: and emancipationism, 9, 15; intellectuals' development of, 35, 45–47, 46n; origins of, 43; and poverty, 135; and privacy, 167; and radicalism, 171; romanticism compared to, 45–46; Weber's awareness of, 260
Bolschewismus, Der (Gurian), 22
Bolshevik Marxism, 29, 84
Bolshevism: American reaction to, 132–33, 136; and civil society, 98; and intellectuals, 18, 65; and representative institutions, 290, 299; Russian Bolshevism, 25; and

expansion of power, 258; planning of, 234; reduction of power, 240; regulatory power of, 244; and scientific knowledge, 233; and universities' autonomy, 283–84, 303

Central Intelligence Agency, 18, 148

Centrally planned economies: in Africa, 241; collectivistic liberals' approval of, 185; and communism, 237, 326; failure of, 32, 98, 101, 352; Soviet Union as, 146; transformation of, into market economies, 32, 353

Charisma: of authority, 252–53, 256, 263; and bureaucracy, 244; and legitimacy, 218; of political leaders, 66; and populism, 48; and religion, 248; and sacred, 108–9, 112; Weber on, 252–53, 255–57, 260–62; and Western Europe, 355

Chekhov, Anton, 132

Chesterton, G. K., 26n

China, 34, 226

Christianity: authority of, 235; disparagement of, 143; and intellectuals, 83; and moral relativism, 167; and philanthropy, 140; and rationalization, 234, 248; and scientific knowledge, 250; and transcendent sphere, 211. See also Millenarianism; Protestant church; Religion; Roman Catholic Church

Churches. See Religion; and names of specific churches

Church-state separation, 284–86

Cicero, 53–54, 270

Citizens and citizenship: and authority, 9; blacks as, 136; civility compared to, 73; civility of, 95, 338, 348, 354; in civil society, 325; collective self-consciousness of state, 74; and consensus, 347; demands on central government, 231; development of, 229–30; idea of, 61; laws' protection of, 343; and liberalism, 136; nationality compared to, 189, 191, 206; rights of, 73, 205–7, 243; and territorial boundaries, 206; virtue of, xi; Weber on, 228, 257

Civility: and antinomy of liberalism, xii; as basis for civil politics, 49–51; of center, 86, 317; citizenship compared to, 73; and civil society, 322, 338–40, 345–46; and collective self-consciousness, 85–86, 340–41; and collectivistic liberalism, 5, 14–15, 170; and common good, 4, 78, 312, 336, 345–46, 350; and conflicts, xi, 4, 75–76, 86, 312, 341, 343; definition of, 17, 49n, 70, 335, 337–38; as developed skill to be free, xi; and education, 153; and emancipationism, 10, 15–16, 19; after French and American

INDEX

276, 277; in Germany, 274, 275; and liberalism, 271, 292; and universities' autonomy, 285–86
Freedom of the press: in civil society, 87, 332–33; demands expressed through, 76–77; expansion of, 230; and privacy, 167; suppressing of, 237
Free trade, 144
French Revolution: and academic freedom, 292; and bohemianism, 46; civility after, 13; ideological politics originating with, 33, 39n.16; and intellectuals, 83–84
French universities: academic freedom of, 276–77, 292; and church-state separation, 285; liberal skepticism of, 270; social sciences in, 297
Friedman, Milton, 345

Galliera, Duchess de, 277
German Democratic Republic, 94
German National Socialism, 25, 64
German universities: academic freedom of, 271–76, 292; central government's control of, 283; and church-state separation, 285; and civil service, 281–82; and empirical social inquiry, 280; and governmental representative institutions, 289, 290; and humanitarianism, 296; and law, 287; and liberalism, 270–72, 274–75; representative institutions of,

289; social sciences in, 297; state universities of, 274, 277
Germany: charismatic authority in, 256; and civil society, 323, 325; communism in, 238; conservative parties of, 239; constitutional patriotism in, 222–23; democracy in, 230; freedom in, 237; ideological politics in, 25; incivility of, 93–94; as liberal-democratic society, 239; and Marxism, 327; millenarianism in, 39; nationalism of, 31, 196, 221; Nazi efforts in, 238, 299; student agitators of, 18; territorial boundaries of, 222–23; terrorism in, 238; as welfare state, 253–54. *See also* Federal German Republic; German Democratic Republic; German universities
Geschichte des Bolschewismus (Rosenberg), 22
Gladstone, William Ewart, 55
Good manners: civility as, 78–80, 321, 324, 326, 337–39, 345; of individuals, 80–81
Government: action of, during Second World War, 134–35; authority of, 73, 230; in civil society, 73–74; and collectivistic liberalism, 128–29, 133–34, 139; corruption of, 141; demands for services from, 76–77, 231–32, 256; efficiency of, 133; and equality, 236–37; ideological

373

Primordial traditionalism, 116–17
Principles of 1789, 194, 195
Printing press, 35, 46, 307
Privacy: in civil society, 127, 333; and press, 166–67; private liberty, 92
Private associations, 129–30, 134, 140, 273, 323, 330
Private business enterprise: abolishing of, 237; and academic freedom, 287; and autonomistic liberalism, 132; civility of, 348; and civil society, 325, 330; and collectivistic liberalism, 130; and conservatism, 124; conservative support for, 239; continuity of, 243; and liberalism, 17; and patriotism, 10; rationalization limited by trade unions, 229; regulation of, 232; and scientific knowledge, 301; and universities, 281, 301; and university training, 304
Private ownership of means of production, 185, 324, 327, 353
Private property: in civil society, 100–101, 214, 323–25, 333; under communism, 101; distribution of, 10–11, 297; and egalitarianism, 10; restrictions on, 104; stratification of ownership, 75
Private universities, 272–74. *See also* Universities
Progressive income tax, 156
Progressivism, 5, 19–20

Property. *See* Private property
Protestant church: authority in, 235; and capitalism, 228; and charisma, 262; and freedom, 111–12; and ideological politics, 35, 39n.16; and intellectuals, 89; millenarianism of, 36; and Protestant ethic, 228, 247, 259–61; and secularism, 234; social gospel of, 163–64; and spark of divinity, 61, 157, 261; and tradition, 103; and universities, 278
Protestant Ethic (Weber), 247
Proudhounist socialists, 83
Psychoanalysis, 8, 308
Psychology, 142
Publicists. *See* Press
Public opinion: and civil society, 322; polls of, 81, 231, 255; rationalism's influence on, 280; and social reform, 142; and social science research, 233

Rabinowitch, Eugene, 21
Radicalism: and antinomy, 312; and bohemianism, 171; and civil libertarians, 132; and class, 127, 170–71; of collectivistic liberalism, 127, 137–38, 148–49, 156–73, 176, 178–80, 185–87; and humanities, 308–9; ideological radicalism, 14–15, 18–20; and liberalism, 148–49, 151, 153, 171, 172; and Marxism, 149, 170; and poverty, 135; recession

This book is set in Minion, a contemporary digital type designed by Robert Slimbach and issued by Adobe Systems in 1989. A neohumanist text face, Minion has no single source but is inspired by the classic typefaces of the late Renaissance. Slimbach called his typeface *Minion* after a word that denoted typeface size in early printing. The word *Minion* means a beloved servant.

Printed on paper that is acid-free and meets the requirements of the American National Standard for Permanence of Paper for Printed Library Materials, Z39.84-1984. ∞

Book design by Sandra S. Hudson, Athens, Georgia
Typography by Monotype Composition Company, Inc., Baltimore, Maryland
Printed and bound by Worzalla Publishing Company, Stevens Point, Wisconsin